MARKETING MISTAKES

MARKETING MISTAKES

FOURTH EDITION

Robert F. Hartley
Cleveland State University

WILEY

JOHN WILEY & SONS

New York Chichester Brisbane Toronto Singapore

Library of Congress Cataloging in Publication Data:

Hartley, Robert F., 1927–
  Marketing mistakes.

  Bibliography: p.
  1. Marketing—United States—Case studies.
I. Title.
HF5415.1.H37   1989   658.8′00973   88-26101
ISBN 0-471-61665-6

Printed in the United States of America

10 9 8 7 6 5 4 3 2

Contents

CHAPTER 1

Introduction

In this fourth edition, a somewhat different approach is taken in Part Two, the major part of the book. Although as in previous editions we will examine classic marketing mistakes to discover what can be learned—that is, the implications that are transferable to other firms, other times, and other situations—perhaps we can gain more insights through comparisons.

Consequently, where possible we have paired notable mistakes with notable successes of firms with similar resources and opportunity in the same industry. We will explore the intriguing question of *why* such firms in the same or similar environments moved in directions that had such different outcomes. What key factor(s) produced a monumental mistake for one and a resounding success for the other? Where such contrasts are possible, we are given an unsurpassed opportunity to gain insights into the intriguing challenge of marketing decision making, and how to improve the batting average for correct decisions.

A variety of firms, industries, problems, and mistakes are presented. Most of the firms are familiar to you, although the details of their problems may not be. The time span ranges over several decades, although most of the cases involve fairly recent events. Where the mistakes occurred several decades ago—such as the Edsel, and Harley Davidson—the circumstances and what can be learned nevertheless are far from dated.

These cases have been specially chosen to bring out certain points or caveats in the art of marketing decision making. They have been selected to give a balanced view of the spectrum of marketing problems. We have sought to present examples that provide somewhat different learning experiences, where the mistake or success, or at least certain aspects of it, differs from others described in the book.

Now let us consider what learning insights we can expect to gain from examining the mistakes and successes of well-known firms. What can we learn with the benefit of hindsight that may help avoid mistakes and increase the success factor?

LEARNING INSIGHTS

Analyzing Mistakes

More has been written about mistakes; successes, unless they are outstanding, receive less public attention, are less sensational, and often are not as interesting to the general and business public.

In looking at sick companies, or even healthy ones that have experienced failures of certain parts of their operations, the temptation is to be unduly critical. It is easy to criticize with the benefit of hindsight. Mistakes are inevitable, given the present state of the art of decision making and the dynamic environment facing the business organization.

Mistakes can be divided into errors of omission and of commission. *Mistakes of omission* are those in which no action was taken, and the status quo was contentedly embraced amid a changing environment. Such errors, which often characterize conservative or stodgy management, are not as obvious as the other category of mistakes. They seldom involve tumultuous upheaval. Rather, the company's fortunes and market position slowly and unspectacularly fade, until years later the sudden realization comes that mistakes having monumental impact have been allowed to happen. The firm's fortunes usually never regain their former glory. A number of examples in this book involve such mistakes of omission: Woolco, Harley Davidson, Adidas.

Mistakes of commission are more spectacular. They involve bad decisions, wrong actions taken, misspent or misdirected expansion, and the like. While the costs of the erosion of market position coming from errors of omission are difficult to calculate precisely, the costs of errors of commission usually are fully evident. The write-offs associated with the Edsel, for example, are estimated to be $100 million in operating losses and another $100 million in unrecoverable investment. (The losses would have been still greater except that $150 million of plant and tools were recovered and used in other Ford divisions.)

Granted that mistakes of omission and commission will occur, alert and aggressive management is characterized by certain actions or reactions when probing their own mistakes or problem situations:

1. Looming problems or present mistakes should be quickly recognized.
2. The causes of the problem(s) should be carefully determined.
3. Alternative corrective actions should be evaluated in view of the company's resources and constraints.
4. Corrective action should be prompt. Sometimes this may require a ruthless axing of the product, the promotional approach, or whatever is at fault.
5. Mistakes should provide learning experiences, the same mistakes should not be repeated, and future operations should be improved.

Slowness to recognize emerging problems suggests that management is either lethargic and incompetent, or that controls have not been established to provide prompt feedback at strategic control points. For example, a declining market share in one or a few market areas should be a red flag to management that something is amiss and prompt corrective action is needed. To wait months before taking action may mean a permanent loss of business.

Just as problems should be quickly recognized, the causes of these problems—the "why" of the unexpected results—must be determined as quickly as possible. It is the height of foolishness to take action before knowing where the problems really lie. To go back to our market share example, the loss of competitive position in one or a few geographic areas may be due to circumstances beyond the firm's immediate control, such as an aggressive new competitor who is drastically cutting prices to "buy sales." In such a situation, all the competing firms in that area will likely lose some market share, and there is little that can be done except to remain as competitive as possible with prices and servicing. On the other hand, closer investigation may disclose that the erosion of business is due to unreliable deliveries, poor quality control, or poor servicing and deteriorating customer relations because of the sales representation in the area.

With the cause(s) of the problem identified, various alternatives for dealing with it should be defined and evaluated, and the corrective choice of action made as objectively and prudently as possible. This may require further research, such as obtaining feedback from customers or from field personnel. If drastic action is needed, there usually is little rationale for procrastination. Serious problems do not go away by themselves; they fester and become worse.

Finally, some learning experience should result from the misadventure. A vice president of one aggressive firm told me:

> I try to give my subordinates as much decision-making power as possible. Perhaps I err on the side of delegating too much. In any case, I expect some mistakes to be made, some decisions that were not for the best. I don't come down too hard usually. This is part of the learning experience. But God help them if they make the same mistake twice. There has been no learning experience, and I question their competence for higher executive positions.

Analyzing Successes

As we noted before, successes seldom command the attention of mistakes; yet they too should provide learning insights. They deserve as much analysis as mistakes, although admittedly the urgency is certainly less than with an emerging problem that requires preventive action lest it spread.

Any analysis of success should seek answers to at least the following questions:

Why were such actions successful?

Was it because of the nature of the environment, and if so, how?

Was it because of marketing research, and if so, how?

Was it because of any particular element of the strategy—such as products and/or services, promotional activities, or distribution methods—and if so, how?

Was it because of the specific elements of the strategy meshing well together, and if so, how?

Was the situation unique and unlikely to be encountered again?

If not, how can we use these successful techniques in the future, or in other operations at the present?

ORGANIZATION OF BOOK

The book is divided into three parts. Part One is devoted to public image problems of firms; that is, problems with a faulty or worsening reputation. Part Two contrasts mistakes with successes. In Part Three a potpourri of cases is discussed: Coca-Cola and its problems with New Coke, A & P's price-cutting fiasco, and Penney's reluctance to change. Finally, in Chapter 15 we classify and summarize the learning insights to be gained from these mistakes and, where possible, the contrasting successes.

Mishandling the Public Image

In studying the mistakes and successes of firms over the last two decades, I have become more and more convinced that the reputation or public image of a firm— how it is perceived by its various publics—can play a crucial role in success or failure. Here, as in the third edition, we will look at examples of mistakes that illustrate serious deficiencies in the handling of the public image.

In light of the importance of public image considerations, Chapter 2 is devoted not to a specific case but to a presentation of the constraints and implications of the public image. The idea is proposed that public image be considered as a "fifth P," an additional element of the marketing mix, controllable by the firm to a considerable degree, just as are the recognized "four P's" of product, price, promotion, and place.

While a number of the mistakes described in this book owe part or most of their problems to a mishandled or misunderstood public image, we have singled out three where image played a particularly significant role. The Nestle case shows the impact of image problems stemming from callousness regarding social responsibility. The firm marketed its infant formula in underdeveloped Third World countries that did not have the sanitation necessary to make the product safe. Nestle's stubborn persistence in doing so generated worldwide criticism, and eventually boycotts and profit damage. Surprisingly, Nestle was more recently involved in another public scandal, that of its Beech-Nut subsidiary, in which corporate executives pleaded guilty to willful violations of the food and drug laws by selling adulterated apple products.

The Coors case shows how a great image can be lost through inattention. It is an object lesson on how important marketing really is. Coasting on a mystique that had somehow built up for its brand, Coors had enjoyed great success. But this mystique began fading. With little advertising, a disregard for basic marketing ideas, and aloof public and employee relations, the company's fortunes faltered badly in the face of aggressive competition. The mystique that had been Coors' proved to be ephemeral.

The last case in this section, that of the toymaker, A. C. Gilbert Company, illustrates practically every mistake imaginable, from not recognizing drastically changing conditions in the industry to successive rash decisions aimed at correcting the problem. But the most serious mistake, permeating all aspects of the operation, was permitting a quality image built up over decades not merely to fade, but to be destroyed, in just a few years. These mistakes caused the 58-year-old company to fail.

Contrasts of Blunders and Bullseyes in the Same Industry

In Chapter 6 we look at the Edsel and the Mustang, major contrasting developments of the same firm in the space of less than five years. How could the Edsel have been such a monumental failure and the Mustang the most successful new car introduction of all time? What are the secrets behind this contrast, and what can we learn from them?

In the early 1960s, Harley Davidson dominated a static motorcycle industry. Suddenly, Honda, a newcomer from overseas, burst on the scene and vastly changed the industry. Harley Davidson's market share dropped from 70 percent to 5 percent in only a few years. The inroads by Honda were a precursor of what was to happen with Japanese imports of all kinds. At the time Japanese products did not have the image of quality and dependability that they have today, making the quick success of Honda all the more remarkable. In Chapter 7 we examine the mistakes of Harley Davidson and the keys to Honda's success.

Chapter 8 compares K mart, the biggest discounter of them all and one of the largest retailing organizations in the United States, and three other well-known firms that fell by the wayside: Korvette, Woolco of Woolworth, and W. T. Grant. How could these three fail so miserably (W. T. Grant, when it went into bankruptcy and eventual liquidation, was the second biggest U.S. company ever to do so) when they had longer experience and greater resources than K mart? What were the keys to K mart's success, the ingredients of failure, and what can be learned that other firms can use to advantage?

In Chapter 9 the great success of McDonald's is compared with the lackluster Burger Chef, an acquisition of General Foods, supposedly one of the foremost marketers of food products in the world. Why did a fast-food restaurant operation bedevil them? And why didn't they learn from the successful and visible experience of McDonald's?

Chapter 10 deals with the rapidly growing market for running shoes, long dominated worldwide by Adidas. Its strategy seemed hardly assailable. But somehow, Nike, using essentially the same strategy and starting from scratch decades after Adidas was well established, drove the old master to the sidelines.

Chapter 11 describes two young computer firms, Apple and Osborne. Both were growing rapidly, spearheading the avalanche of demand for personal computers. But one firm, Osborne, after seeing its sales jump from nothing to $100 million in only 18 months, suddenly plummeted even faster. What led to such a violent roller coaster experience, and why didn't something similar happen to Apple?

A Melange of Mistakes

In Part Three we examine a variety of mistakes, capped by the great Coca-Cola debacle when the company tried to change the flavor of its cola, this despite intensive marketing research that seemed to confirm the correctness of the decision to change.

In these cases we are particularly interested in identifying the errors that led to the mistake. For example, with Coca-Cola, how could marketing research efforts be so badly misread? And how could Penney's management have been so unaware of a greatly changing enviroment? How could A & P have so badly miscalculated the lasting effectiveness of major price cutting?

A caution lest we give the impression in these cases that bullseyes, or blunders, are long lasting: the pendulum can swing quickly. The successful firm of today may be mediocre tomorrow, or even a failure. Success does not guarantee continued success. A faltering Nike may not be inspiring today, but at a certain period it showed an unusual pattern of success. But we will also encounter other intriguing cases, McDonald's and K mart, for example, where the pattern of success has scarcely slackened. Why?

Where possible in these cases we have depicted the major personalities involved at the time. We invite you to imagine yourself in their position, confronting the problems and decisions they faced at their point of crisis, or at the time when actions or lack of action led to a subsequent crisis. What would you have done differently, and why? We invite you to participate in the discussion questions and role-playing episodes appearing at the end of each case. We urge you to consider the pros and cons of alternative actions.

For Thought and Discussion

1. Do you agree that it is impossible for a firm to avoid mistakes? Why or why not?
2. How can a firm speed up its awareness of emerging problems so that it can take responsive action? Be as specific as you can.
3. Large firms tend to err more often on the side of conservation and are slower to take corrective action than smaller firms. Would you speculate as to why this is so?
4. Which do you think is likely to be the more costly to a firm: errors of omission or errors of commission? Why?

One

MISHANDLING THE PUBLIC IMAGE

2

The Public Image—
An Addition to the
Marketing Strategy

A firm's reputation or public image tends to be taken for granted—until something untoward occurs, and an organization is brought to painful awareness that an image problem exists. Yet, as we will explore in this chapter, the public image for the most part is controllable. It can and should be protected, but it can also provide powerful strategic thrust. It deserves to be considered as one of the elements of the marketing mix: an active tool, not a passive appendage.

THE "FOUR P's" OF THE MARKETING MIX

Marketing strategy has been viewed as manipulating the "four P's," the elements of the so-called marketing mix, in such a way as to best appeal to those customers the firm seeks: i.e., the target market. Subject to certain constraints—of customer acceptance, of competition, of company resources, of governmental regulations, for example—the marketer has been seen as able to control or direct only four variables. These are the *product,* its quality level, and particular features; the *price* to be charged; the product's *promotion;* and its *placement,* or how it will be distributed in the market.

The four P's are interdependent. Decisions regarding one of the P's will impact on the others. For example, if a product is to be distributed as a prestige item, the pricing must reflect this, as should also the distribution structure and the promotional efforts.

Many alternatives are possible for each of the P's, and they may be mixed or blended in endless combinations. But if the strategy is to be effective, the P's should be *tailored, compatible,* and *coordinated,* as described in the following guidelines:[1]

1. A mix should be specially *tailored* to a product or campaign, keeping in mind particular target markets the firm most wishes to attract.
2. The various elements of the mix must be screened for *compatibility.* For example, if the firm wants to appeal to those consumers interested in economy, its choice of dealers, prices, promotional efforts, and of course the product itself should be geared to this objective. In this instance, distributing an attractively priced product through discount stores with sufficient advertising to presell customers might seem indicated.
3. Decisions regarding the P's should be *coordinated* and the complete marketing mix strategy made at one time. Some tradeoffs may be desirable. For example, a decision might be made to spend more money on advertising and reduce the sales force because the advertising should make the product easier to sell. If the price is made low enough and if distribution is through discount stores, then sales personnel may also be reduced because these customers have central buying for the entire chain concentrated at their headquarters.

In order to meet these guidelines, the marketing strategy is generally best selected by one person or group, rather than having each element decided independently. Most firms accomplish this by placing authority for all elements of the marketing mix under the control of a marketing manager or marketing vice president.

THE "FIFTH P"

An additional P, a "fifth P," deserves consideration as another element of the marketing mix. This is the firm's *public image,* that is, its reputation, how it and its output (products and/or services) are perceived. Figure 2.1 depicts the idea of the public image being added to the other P's and interrelating with them.[2] In the balance of this chapter we will furnish support for the inclusion of the public image as part of the marketing mix, and of the implications of this. But first let us examine the dimensions of the public image.

[1]Some of the material to follow has been adapted from my book, *Marketing Fundamentals* (New York: Harper & Row, 1983), pp. 38–41, and 477–501.

[2]A few marketing scholars have begun to question the adequacy of the traditional notion of the four P's. Philip Kotler, for example, has recently proposed that the four P's should be increased to six P's, by adding *Political Power* and *Public-opinion Formation.* (Kotler: "Rethink the Marketing Concept," *Marketing News,* September 14, 1984, pp. 1, 22, and 24.) Public image would seem to be more of an umbrella concept that easily covers these and other controllable factors impacting on a firm's success in the marketplace.

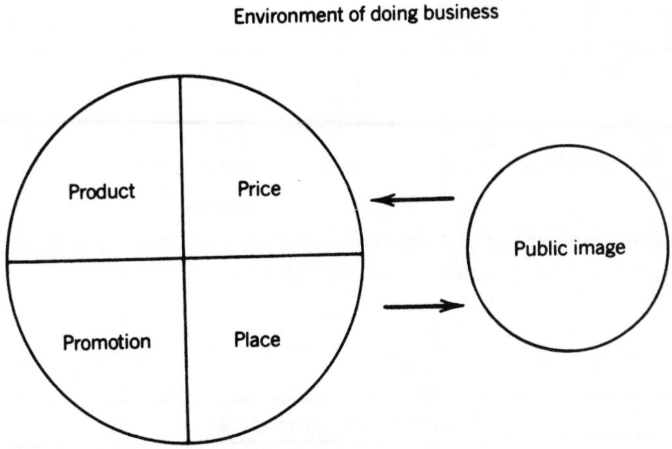

Environment of doing business

Figure 2.1. A firm's marketing mix (the five Ps).

A *public image* is a composite of how an organization is viewed by its various publics: its customers, suppliers, employees, stockholders, the financial institutions, the communities in which it dwells, and the various governments, both local and federal. And to these groups must be added the press, which cannot always be relied upon to deliver objective and unbiased reporting, but is influenced by the firm's reputation.

Two other terms, publicity and public relations, are related to public image development. *Publicity* is communication about the firm, sometimes, but not always, initiated by it, which is disseminated by the media without charge and with little control by the firm. *Public relations* involves a broad set of planned communications about the company, including publicity releases, designed to promote goodwill and a favorable image.

Publicity then is part of public relations when it is initiated by the firm. However, it can also come about through no planned efforts of the firm; in such cases it can be adverse and bring notoriety because of some controversial action or happening. Since public relations involves communications with stockholders, financial analysts, government officials, and other noncustomer groups, it is usually placed outside the marketing function, perhaps in the form of a staff department or an outside consultant who reports to top management.

Types of Images

The general impressions of a firm or organization and of its output, be this product, services, or even future expectations, can range from strongly positive to neutral to strongly negative. The degree or intensity of positive or negative feelings toward a firm can be depicted on a scale or continuum as shown in Figure 2.2.

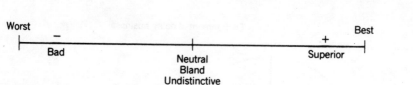

Figure 2.2. Intensity of public image perception of an organization.

Following are some representative images or perceptions that can be categorized as negative, as neutral, and as positive:

Negative Perceptions of Image	
A polluter	I just don't like their attitude
Unfriendly	I don't trust them
Junky	Not a sharp operation
Low quality	Inefficient
Poor servicing	Not on top of things
Not a good neighbor	Fading in their industry
Could care less	Too demanding
Stodgy	Bound up in red tape
Always understaffed	Second rate
Insulting advertising	
A dirty store	
Distant	

Neutral and Undistinctive Perceptions of Image	
Haven't heard of them	Who?
Just another _____	OK, I guess
Boring ads	An unknown quantity
They haven't proven themselves	

Positive Perceptions of Image	
A good neighbor	An efficient operation
A good place to work	I trust them
Maker of quality products	In the front of the industry
Provides good values	Honest, dependable services
Has the customer's interest in mind	They care
Friendly	Courteous and helpful employees
Interesting and entertaining advertising	A "fun" place

The public image may not necessarily be valid. For example, a firm may be viewed as a polluter despite strenuous and effective efforts to remedy the problem.

Furthermore, not everyone will have the same opinion of an organization and of its output. Perceptions of the firm by its own executives may differ considerably from how its employees, customers, and the general public see it. But even among one group, such as customers, some will be more favorable, others more negative. But if an unfavorable opinion is common, this is a serious problem and needs drastic corrective action. Even if only a few people are negatively inclined, this should not be ignored. Such people are likely to switch to competitors soon—if they have not already done so. And their negative attitudes tend to become contagious as they spread bad word-of-mouth publicity.

How Controllable is the Public Image?

Within certain limits, image is controllable just as are the original four P's. (Of course, when a disaster occurs, such as that at Union Carbide's Bhopal, India plant, some would maintain that the resulting poor image is for the most part uncontrollable.) Now skeptics would argue that the public image cannot be changed or manipulated as readily as the other P's, such as promotional efforts and prices. A firm's reputation, after all, would seem rather durable. Therefore, how can image be considered part of the marketing strategy?

The public image is not quickly changed for the better—although it can be torn down easily enough as we will see in the Gilbert case. But while several of the original four P's are readily changed, others may not be more quickly changed than the public image. For example, the product and place elements of the marketing mix.

Some products take years to develop sufficiently to bring on the market. For example:[3]

Crest fluoride toothpaste—10 years

Hills Brothers instant coffee—22 years

Lustre Creme liquid shampoo—8 years

Minute rice—18 years

Xerox copying machine—15 years

Automatic washer—12 years

Place or channel decisions often are not easily or quickly changed. They involve relationships built up with other members of the channel of distribution and may be broken, but often with hard feelings. Even such huge firms as General

[3]Lee Adler, "Time Lag in New Product Development," *Journal of Marketing*, January 1966, pp. 17–21.

Motors would incur severe financial strains and even legal difficulties in changing the distribution—for example, the task of GM in buying out its 18,000 independent dealers or of supporting them in some other endeavor would be monumental.

Consequently, decisions that deal with distribution and with at least some products must be regarded as long-term and capable usually of only gradual modification. And the public image is no different.

Until the last several decades, a firm's public image could more easily be taken for granted as of no major consequence, even though the reputation of a firm and its products has affected demand, almost from the beginning of time. In today's skeptical and critical environment, however, few firms can disregard their public image anymore, at least as far as the public relations aspects of it. And this image or reputation can be a strength or a weakness.

Aggressive Use of Image The public image as an element of the marketing mix is delimiting if it is viewed—as it often is—only as something to protect and, if necessary, to try to restore. These are defensive moves, reactive and not aggressive. But an image can be used more positively, even aggressively, if it is in good shape, or if it can rather quickly be brought to a favorable public awareness. Take Sears, for example:

> Sears has capitalized on its long-established image of dependability and fair dealing by successfully diversifying into a variety of consumer services, such as insurance, investment counseling, even dental clinics.

An example of a most effective building of an image for a new enterprise, and using this as the vital element of the marketing mix, has been Hyatt Legal Clinics:

> Joel Hyatt, in his TV commercials featuring himself as the founder, has conveyed a warm, helpful, and concerned image for his Hyatt Legal Clinics. That this is so different from the general public's impression of law firms and lawyers has enabled the firm, first established in 1978, to grow to the largest law firm in the U.S.

Importance of the Public Image

A firm's public image plays a vital role in the attractiveness of the firm and its products to employees, customers, and to such outsiders as stockholders, suppliers, creditors, government officials, and the news media, as well as diverse special groups. In some situations it is impossible to satisfy all the diverse publics: for example, a new, highly automated plant may meet the approval of creditors and stockholders, but it will undoubtedly find resistance from employees who see jobs threatened. On the other hand, high-quality products and service standards should bring almost complete approval and pride of association—given that operating costs are competitive—while shoddy products and false claims would be widely decried.

A firm's public image, if it is good, should be cherished and protected. It is a valuable asset that usually is built up from a long and satisfying relationship of a firm with its various publics. If a firm has developed a quality image, this is not easily countered or imitated by competitors. Such an image may enable a firm to charge higher prices, to woo the best distributors and dealers, to attract the best employees, and to expect the most favorable creditor relationships and the lowest borrowing costs. It should also enable a firm's stock to command a higher price–earnings ratio than other firms in the same industry not having such a good reputation and public image. All these factors can give a competitive advantage.

Consequences of a Negative Image. A bad image hurts a firm with all the different publics with which it deals. All can turn critical and even litigious, depending on the source and extent of the bad image. At best, present and potential customers may simply seek alternative sources for goods and services and switch to competitors wherever possible.

At the worst—the Bhopal disaster, or Love Canal and Agent Orange, or the MGM Grand Hotel fire in Las Vegas—major liability suits can cost hundreds of millions of dollars, bring new governmental regulations, greatly increase the costs of liability insurance, and even spread a badly tarnished image to other firms in the industry. Years may be required to mute the negative perceptions, and millions of dollars of advertising may be committed to try to improve public impressions. For example, after Love Canal and Agent Orange triggered a wave of adverse publicity, the chemical industry launched an advertising campaign to try to allay the image. Monsanto alone spent millions on a campaign with the theme, "Without chemicals, life itself would be impossible."

The consequences, of course, of a bad image translate directly to the bottom line, to reduced profits, or worse.

THE PUBLIC IMAGE MIX

Figure 2.3 shows the major inputs in creating an image, and also the outputs or consequences of the resulting image on the various publics. Notice that some of the factors are both inputs and outputs—employees, for example. Employees can help foster a negative or a positive image; but they are also affected by their firm's image, with the more able only attracted to the firm with a good reputation. Similarly, dealers both affect image and are affected by it.

So many variables or inputs can be involved that we can hardly identify everything. For example, warranties ("Satisfaction guaranteed or your money back"), and packaging should be included for some firms. Even the brand name

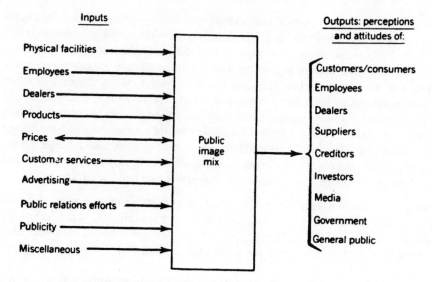

Figure 2.3. Major inputs and outputs of the public image mix.

conveys an image, although this will generally reflect past actions affecting customer satisfaction or dissatisfaction. However, sometimes the name itself can be instrumental in fashioning an image:

> A classic but little known example of this dates back to the late 1800s in England. William Lever, a grocer's son, was a traveling salesman when he entered the soap business with a yellow soap that he called "Sunlight." The name caught on in a dreary, sun-starved England, and in three years the foundation was laid for what was to become one of the largest firms in the world, Unilever, Ltd.[4]

And then there is Cracker Jacks, which built its good reputation with children by "generously" giving a gift in every package.

You can see that most of the inputs or factors that affect the public image are controllable to a considerable extent. A firm certainly can determine its facilities, products, use of advertising, customer service practices, and prices relative to competing products, as well as the efforts of public relations and publicity to favorably affect the image. And a firm can hardly escape blame for such things as poor customer service, or bad publicity about pollution, or disregard for product

[4]For more details of the early days of Lever, and a subsequent encounter with Procter & Gamble, see Robert F. Hartley, *Marketing Successes: Historical to Present Day* (New York: Wiley, 1985), pp. 63–72.

safety, or poor quality control, which can badly harm the image—despite all the public relations pronouncements and staged community involvement efforts.

Effect of Facilities on Public Image

The total combination of facilities and the visible accounterments of the firm can create an impression that ranges from positive to neutral to negative. Facilities include trucks, plants, stores, office buildings, the company logo and signs, and any other publicly visible aspects of the firm.

Factories can be eyesores and unpleasant places to work in, as well as they can be neighbors. They can have a bad environmental impact and can create air and/or water pollution—and worse. Or they can be neatly landscaped, pleasing to the eye, and have strict pollution control. Of course, type of industry plays a major role. Steel mills, paper mills, oil refineries, and chemical plants, by their very nature, are dirtier, less desirable neighbors than electronics factories or, indeed, factories of most other industries. In any industry, the firm with an old plant may not be able to invest millions to modernize and improve its appearance. But even in heavy industry a firm can have a good reputation or a bad one, can be a good citizen and neighbor to the community, or a disgrace. As an example of the latter:

> Some years ago a paper mill, in attempting to improve its public image, had an advertising campaign showing the clean waters of a river supposedly downstream from its plant. It fell into disgrace when some diligent investigative reporter found that the idyllic scene in the commercials was upstream from the plant.

Where a firm is a dominant employer in a community, the possibility of real public image problems looms very important when layoffs are necessary, whether temporary or permanent. The layoffs of some no-longer-competitive steel mills in the Mahoning Valley of northeastern Ohio devastated the cities involved, of which the largest was Youngstown. Regardless of the necessity, the bad publicity emanating from such closings blackened the public image of the entire steel industry. Perhaps one of the worst closings in recent years was that of the Insulite Division of Boise Cascade Corporation in International Falls, Minnesota, a community of 6000 people on the Canadian border.

> The announcement of the permanent closing came in a statement December 6, 1984, "The closure affects approximately 500 employees in the International Falls area and another 65 associated with Insulite's sales staff." Workers had about 48 hours to clean out their lockers. There was also a domino effect as another 150 loggers who supplied wood for the siding produced also were out of work. Newspapers throughout the nation picked up on this closing which threw well over 10 percent of the population out of work with no alternative employment opportunities. Headlines such as these appeared: "A Little Town on the Ropes," "Mill Closing a Kick in the Economic Gut," and

"Closing Shock: A Child Lies Awake."[5] What made the closing particularly newsworthy, and the public image of Boise Cascade blacker, was the timing: 19 days before Christmas.

If a firm uses its own trucks, this can impact on the image. Retail firms in particular often have their own delivery system, and this can add prestige and advertising for the store, especially if it is well maintained and if the drivers are uniformed. As we noted before, the choice of dealers—their reputations and facilities—will also rub off on the manufacturer's image, and vice versa.

Many major firms, especially those that have widely diversified into unrelated areas, have undertaken corporate identity programs to improve their images through new logos, new signs, and distinctive business forms. However, face-lifting alone, without more fundamental changes where there is a problem, is seldom enough to change an image in a positive fashion.

Effect of Company Employees

Contacts of employees with outsiders, be they customers, suppliers, or others, convey positive or negative impressions of the firm. Even the way the telephone is answered casts an impression. Smart firms devote attention to this aspect of the image. Special employee training may be needed, special policies established, and some type of follow-up used to ensure that the company's image efforts do not deteriorate. The Bell Telephone Company was one of the pioneers in emphasizing this aspect of the public image:

> Servicemen were inbued with the need to leave customers' premises neat, and courtesy was stressed. Telephone operators were trained with the objective, "Voice with a Smile." Company representatives in business offices learned the technicalities of handling many different kinds of customer contacts through role playing, and they were judged on the quality of their speech, their understanding, explanations, and interested and helpful manner. Periodic retraining was used to ensure continuous high quality.[6]

Product Quality and Dependability

The product, its level of quality compared with competing brands, and particularly its dependability or freedom from defects, is another aspect of the marketing program that can strongly affect the image. The American auto industry has long been plagued with product defects, and although concerted efforts have been made to try

[5]For example, the *Cleveland Plain Dealer,* December 16, 1984, pp. A1 and A10.
[6]Described by Alfred R. Oxenfeldt, *Executive Action in A Marketing* (Belmont, Calif.: Wadsworth, 1966), p. 639.

to lessen defects in new cars, these have not been wholly successful, as most of us know from personal experience.

In the interests of improving product dependability and freedom from defects, quality control may have to be improved. Most firms use statistical quality control which accepts a predictable number of defective units, with only every *nth* item checked. This is far less expensive than complete quality control that accepts zero defects. But the latter perhaps ought to be considered for some items in which serious servicing problems cannot otherwise be eased. Multiple inspections of critical parts are rejected by most firms as too costly, but compared to the costs of customer brand switching and costly callback programs, improved quality control might sometimes offset the increased costs. It would certainly favorably affect the public image.

The intrinsic nature of the products or type of business that a firm handles will also affect the image. For example, consider these extreme examples: diamonds versus prunes; a garbage collection versus air express; a salvage store versus a department store. For certain lines of business, the public image will be more negative than for others, not because of the efforts of the personnel involved but because of the nature of the business and of the products or services.

The Price Component

Note in Figure 2.3 that price has a two-way arrow. This reflects that prices of a firm's products relative to competing brands tend to be a rather powerful conveyor of image, particularly as to whether the firm is a maker of high-quality or low-quality products, or something in between. A higher price than other brands usually connotes higher quality. Of course, if there is a serious discrepancy between a high price and the realized quality of a product, image is affected adversely.

The perceived image of a firm also helps determine the prices that it can realize for its products. With a favorable image, especially regarding product dependability and customer service, relatively higher prices will be accepted by customers.

For example, the Maytag Company is located in a small town, Newton, Iowa. Compared to its competitors, the likes of General Electric and Whirlpool, it is a small company. But through the years it has achieved and maintained a reputation for quality and dependability at a premium price—an image reinforced since 1967 by famous TV commercials showing a forlorn Maytag repairman with nothing to do.

Lately Maytag has had to worry about its mature appliance market in which the replacement cycle for the industry is 10 to 12 years, and in Maytag's case, often more. Maytag needs to diversify outside the appliance business, and is attempting to do so. It must be careful, however, not to compromise its quality reputation by acquisitions that will not be compatible with its long-established public image.

Importance of Customer Service

Viewed in the broadest sense, customer service includes all offerings to a firm's customers beyond the product itself. Repair and warranty service usually receives the most attention (and complaints), but customer services include such diverse things as return-goods privileges extended by retail stores, and conveniences such as delivery, telephone ordering, customer parking, credit, and so on.

The effect of a firm's reputation for good service in attracting potential customers and preventing the loss of existing customers is obvious. It results in customer satisfaction, in loyal customers and repeat business, and in word-of-mouth influence, which is potent, if not easily measured. Less obvious is the protection from price competition that a good reputation for service can provide. Although some customers are swayed by a better price, many place a higher value on a firm's reputation for dependable service. Some services, such as extended warranties, are easily imitated. Others, such as prompt and dependable delivery and high-caliber maintenance and repair facilities, are less easily matched, and their effective performance slowly builds reputations.

Indirect benefits can come from a customer service program as a major part of the public image mix. A firm's good reputation for service can make customers easier to sell to. Recruiting salespeople tends to be easier, and higher morale and lower personnel turnover often result from the harmonious customer relations that good service engenders.

Rather than giving customer service the attention it deserves, in many firms executive time is directed elsewhere. Operational crises and problems claim attention: for example, making a decision on promotional scheduling that cannot be delayed, breaking in a salesperson in a new territory, or devoting immediate attention to several territories in which planned sales were not reached. And the customers who are antagonized, who are ill treated, whose special requirements are disregarded, who quietly fade away, never to return—all these are overlooked in the pressure of "more important" matters.

A good part of the reason that many firms neglect the customer relations aspect of their business is a lack of awareness of how serious such problems might be. The extent of customer dissatisfaction often cannot be detected by sales and profit figures, at least not until such problems may have assumed major proportions. Moreover, because only a small proportion of total complaints ever reach the ears of responsible executives, expressed dissatisfactions tend to be viewed as involving only a few customers with mostly unjustified complaints.

Procedures should be established for prompt feedback on service problems and customer complaints to responsible executives. Usually some centralized and standardized procedures need to be established, both to obtain service feedback and to handle complaints. Some firms have found that "hot lines," toll-free direct lines to company headquarters for customers whose problems are not being handled to their satisfaction, are effective both as a service and a sales tool. Even such a simple thing as keeping customers informed of the status of their orders, especially when shipments will be delayed or reduced as a result of shortages, strikes, or other unforeseen circumstances, can improve the customer-service aspect of the public image.

The Role of Advertising in the Public Image Mix

Advertising can play both a positive and a negative role with a company's image. It can and often does contribute to an existing image, and this may be subtle or more direct. It can also be used to establish a new image.

Contribution to a Present Image. The type of media used, the message and how it is presented, the TV programs sponsored, the persons who deliver any testimonials, even the repetitiveness of the message—all can affect the image of the company. Advertising can be dignified and in good taste, or it can be petty, raucous, obnoxious, belittling, and insulting to the intelligence. Just as a person is, so is a firm judged by the company it keeps, that is, by the way it advertises and its public display of doing business. For example, we can contrast the dignity of high-quality retail department or specialty store advertising with that of the typical discount store or promotional department store; in the former only one or a few items will be advertised, with considerable white space in the ad; the latter will be cluttered and heavy type ads. The situation is similar for TV commercials. We can contrast the Xerox, IBM, and Hallmark-type of advertising with commercials for toothpastes, detergents, deodorants, and cold remedies.

Defending or Establishing a New Image. *Institutional advertising* is the main promotional vehicle used to try to influence the company image directly. Institutional advertising is nonproduct advertising that seeks to create a favorable image with the general public.

Some industries and firms have been subjected to considerable criticism by the media, by consumer groups, and by politicians. Particularly during inflationary times, firms that deal with basic necessities and keep raising prices are most vulnerable to criticism, whether justified or not. Thus the oil companies and the public utilities have been castigated. The supermarket and auto industries have also been vulnerable. In order to defend their image and restore some semblance of good public relations, some large firms have turned to advertising to tell their side of the story. This has been termed *advocacy advertising*. Mobil Oil has been particularly aggressive in using advocacy advertising, not only in defending itself, but also in preaching for its point of view in other public and governmental issues.

Image-developing advertising is more common. A firm may find that it is stuck with an image that at one time was appropriate and that appealed to a substantial target market but now does not, and so wishes to change the image. For example:

> Timex for several decades by reason of its advertising had gained the image for watches that "take a licking and keep on ticking." But it found that this formerly successful utilitarian image was wanting in today's watch market dominated by foreign imports. A better image, it seemed to Timex, would be one of more fashion and higher price. To push its image beyond that of a "less expensive brand," Timex in 1981 increased its advertising expenditures some 15 percent.[7]

Whether the efforts of Timex to upgrade its image will be successful is too soon to tell; the task could require a decade. However, there is a classic model of success in changing an image as described in Chapter 7, but the image to be changed was not the company's but the activity for which it was gearing its products:

> In the late 1950s, the U.S. motorcycle industry was dominated by large high-powered machines. The major producer, Harley Davidson, had completely captured the market for police and delivery motorcycles and was secure with the other major market segment, the "hard core motorcyclists."

> Honda Motor Company started in 1948 as a small Japanese motorcycle manufacturer. As its domestic market was secured, Honda looked to overseas markets and established its first U.S. branch in California in 1959. It correctly assessed market opportunity as existing among first-time riders who wanted a lightweight, inexpensive machine that would solve traffic problems.

> An image problem impeded creating such a new market: a mental picture of black leather jackets and *The Wild Ones*. An intensive national advertising campaign sought to win social acceptance for the motorcycle and its rider, and the theme became "You meet the nicest people on a Honda."

> Motorcycle registrations jumped from 500,000 in 1960 to nearly 1.9 million in 1966. A survey of Honda owners in 1964 showed that most had never ridden a motorcycle before they bought the Honda. Advertising had changed the image of the motorcycle and made it acceptable.

PUBLIC IMAGE FOR NONPROFIT ORGANIZATIONS

Not only should product-oriented firms be concerned and protective of their public image; so too should nonprofit organizations such as schools, charitable drives, police departments, hospitals, even politicians. Let us consider here the importance

---

[7]For more detail, see "Falling Profits Prompts Timex to Shed its Utilitarian Image," *Wall Street Journal,* September 17, 1981, p. 27.

of public image and how it might be improved or built by several nonproduct organizations and persons.

Large city police departments frequently have a poor image among important segments of the population. The need to improve this image is hardly less important than for a manufacturer faced with a deteriorating brand image. A police department can develop a "marketing" campaign to win friends; examples of possible activities aimed at creating a better image are promoting tours and open houses of police stations, crime laboratories, police lineups, cells, and so forth; speaking at schools; and sponsoring recreation projects, such as a day at the ballpark for youngsters.

Public school systems, faced with taxpayers' revolts against mounting costs of education and with image damage due to teacher strikes need conscious effort to improve their image in order to obtain more public support and funds.

Many nonbusiness organizations and institutions, such as hospitals, schools, governmental bodies, even labor unions, have grown self-serving, with a bureaucratic mentality dominating, so that perfunctory and callous treatment is the rule and the image is in the pits. Improving the image can only come through a greater emphasis on satisfying customers' or the public's needs.

Building images of political candidates represents the most extensive use of marketing techniques in nonbusiness areas. Two marketing tools are commonly employed; public opinion research and mass media, especially television, advertising. Using these tools, and especially the latter, to win elections almost precludes the candidate without much money from effectively competing. With money, a candidate may bypass political party organizations, challenge entrenched incumbents, in fact manufacture an instant public image.

TYPES OF IMAGE PROBLEMS

Image problems can be categorized as: (1) overcoming a dull image; (2) trying to upgrade an image; (3) combating a fading image; and (4) overcoming a bad image. We will briefly discuss each of these.

Almost three decades ago, this statement was made by an eminent researcher:

> What happens to the retail store that lacks a sharp character, that does not stand for something special to any class of shoppers? It ends up as an alternative store in the customer's mind. The shopper does not head for such a store as the primary place to find what he or she wants. Without certain outstanding departments and lines of merchandise, without clear attraction for some group, it is like a dull person.[8]

[8]Pierre Martineau, "The Personality of the Retail Store," *Harvard Business Review* (January–February 1958), p. 50.

Certainly a dull or innocuous image is a millstone around the neck of any firm and a major competitive drawback. The only thing worse is having a decidedly negative image. Image is not an easy thing for a firm to improve or change, but efforts certainly need to be made by such a firm.

Sometimes a firm wants to upgrade its image. Perhaps it had originally formulated its niche as a low-price, bargain operation, and now wants to attain more of a quality image. But upgrading an image is not easily done, as described in the Korvette case. Some firms that attempt this fail because they expect results too quickly. But other firms might be better advised to change their name—start afresh, perhaps with a new division—rather than try to upgrade a long-established name and image.

Even mighty Sears, in 1974–1975, attempted to upgrade its image—and its profit margins—with higher-price goods and higher-fashion women's apparel. Its earnings tumbled 28 percent as its traditional price-conscious customers became disillusioned by the emphasis on higher prices. Sears soon abandoned the attempt to change its image, but the damage had been done and sales and profits were slow in recovering.

Combating a fading image would seem easier than upgrading a long-established one. However, aggressive and effective efforts need to be taken to reverse the fading trend, as Coors found out. Reversing an established trend is not easily done, and may never succeed in recouping all the lost ground.

Overcoming a bad image normally is the most difficult problem. This is the extreme position of image illness, and it could even be the death knell. It is far worse than a dull image, an image of low quality, or a formerly good image that is now fading.

A bad image may be formed slowly by a history of questionable practices that have become widely publicized: for example, unsafe products, deceptive advertising, illegal payoffs, callousness toward community relations and employees, and so on.

Occasionally something catastrophic will bring down an image. The calamity of Union Carbide has, of couse, been widely publicized. But firms have been known to be more directly involved in their own violent image destruction, as we will examine with the A. C. Gilbert Company case.

ERRORS IN HANDLING THE PUBLIC IMAGE

Firms can do a great injustice to their image. They may:

1. Blatantly ignore matters that have a probability of affecting it adversely.
2. Disregard the constraining consequences of their image.
3. Abdicate their image-building and image-maintaining efforts to public relations.
4. Not coordinate all aspects of the operation that can affect the image.

Ignoring Possible Negative Image Consequences

Sometimes a firm naively disregards possible negative public reactions:

> Columbia Gas of Ohio faces competition for heating homes not only from electric companies but also from cost savers such as heat pumps, solar systems, wood stoves, and kerosene and quartz room heaters. During a period when energy costs were rapidly rising, with much publicity about the need to conserve energy—placing this need even on a patriotic level—Columbia found that all this conservation was resulting in a cut in usage and less revenue. So what did Columbia do? It sought to impose a surcharge on consumers who had heat pumps and other energy-saving devices.

> There was immediate public outrage. Responding to public opinion, the Ohio legislature hastened to introduce bills to block surcharges on heat pumps and similar systems. In the face of widespread opposition, Columbia doggedly went ahead and triggered further controversy by trying to block service to homebuilders who planned to install heat pumps in new houses. The Public Utilities Commission finally had to order Columbia to provide service; the firm, now beginning to realize the seriousness of the resentment against it, backed off. As one legislator tersely summarized the situation: "It does not make much sense, when the federal government gives tax credits for insulation, to penalize people for doing what we asked them to do, which is conserve."[9]

The Nestle case, described in Chapter 3, also illustrates this unseemly myopia regarding public image.

Why do firms ignore their image, or at least greatly underestimate the consequences of their actions on it? Several factors usually account for this. First, a firm's public image generally makes a nonspecific impact on company performance. The cause and effect relationship of a poor or deteriorating image is virtually impossible to assess, at least until and unless image problems worsen. The inability to be able to point the blame directly to the intangible image results in other areas of performance being given the closer scrutiny and the efforts at corrective action.

Second, an organization's image—how it is perceived by the various publics—is not easily and definitively measured. While some tools are available for tracking public opinion, they tend to be imprecise and of uncertain validity. Consequently, image studies are often ignored or given short shrift relative to more quantitative measures of performance.

Third, it is difficult to determine the effectiveness of image-building efforts. While firms may spend thousands, and even millions of dollars, for institutional and image-building advertising, measures of the effectiveness of such expenditures are inexact and also of questionable validity. For example, a survey may be taken of

[9]Reported in a number of sources across Ohio, of which one example is William Carlson, "Columbia Gas Faces Horde of Challengers," *Cleveland Plain Dealer,* May 24, 1981, p. 27A.

attitudes of a group of people before and after the image-building campaign is run. Presumably, if a few more people profess to be favorably disposed toward the company after the campaign than before, this is an indication of its success. But an executive can question how much this really translates into sales and profits.

Disregarding Constraints

A firm's present image ought to be considered and recognized as a factor affecting strategy options. Public image is a resource, just as much so as personnel, facilities, and finances. But it is also a constraint. Most firms do not have unlimited resources, so their planned strategies must be geared to what is realistic and practical. So it is with the image. To expect a Korvette or a K mart to be on the same status level as a Neiman Marcus in a few years is unreasonable, as is the expectation that a Volkswagen can soon achieve the status of a Mercedes-Benz.

Two generalizations can be made about the constraining influences of a firm's public image:

1. A dull, a negative, or a low-quality image is extremely difficult to upgrade. Massive advertising efforts and years of persistence may be necessary to overcome such an image.
2. A favorable image can be quickly torn down if a firm is careless with its product quality, service, or other aspects subject to public scrutiny.

Abdicating Image Efforts

In many firms a public relations department, either in-house or through an advertising agency or other outside consultant, is responsible for all image-related matters.[10] This supposedly places public relations in expert hands, as well as under the control of those who can have the detached objectivity that supposedly no operating executive can have.

Some firms are beginning to move in the direction of greater participation by marketers. This is hardly meeting with the approval of all concerned. Public relations practitioners tend to view such a move as "encroachment," and the marketers as "carpetbaggers": "Marketing people are making inroads. They are like 'carpet baggers' . . . who move into an organization, then pull out and let PR pick up the pieces."[11]

Yet we know that many other aspects of a firm's operation affect the public image—public relations pronouncements and publicity releases are just two of the factors. A firm that recognizes the importance of its public image, not only as

---

[10]For a discussion of the relationship between marketing and public relations, see Philip Kotler and William Mindak, "Marketing and Public Relations," *Journal of Marketing*, October 1978, pp. 13–20.

[11]Based on a survey of 4400 PR practitioners released by "pr reporter" newsletter, "Twentieth Annual Survey of the Profession," reported in *Marketing News*, December 21, 1984, p. 12.

something to be protected, but also as a valuable tool for opening up new o͵ tunities and guiding the marketing strategy, would do well not to totally abd͵ this important resource to a staff department.

Not Coordinating Internal Image Inputs

From the public image mix we know that a good many aspects of a firm's operation have at least the potential of affecting the firm's public image, for good or for bad. To protect or to build an image, all the various contributors should be in close communication and working with coordination. For example, a sales department's effectiveness is sure to be undermined if servicing of orders or quality control is deficient.

Kotler puts it this way: "Marketers typically think of their jobs as manipulating the 4 P's . . . This is the outside job of the marketer. But marketers also have an inside job to do. That is, they have to make other company departments marketing- and consumer-oriented."[12]

Now we will examine in considerable detail three examples of firms that had image problems, and did a poor—and in one case, even fatal—job of coping with them. There is a major learning experience in this: the importance of the public image should not be taken lightly.

For Thought and Discussion

1. "Good customer service doesn't do you much good, but poor customer service can kill you." Evaluate this statement.
2. Evaluate the effectiveness of advertising in enhancing the public image.
3. Give some specific examples of how a firm's public image is both affected by and affects the components of the marketing mix.
4. Discuss the pros and cons of having the public relations function under the control of the marketing department.

Invitation to Role Play

"Our public image is not very good," your boss confides to you one morning. "In a survey our marketing research department just finished, customers rated us below average in service. They also thought we were old-fashioned and not progressive."

"Our appliances still get good ratings for dependability, don't they?" you respond.

"Yes, but that's not enough today. I want you to have on my desk by next Monday a proposal I can present to the board of directors on some concrete ways to improve this image."

Prepare a program to improve the image of a small appliance manufacturer. Also point out what difficulties you would expect in making such an image change.

---

[12]"Kotler: Rethink . . ." p. 24.

3

Nestle's Infant Formula— The Consequences of Spurning the Public Image

When a firm is a huge international conglomerate, with diversifications into many product lines, bad publicity and negative public reactions about a single product seemingly should be no particular cause for alarm. The inclination is to ignore such a "minor" problem and it should go away.

But the expectations of Nestle went awry. The attitudes of the general public toward the firm continued to worsen, exacerbated certainly by a negative press and vocal protestors. Far from diminishing over a few weeks and a few months, the situation worsened over years. And far from affecting only the particular product involved—infant formula marketed to underdeveloped countries—other products and other divisions of the company became the object of virulent protests. Nestle had for too long ignored assaults on its public image, and now the road back to public acceptance was slow and rocky.

BACKGROUND

The Trouble Begins

By the early 1970s, suspicions were arising that powdered infant formula manufacturers were contributing to the high rate of infant mortality in less developed Third World countries by their aggressive marketing efforts directed to people unable to read the instructions or use the product properly due to their living conditions. The possible linkage between infant formulas and mortality through product misuse began to be discussed by medical professionals, industry representatives, and government officials at a number of international conferences. But public awareness of the problem had not surfaced as yet.

Then in 1974, a British charity organization, War on Want, published a 28-page pamphlet, *The Baby Killer*. In it, two multinationals, Nestle of Switzerland, and Unigate of Britain, were criticized as engaging in ill-advised marketing efforts in Africa. With the printing of this short publication, the general public became not only aware of the problem, but increasingly concerned.

This concern was to intensify less than a year later. A German-based Third World Working Group reissued a German translation of *The Baby Killer*, but with a few changes. While the British version criticized the entire infant formula industry, the German activists singled out Nestle for "unethical and immoral behavior" and retitled their version *Nestle Kills Babies*.

The accusation enraged executives at Nestle headquarters and they sued the activists for defamation. The trial lasted two years and focused worldwide attention on the issue. Though Nestle won the lawsuit, the court advised the firm to review its current marketing practices. "We won the legal case, but it was a public-relations disaster," one Nestle official admitted. The baby-killing accusation was a natural for antiwar groups and others looking for a cause. The company was dealing with the situation on a scientific and nutritional level, but the protestors were dealing on an emotional and political level.[1]

The Nestle Company

The Nestle Company, formally known as Nestle Alimentana, S.A., is headquartered in Vevey, Switzerland. It is a giant, worldwide corporation with sales of $12.5 billion in 1983. It owns or controls extensive interests in numerous companies of the food and cosmetics industries in various parts of the world. Products include instant drinks (coffee and tea), dairy products, cosmetics, frozen foods, chocolate, and pharmaceutical products. In addition it holds interests in catering services, as well as restaurant and hotel operations such as the Stouffer Corporation, which was acquired in 1973. By 1980, Nestle was marketing its products in Europe, Africa, North America, Latin America, the Caribbean, Asia, and Oceania. Its three top product groups were dairy products, instant drinks, and culinary/sundry products. Infant foods, including the controversial infant formula, and dietetic products accounted for considerably less than 10 percent of total conglomerate sales.

Nestle's appetite for acquisitions has continued unabated in recent years. In 1975 it purchased food processor Libby, McNeill & Libby. In 1979 it acquired Beech-Nut, the baby-food producer. Other purchases of note include CooperVision,

---

[1] "Infant Formula Protest Teaches Nestle a Tactical Lesson," *Marketing News,* June 10, 1983, p. 1.

a contact-lens maker; such well-known candy brands as Chunky, Bit-O-Honey, Raisinettes, Oh Henry, Goobers, and Sno Caps; and most recently Hills Bros. Coffee Company and Carnation.

The Infant Formula Industry

Nestle first developed and marketed a milk food used to nourish premature infants in 1867. This was in response to an urgent need of a premature infant who was unable to take any food. Borden also introduced a similar sweetened and condensed milk.

Infant formula foods are somewhat more recent, being developed in the early 1920s as an alternative to breast feeding. Infant formula is a specially prepared food for infants (under six months) and is based on cow's milk. It is scientifically formulated to approximate the most perfect of all infant foods, human breast milk. Today a number of different artificial milk products are available for infants, and these range in nutritional value from very high (humanized infant formula) to very low (various powdered, evaporated, and sweetened condensed milks).

Sales of infant formula had increased sharply after World War II and hit a peak in 1957, with 4.3 million births in developed countries. From this point on births started a decline that continued into the 1970s. The result was a steep downturn in baby formula sales and profits. Therefore, the industry began searching for new business. This was found in the Third World countries where the population was still increasing—the less developed countries of Africa, South America, and the Far East.

Total industry sales for infant formula alone, excluding all other commercial milk products, is about $1.5 billion. Of this, an estimated $600 million comes from the less developed countries. Hence, this market segment comprises a significant total market potential.

Nestle maintained a strong market share—some 40 to 50 percent of the Third World market for baby formula. Competitors included three U.S. firms, American Home Products, Bristol Myers, and Abbott Labs, which shared 20 percent of the market. Foreign firms accounted for the remainder. In 1981 the market was estimated to be growing at 15 to 20 percent per year.[2]

THE ISSUE: MISUSE OF THE PRODUCT, AND MARKETING PRACTICES

> If your lives were embittered as mine is, by seeing day after day this massacre of the innocents by unsuitable feeding, then I believe you would feel as I do that misguided

2Kurt Anderson, "The Battle of the Bottle," *Time*, June 1, 1981, p. 26.

propaganda on infant feeding should be punished as the most criminal form of sedition, and that these deaths should be regarded as murder.[3]

This lone indictment from a doctor back in 1939 evolved from a single cry into a crescendo of protest against the infant formula industry.

Incapability of the Market to Use the Product Correctly

A large number of Third World consumers live in poverty, have poor sanitation, receive inadequate health care, and are illiterate. Therefore, the misuse of the infant formula would seem inevitable. Water is obtained from polluted rivers or a common well and is brought back in contaminated containers. A refrigerator is considered a luxury item, and fuel is very expensive.

Consequently, the powdered formula may be mixed with contaminated water and put into unsterilized bottles and nipples. In addition, the mothers are tempted to dilute the formula with excess water so that it will last longer. An example was cited by one physician at a Jamaican hospital of the malnutrition of two exclusively bottle-fed siblings, 4 months and 18 months old, respectively. A can of formula would adequately feed a 4-month-old baby just under three days. However, this mother so diluted the formula as to feed the two infants for 14 days. This mother was poor and illiterate, had no running water or electricity, and had 12 other children.[4]

Studies have given three reasons for the trend to less nursing and more bottle feeding in the less developed countries.[5]

First, a changing sociocultural environment. This consists of urbanization, changing social mores, and increased mobility in employment. Infant formula was seen as representing social mobility and as a symbol of highly regarded modern products and medical expertise. The smiling white babies pictured on the fronts of formula tins suggested that rich white mothers feed their babies this product and that therefore it must be better. The high-income consumers in these less developed countries were the first to use infant formula in imitation of western practices. Bottle feeding was looked upon as a high-status practice, and the lower income groups readily followed along.

[3]As quoted in Cicely D. Williams, "The Marketing of Malnutrition," *Business and Society Review,* Spring 1980–81, p. 66.

[4]U.S. Congress, Senate, Committee on Human Resources, Subcommittee on Health and Scientific Research, *Marketing and Promotion of Infant Formula in the Developing Nations,* Hearing, 95th Congress, 2nd Session, May 23, 1978 (Washington, D.C.: Government Printing Office, 1978), p. 6.

[5]Prakash Sethi and James E. Post, "Public Consequences of Private Action: The Marketing of Infant Formula in Less Developed Countries," *California Management Review,* Summer 1979, pp. 35–48.

Second, the health care professional. Many hospitals and clinics endorsed the use of infant formula. A mother's first experience with a hospital may be to deliver a baby. Therefore, any products or gifts received there carry medical endorsement. Also, hospital practices are perceived as better and deserving of emulation. Babies are routinely separated from their mothers for 12 to 48 hours and are bottle fed whether or not the mothers plan to breast feed.

Third, the marketing and promotional practices of the infant formula manufacturers, which we will discuss shortly.

In 1951, approximately 80 percent of all 3-month-old babies in Singapore were being breast fed; by 1971, only 5 percent were. In 1966, 40 percent fewer mothers in Mexico nursed 6-month-old babies than had done so six years earlier. In Chile in 1973 there were three times as many deaths among infants who were bottle fed before 3 months of age than among wholly breast-fed infants. Other statistics of increased illnesses and higher death rates of bottle-fed infants were plentiful.[6]

Quality Control Problems

Nestle had some serious quality-control problems in its production of the formula in its far-flung plants:

In April 1977, the Colombian General Hospital encountered an increase in mortality in the premature ward. Bacteria were traced back to a Nestle factory, but 25 deaths occurred before the cause was found.

Also in 1977, the Australian Department of Health reported that 134 infants had fallen seriously ill as a result of being fed contaminated infant milk formulas produced by Nestle. Government officials estimated 20 million pounds of contaminated milk had been exported to the Southeast Asian countries.

The Australian story started in 1976. The Nestle Tongala plant noticed an increase in bacterial counts in samples of infant milk powder. Inspection revealed cracks in the spray dryer used to turn liquid milk into powder form. The bacteria were found to be a variant of salmonella that causes severe gastroenteritis. The State Health Department was not informed, and Nestle attempted sterilizing the equipment without halting production, but the bacteria continued to be discovered. The dryer was kept in operation for a full eight months after the contaminates were found.[7]

Perspective of Criticisms of Misuse

In fairness to Nestle, the critics who condemned the company and other infant food manufacturers for even attempting to market in the underdeveloped countries dis-

---

[6]For more such statistics, see Leah Margulies, "Bottle Babies: Death and Business Get Their Market," *Business and Society Review*, Spring 1978, pp. 43–49.

[7]Reported in Douglas Clement, "Nestle's Latest Killing in Bottle Baby Market," *Business and Society Review*, Summer 1978, pp. 60–64.

regarded any benefits of such products over the alternatives. The problem of water contamination also affects the alternatives to the commercial infant foods, which are various "native" cereal gruels of millet/rice used as weaning foods. The nutritional quality of these gruels tends to be low, and this deficiency is in addition to contamination of the water and containers used to cook the material. Furthermore, the millet/flour often has microbiological contamination. While it is true that infant formula mixed with contaminated water and containers presents dangers, the commercial formulas are more nutrituous than local foods and are closer to breast milk than native weaning foods and are therefore easier to digest. A further rebuttal to the critics is that not all people of the less developed countries face water contamination. Millions can safely mix powdered formula with local water without water contamination.[8]

Criticisms of Nestle's Marketing Practices

Nestle has undoubtedly been an aggressive marketer in many Third World countries. Its promotional efforts have been directed to physicians and other medical personnel as well as consumers. Direct consumer promotion of infant formula has taken many forms. Media have included radio, newspapers, magazines, and billboards—and even vans with loudspeakers have been used. It has widely distributed free samples, bottles, nipples, and measuring spoons. In some countries direct customer contacts have been made through "milk nurses," who have been the subject of particular criticism.

Nestle employed about 200 women who were registered nurses, nutritionists, or midwives. These professionals were often nicknamed "milk nurses." Critics maintained that these milk nurses were actually sales personnel in disguise who visited mothers and gave product samples in an attempt to persuade mothers to stop breast feeding. With their uniforms giving them great credibility, this practice was condemned as being too persuasive for naive consumers.

Promotion to physicians and other medical personnel has also been controversial. This type of promotion has generally involved the use of detail people who discuss product quality and characteristics with pediatricians, pediatric nurses, and other related medical personnel. (The use of detail people, who are a type of missionary sales representative, is common practice, as we will describe in the accompanying "Information Sidelight.") Materials such as posters, charts, and free samples were made available to physicians, hospitals, and clinics without charge. Physicians and other hospital personnel have also received company-sponsored travel to medical meetings.

Critics felt that the promotion of infant formula had been too aggressive and had contributed to the decline in breast feeding. Despite increased criticisms, how-

[8]John Sparks, "The Nestle Controversy—Anatomy of a Boycott," Public Policy Education Fund, Inc., June 1981.

INFORMATION SIDELIGHT

THE USE OF MISSIONARY SALESPEOPLE (DETAIL PEOPLE)

Missionary salespeople—these are called detail people in the drug industry—
are commonly used by many firms to provide specialized services and cultivate
customer goodwill. They generally do not try to secure orders.

Missionary salespeople are employed by manufacturers to work with their
dealers. They may put up point-of-purchase displays, train dealer salespeople,
provide better communication between distributor and manufacturer, and in general try to have their brand more aggressively promoted by the dealer. In the drug
industry the detail people leave samples, and explain research information about
new products to the medical professionals so as to encourage prescriptions and
recommendations for their brands.

---

ever, sales of infant formula in poor countries continued to escalate. It had become
the third most advertised product in the Third World, after tobacco and soap. And it
was generally recognized that new mothers in such countries were most susceptible
to advertising. A 1969 study of 120 mothers in Barbados found that 82 percent of
the ones given free samples later purchased the same brand—this, whether the
samples were received from the hospital or at home.[9]

In summary, the criticisms of promotional practices were:

- Bottle feeding contributes to infant mortality in less developed countries.
- Baby booklets ignore or de-emphasize breast feeding.
- Media promotions are misleading in encouraging poor and illiterate moth-
  ers to bottle feed rather than breast feed their infants.
- Advertising portrays breast feeding as primitive and inconvenient.
- Free gifts and samples are direct inducement to bottle feed infants.
- Posters and pamphlets in hospitals, and milk nurses are viewed as "en-
  dorsement by association," or "manipulation by assistance."
- The prices of formulas at the milk banks are still too expensive for many
  consumers who are tempted then to dilute the formula.

THE SITUATION WORSENS FOR NESTLE

With the publication of the two articles, *The Baby Killer* and *Nestle Kills Babies*,
and the subsequent lawsuit by Nestle which received worldwide publicity, two
groups were formed and solidified their opposition that was eventually to lead to the

---

[9]Reported in "A Boycott Over Infant Formula," *Business Week*, April 23, 1979, pp. 137–140.

boycotting of Nestle products and services: The Interfaith Center on Corporate Responsibility, and the Infant Formula Action Coalition (INFACT).

Since the early 1970s, various agencies had been trying to reduce the promotion and advertising practices of the infant formula companies. These agencies included the Protein Advisory Group in 1970 and 1973, the World Health Assembly in 1974, and the World Health Organization (WHO) in 1978.

As a by-product of the growing condemnation of the industry, Nestle and other firms began to make some changes in their promotional practices, at least on paper. The changes were brought about through the auspices of the International Council of Infant Food Industries (ICIFI), which was formed in 1975 by nine infant food manufacturers, including Nestle. The changes included: product information would always recognize breast milk as best; infant formulas would be advertised as supplementary, and that professional advice should be sought; and nurse uniforms would be worn only by professional nurses.

But the self-regulation apparently did not work sufficiently to allay the criticisms. Documentation by the International Baby Food Action Network confirmed over 1000 violations of the "code" since 1977. Some critics compared "asking for self regulation was like asking Colonel Sanders to babysit your chickens."[10]

With continued reported violations, a boycott was organized in the United States in July 1977, and soon spread to nine other countries. It was to last until January 26, 1982 in the United States and Canada, with other countries following suit over the next two years.

Nestle was singled out as the sole object of the boycott due to its 50 percent worldwide market share along with the adverse publicity that had centered on it more than other firms who were engaged in the same marketing practices.

The demands of INFACT and the boycotters were:

1. Stop altogether the use of milk nurses.
2. Stop distributing all free samples.
3. Stop promoting infant formula to the health care industry.
4. Stop consumer promotion and advertising of infant formula.

The boycott soon had the support of over 450 local and religious groups across America, and proponents claimed it was the largest non-union boycott in U.S. history. Boycott activity was strongest in Boston, Baltimore, and Chicago, where INFACT established an office with five full-time staffers. Thousands of signatures were gathered on various petitions urging removal of Nestle products from supermarket shelves. Some grocers acquiesced, agreeing to remove such products as Taster's Choice from their shelves. The boycott also hit college campuses. With the slogan, "Crunch Nestle," boycotts were encouraged on products ranging from milk chocolate to tea, coffee, and hot chocolate. The college boycott reportedly

---

[10]"Killer in a Bottle," *The Economist*, May 9, 1981, p. 50; and Douglas Clement, pp. 60–64.

began at Wellesley College and soon spread to others, such as Colgate, Yale, and the University of Minnesota.

This boycotting undoubtedly was effective, not only directly in causing lost business and profits for the company, but also indirectly in crystallizing public opinion against the company, and in invoking governmental response. For example:

The government of New Guinea enacted stringest laws to curb the artificial feeding of babies in the summer of 1979. Bottles and nipples now could only be obtained by prescription. Other countries also began introducing legislation to reduce the marketing and advertising of breast-milk substitutes.

The World Health Organization (WHO) in May 1981 adopted a restrictive ad code that applied only to the infant food industry. A portion of Article 5 of the code states, "There shall be no advertising or other forms of promotion to the general public of products within the scope of this code."[11] The products covered were infant food formulas and other weaning foods.

The European Parliament in France voted overwhelmingly for strict enforcement of the WHO code throughout the 10-nation Common Market. The European Parliament also placed responsibility on common market firms for the actions of their subsidiaries abroad in observing the WHO code.

NESTLE FIGHTS BACK

Nestle's first efforts to combat vituperative accusations resulted in more harm than good, as we have seen. As its public image continued to worsen, the worldwide boycott finally surfaced in 1977. Now Nestle could no longer ignore the protests and hope they would go away. Obviously they were not going to go away. Initial strategy at this point was to treat the boycott and widespread protests as a public relations problem. The public relations department of the firm was upgraded into the Office of Corporate Responsibility. The world's largest public relations firm, Hill & Knowlton, was hired to assist. Over 300,000 packets of information were mailed by Nestle to U.S. clergymen, informing them that they were wrong in their denunciations of Nestle. Finally, Daniel J. Edelmon, a renowned public relations specialist, was hired. He advised the company to keep a low profile and to try to get third-party endorsements of its actions.

Finally, in 1981, after failing to improve its image and mute the critical cries against it, Nestle dismissed its two public relations firms and took on itself the task of reestablishing its reputation. Ignoring the situation had not helped; public outcries, rather than lessening, had increased. And efforts to angrily denounce the

---

[11]"World Health Organization Drafts Restrictive Ad Code," *Editor & Publisher,* April 11, 1981, p. 8.

critics had only exacerbated the situation. Now the firm was ready to try a new tack in efforts to establish its credibility as a humane and responsible corporate citizen.

One of the first steps was to endorse the World Health Organization's Code of Marketing for Breast Milk Substitutes—a step three other U.S. manufacturers did not make until two years later. The code, which imposed only voluntary compliance, banned advertising to the general public, as well as distribution of samples to mothers.

Next, Nestle sought an ethical group to work with in vouching for its compliance with the code, and found it in the Methodist Task Force on Infant Formula.

Nestle's relations with the press had been abysmal. For example, in the first six months of 1981, the *Washington Post* published 91 articles critical of Nestle. In the company's multifaceted attempt to rebuild its image, the policy dealing with the media was changed to an "open-door, candid approach."[12]

The most effective restorative strategy finally adopted was the establishment of a 10-member panel of medical experts, clergy, civic leaders, and experts in international policy to publicly monitor Nestle's compliance with the WHO code and to investigate complaints against its marketing practices. This Nestle Infant Formula Audit Commission (NIFAC) gained credibility with the acceptance of the chairmanship by Edmund S. Muskie, former Secretary of State, vice-presidential candidate, and Democratic senator from Maine. The Commission was established in May 1982.

This so-called Muskie Commission worked with representatives of WHO, International Nestle Boycott Committee (INBC), and UNICEF to resolve conflicts in four areas of the WHO code. Points of contention were educational materials, labels, gifts to medical and health professionals, and free or subsidized supplies to hospitals. These were resolved, and Nestle agreed that, on educational material it intended to distribute, the social and health aspects of formula vs. breast feeding would be addressed. Its infant formula labels would clearly state the dangers of using contaminated water and the superiority of mother's milk. Personal gifts to health officials (which smacked of bribery and seeking of preferential treatment) were banned. Finally, free samples of formula distributed to hospitals were to be limited to supplies that would go to mothers incapable of breast feeding their children.

At last, after years of an adversarial posture, which had only resulted in a growing crescendo of criticisms and boycotts, with bitter accusations that the company was causing the deaths of millions of Third World babies because of its marketing practices, the situation was improving. "We have all learned a lesson . . . ," said Rafael D. Pagan, Jr., president of the Nestle Coordination Center for Nutrition. "Companies should be sensitive and listen carefully to what con-

[12]"Fighting a Boycott," *Industry Week*, January 23, 1984, p. 54.

**Table 3.1   Nestle Sales and Profits, 1974–1980
(In Thousands of Swiss Francs)**

Years	Sales	Profits
1974	16,624,000	742,000
1975	18,286,000	799,000
1976	19,063,000	872,000
1977	20,095,000	830,000
1978	20,266,000	739,000
1979	21,639,000	816,000
1980	24,479,000	638,000

Sources: Company annual reports.

sumers and members of the general public are saying. When problems surface, they should seek a dialogue with responsible leaders and try to work out the problems together."[13]

After a decade of confrontation with protestors and seven years of boycotting, early in 1984 most groups agreed to a suspension of their boycott. While some diehards refused to accept the conciliatory efforts of Nestle, several large groups— for example, the American Federation of Teachers, the American Federation of Churches, the Federation of Nurses & Health Professionals, the United Methodist Church, and the Church of the Brethren—had either withdrawn from the boycott or decided not to join it.

The company admitted, however, that perhaps 20 obdurate boycott leaders and 50,000 followers in the U.S. may never stop ostracizing the company no matter what Nestle does.[14]

The results in lost business for Nestle from the infant food controversy are difficult to pinpoint. Company estimates ranged up to $40 million in lost profits as direct results of the boycotts. However, lost business was probably far greater than this, with some coming in the years before the boycotts began as consumers turned to alternative brands from firms with better reputations. Even during the years of boycotts, not all consumers were militant protestors; but they could certainly take their business elsewhere, as sort of a silent protest. Admittedly, infant food business accounted for only 3 percent of total Nestle sales worldwide. But other Nestle products were blackened to an unknown degree by the destroyed public image of this one minor part of the total business. One of the most obvious negative consequences of the boycotts was the loss of meetings and convention business at Stouffer facilities, with some planners opting to schedule at other locations as a means of avoiding any association with negative publicity.

[13]"Nestle Gains Formula Accord: Product Boycott is Suspended," *Marketing News*, February 17, 1984, p. 5.
[14]"Fighting a Boycott," p. 55.

Table 3.1 shows the sales and profits for the Nestle conglomerate during some of these years. It shows profits declining from the years before the protests had become so pronounced. But we really cannot measure how much is the direct effect of the confrontation; more important, we can only guess at the extent of unrealized potential.

WHAT CAN BE LEARNED?

The Nestle debacle should be sobering for many firms. It should raise some real concerns about the possibility of damage to the public image, damage that can be difficult to rebuild. Specifically, these are major points to be learned from this experience:

- The vulnerability of the public image. A reputable image, or at least one that is neutral and not negative, can be quickly besmirched. A firm should not underestimate the power of social awareness and activist groups. Furthermore, the large firm is the most vulnerable—even if other firms in the industry are engaged in the same practices—and is the most desirable target for activist groups. Size brings with it greater visibility and public recognition than is the case with smaller competitors. This makes the larger firm the target of choice: to bring down the giant. And public sentiment—whether on the athletic field, in business, or wherever—is not on the side of the big and powerful.
- The power of a hostile press. A bad press can both arouse and intensify negative public opinion. It can fan the flames. A firm cannot plan on the press being objective and unbiased in such reporting. The press tends to be eager to find a "fault object," and when this is a large and rather impersonal firm, the likelihood is all the greater that bad actions or the negatives of a particular situation will be emphasized far more than the positive and helpful side of the issue. While infant formulas had many benefits and were a very positive health influence in many situations, still, publicity focused almost exclusively on alleged marketing abuses and customer misuses.
- The longevity of a besmirched reputation. Nestle's expectations that the controversy would die out were certainly squashed by the duration and increasing virulence of the protest movement. Without constructive efforts by Nestle in the early 1980s, the gathering strength of the protest movement probably would have resulted in ever-greater boycotting, and most likely in restrictive legislation by many countries. Thus, a tarnished reputation is not suddenly going to become bright and shiny just because of the passage of time. Some sort of strong positive efforts must be made by the firm to try to restore its image, or it will not be improved.
- Public relations deficiencies. Public relations is not the answer when certain

aspects of a firm's operation are the focal points of criticism. The act must be cleared up first. The public relations efforts of Nestle were notoriously impotent, despite hiring two of the largest and most expensive public relations firms in the world. Without improving the operations under question, no amount of public relations statements—even mailing to clergy some 300,000 pamphlets propagandizing Nestle's position—is likely to produce positive and lasting results.

- The potential of marketing efforts to impact on the public image. We maintain that marketing inputs (see Figure 2.3 in Chapter 2) have the greatest potential for affecting the public image, positively or negatively. Here, all the problems of Nestle emanated from its marketing efforts in the Third World countries. Normally such marketing efforts would be viewed as effective; under different circumstances they could well have been lauded as models for the effective use of marketing for a new and improved product. Alas, of course, the marketing efforts were seen as far too effective—too aggressive in swaying a naive population in not wholly desirable directions. A firm's marketing efforts are the most visible aspects of its operation. This visibility can be a curse sometimes, as it was with Nestle. The caveat is to consider marketing efforts as part of the important public image mix, and be guided accordingly.

Suggested Reactions with a Darkening Public Image

The Nestle example gives us helpful insights as to how best react to smears and protests. Ignoring the problem seems ill-advised, if the protests are severe enough and if the issue is inflammatory enough. And certainly alleged culpable loss of life—whether from chemical dumps or spills, or from the ill-advised use of infant formula—is usually inflammatory enough.

Direct confrontation and an adversarial stand is seldom effective either. As Nestle found out the hard way, its court case, even though won by Nestle, only increased the negative publicity and fueled the protestations. Even if the weight of evidence is on the firm's side, the propaganda and one-sided criticisms of the opposition will likely win over the general public.

So it seems more prudent for the firm that unwittingly falls into the snare of public image problems regarding its social role to approach the situation with a spirit of cooperation and constructive participation with opposing groups, despite some diehard activists who may refuse all efforts at conciliation. We cannot fault the efforts of Nestle in 1981–1983 in working with the more reasonable critics. But we can severely fault the company for waiting so long to take such constructive actions.

Many firms need a greater sensitivity to potential problem areas involving corporate social performance. They need to try to anticipate potential problems and nip them quickly. Failing this, an organization should strive to resolve as many of the objections as it can—even if this means assuming the burden of an inequitable compromise position. The consequence otherwise may be a gradually deteriorating image problem, even if the negative public perceptions are not fully based on facts.

A firm doing business in sensitive areas needs to prove that it is a responsible corporate citizen and not an insensitive giant organization. More attention to the public image mix may well prevent the type of image problems that bedeviled Nestle for years.

ADDENDUM: ANOTHER NESTLE SCANDAL

On February 17, 1988, two former top executives of the Beech-Nut Nutrition Corporation were found quilty of violating federal laws by intentionally marketing phony apple juice intended for babies.

The previous November, the company itself pleaded quilty to 215 felony counts and admitted to willful violations of the food and drug laws by selling adulterated apple products from 1981 to 1983. While the apple juice, the best-selling product of Beech-Nut, was labeled "100% fruit juice," it was actually a blend of synthetic ingredients, a "100% fraudulent chemical cocktail," as one interviewer testified.[15]

Beech-Nut is the second largest U.S. baby food manufacturer and is a subsidiary of Nestle, which acquired it in 1979. The company was founded in 1891, and had always stressed purity, high quality, and natural ingredients in its marketing programs and company philosophy.

How could such a reputable company have strayed so far from its reputation and, indeed, its heritage?

Background. In 1977, Beech-Nut signed an agreement to buy apple concentrate from Interjuice Trading Corporation, a wholesaler whose prices were about 20 percent below the market. Such a low price should have aroused suspicions of adulteration, and it did. Beech-Nut chemists concluded that the Interjuice product was probably extensively adulterated, and maybe even entirely ersatz. In 1978, several Beech-Nut employees were sent to inspect Interjuice's plant, but were not given access to all the facilities, and in particular, the concentrate processing unit. Some years later suspicions were verified that this was a huge national bogus concentrate operation. And Beech-Nut was by far its biggest customer.

While the scientists urged the company to stop buying from Interjuice, top Beech-Nut executives demurred. The company was on the verge of bankruptcy. Products containing apple concentrate accounted for 30 percent of Beech-Nut's sales, and the savings from the cheap concentrate were helping to keep the company alive.

15"What Led Beech-Nut Down the Road to Disgrace," *Business Week*, February 22, 1988, p. 124.

After a desperate search for a buyer, the company was sold to Nestle in 1979 for $35 million. Nestle invested an additional $60 million, and hiked marketing budgets, but the losses continued.

In early 1981, Jerome LiCari, director of research and development, mounted a major effort to improve adulteration testing. By August, he and his fellow scientists believed they had an irrefutable case against their supplier. But their concerns were ignored, and LiCari was even threatened with termination by John Lavery, the chief of operations. LiCari then went to company headquarters and met with the president, Neils Hoyvald, but still no action was taken.

Matters came to a head in June 1982 when a private investigator, hired by apple processors, offered conclusive proof of the bogus concentrate, and asked Beech-Nut to join other juicemakers in a lawsuit against the supplier. But Beech-Nut refused, and continued selling products made from the phony concentrate for months despite warnings by the Food and Drug Administration and the New York State Agriculture Department. The company was later charged with stalling the investigation until it could unload its $3.5 million inventory of tainted apple juice products.

Nestle lawyers vigorously defended Neils Hoyvald and John Lavery, hoping to remove some of the onus of the corporate guilty plea in November, but the efforts failed.

Consequences. The lawsuit and scandal cost Beech-Nut an estimated $25 million in fines, legal costs, and slumping sales. Negative publicity led to market share dropping about 20 percent in 1987, and new record losses resulted for the year.

Fortunately for Nestle, most of the bad publicity focused on Beech-Nut, and not on Nestle as the parent company. None of the legal action involved Nestle or Nestle executives. But, of course, the profit travails of a subsidiary impact on the parent. And Nestle executives must have shuddered at the possibility of its involvement with adulterated apple juice being publicized and related to the infant formula scandal.

Analysis. In probing into what led to this blatant disregard for ethical and even legal considerations and, of course, the public image consequences, we need to determine just what could have led responsible executives to this pathway of destruction. Were they honorable men? There is no evidence that they were not. They were hardly hardened and conscienceless individuals pursuing a program for personal gain. Why then?

We are forced to conclude that unethical and illegal acts can be undertaken by essentially honest and well-respected individuals. This defies our darker musings, but it is true. Here we have a company in serious financial straits. The opportunity is presented to save millions of dollars in adulterated ingredients that would not easily be detected. What a temptation! Health and consumer safety apparently was not a major consideration here: the adulterated ingredients were hardly life-threatening—

just dishonestly promoted. So, if we have a little cheating, how bad is this, really? Such could well have been the reasoning of the executives involved.

In situations like this, it is easy to rationalize. Another flawed rationalization is that there was no good, solid proof that the concentrate was not authentic. Lacking this, why should we suspect the worst? But the clues were there for any objective observer:

- 20 percent lower cost than any alternatives—how would this be, without something amiss?
- The lack of full disclosure by the supplier.
- The almost certain proof of adulteration by the Beech-Nut research and development department.

The defense maintained that positive proof was lacking that the concentrate was bogus. But should not a grave suspicion require further intense investigation? A laissez-faire or hands-off policy by top management of a serious charge—especially when millions of dollars of inventory are involved, suggesting a conflict of interest—can hardly be condoned.

So, the public image can be vulnerable—and should be vulnerable—to less than ethical practices, whether they directly impinge on public health and welfare, as did the infant formula, or whether they involve "merely" a major misrepresentation.

For Thought and Discussion

1. Faced with activist protestors, do you think a firm has any recourse but to yield to their complete demands? Is there any room for an aggressive stance?
2. Could the public relations efforts of Nestle have been used more effectively?
3. Do you think Nestle was unfairly picked on? Why or why not?

Invitation to Role Play

1. As the staff assistant to the CEO of Nestle, you have been asked to develop a position paper as to the desirability of withdrawing infant formula from the market in Third World countries. Discuss the pros and cons of such a move, and then make your recommendations and support them as persuasively as you can.
2. You are the manager of a Stouffer hotel. A delegation of clergy and lay people have approached you with the threat of boycotting your premises. Be as persuasive as you can in trying to dissuade them from doing so.
3. As the research director of Beech-Nut, Mr. LiCari, upon the lack of receptivity of top management, did you have any other recourse?

4

Coors—A Great Image Can Fade

A tragedy occurred in the winter of 1960 that was to have an impact on the fortunes of the Adolph Coors Company, brewers, some 15 years later. On the morning of February 9, Adolph Coors III, 44-year-old chairman of the board of the brewing empire, kissed his wife and four children goodbye, and drove off to the plant 12 miles away. He was never seen again, alive.

For months, one of the most intensive manhunts in Colorado history took place. Finally, on September 26, more than seven months later, tattered clothing and scattered bones were accidentially discovered in a desolate, heavily wooded area of aspen and pine about 40 miles southeast of Denver. Apparently, after the body had been dumped, the remains were scattered by coyotes or hogs. Dental charts confirmed the identification of Coors.

THE GOLDEN YEARS

Adolph Coors III had been sharing leadership responsibilities with his father, Adolph Coors II. After the murder, the father again assumed the sole leadership mantle even though his official title was treasurer, until he died in 1970 at the age of 86. The elder of Adolph Coors III's two surviving sons, William H. Coors, was the chairman and chief executive; the other son, Joseph, was president. There were no formal lines of authority, although Bill generally handled the technical side of brewing and Joe the financial and administrative functions.

Both Bill and Joe (employees called them by their first names) were lean and tall, and rugged outdoorsmen. In fact, they regarded physical fitness and athletic recreation as so important for their employees that executives and workers were sent to outdoor-survival schools. Golf was subsidized for employees. Ski trips were underwritten. But Bill and Joe were concerned with more than the therapeutic benefits of fresh air for their employees: they insisted that employees must not only participate in these programs but also must compete. "If you can't fight competition, you don't need to survive," Bill Coors asserts.[1]

Sensational Growth

By 1970, the accomplishments of Coors in the brewing industry were awesome— all the more so in light of the nonconformity of Coors to existing industry practices. The company produced only one kind of beer, and this in a single brewery, albeit the largest in the world. It sold its beer in only 11 Western states, most of these the most sparsely populated areas of the United States. It refused to build branch plants, and had not expanded its territory in 22 years. The one brewery in Golden, Colorado, was not even close to its biggest market, California—indeed, the average barrel of Coors traveled over 900 miles. Finally, its ads featuring rushing mountain streams, and the slogan, "Brewed with pure Rocky Mountain spring water," had not been changed in 33 years.

Yet, this little regional brewery of Bill and Joe Coors had moved up to the big time. With a 19 percent increase in production in 1969 over 1968, it moved into fourth place in the national beer rankings, the only regional brewer to come close to the national brewers. In 1969, the production of the top four breweries was as follows:

Anheuser–Busch	18.8 million barrels
Joseph Schlitz	13.7 million
Pabst	10.2 million
Coors	6.4 million

Furthermore, in nine of the eleven states where it had distribution, Coors topped all other brands in sales. Among the full eleven states, the market share of Coors was 30 percent. In California, by 1973 it had 41 percent of the market, compared with only 18 percent for the industry leader, Anheuser–Busch; in Oklahoma almost 70 percent of all the beer sold was Coors. Overall demand was so outstripping supply that the company was forced to ration its product among distributors.

---

[1]"Colorado's Coors Family Has Built an Empire on One Brand of Beer," *Wall Street Journal,* October 26, 1973, p. 1.

INFORMATION SIDELIGHT

THE MARKETING CONCEPT

A marketing orientation, commonly known as the marketing concept, is a well-known philosophy of marketing—almost every basic marketing text devotes an early chapter to this. Yet many firms still disregard it—as Coors did for most of its corporate life—in the belief that their products will sell themselves. For a wanted product of exceptional quality that is unique from competing products, such a production orientation may succeed, for a while. But competitively, the firm having the marketing concept will usually win out over the longer period.

We can define the marketing concept or orientation as:

An integration of marketing activities directed toward customer satisfaction.

Essentially this is a change in emphasis within a firm to a customer-oriented type of thinking: finding out consumers' needs and preferences, how these might be changing, how they can be better served. The marketing concept has these basic components:

1. Customer orientation
2. Integrated marketing
3. Marketing research
4. Long-range planning and new-product development

Organizational realignment has sometimes been the most tangible evidence that a firm has adopted the concept. All business functions related to marketing—e.g., sales, advertising, product planning, physical distribution—are integrated under a top marketing executive for coordination and a unified objective. A consumer orientation almost necessitates marketing research in order to keep up with customers' wants, attitudes, and buying patterns. A more formal role for long-range planning is also needed to coordinate a firm's efforts as well as to pursue a vigorous program of new-product development.

In compiling this performance record, the brothers eschewed a marketing orientation. Bill Coors stated this succinctly: "Our top managementthrust is on engineering and production . . . we're production-oriented. Nobody knows more about production than I do."[2] Emphasis was on making a quality beer in terms of

[2]"The Brewery That Breaks All the Rules," *Business Week*, August 22, 1970, p. 60.

processing and raw materials. The product was a mild, light-bodied beer, scientifically tested and brewed, using hops, rice, Rocky Mountain spring water, and a specially developed strain of barley grown by contract farmers. Great pains were taken to preserve the flavor. Pasteurization, which would add greatly to the ease of preserving, was shunned, since it would slightly affect the taste. Eliminating pasteurization greatly increased the logistical problems. The beer had to be canned at near-freezing temperatures and shipped under refrigeration to refrigerated warehouses—otherwise, the natural taste could not be maintained. To further assure perfection of taste, distributors were required to pull Coors cans off the shelves in 30 days, lest there be some fading of the flavor.

Coors had become the beer of celebrities; from President Ford, who packed Coors on Air Force One, to Henry Kissinger, as well as such actors as Paul Newman (who in an *Esquire* interview claimed, "The best domestic beer, bar none, is Coors") and Clint Eastwood. In these years, the famous, as well as the rank and file, all were contributing to the Coors "mystique." Some 300,000 Coors fans a year toured the brewery; others made "pilgrimages" to a waterfall near Grand Lake, Colorado, which was supposed to be the one pictured on Coors bottles and cans. T-shirts and sweatshirts emblazoned with "Coors—Breakfast of Champions" were being sold by entrepreneurs hoping to cash in on the Coors mystique. And in the East, where Coors was not directly distributed, it could sell for three times the regular price.

Besides the product, the company was unique from the rest of the industry in certain other respects. In the heady years of the 1960s and early 1970s, Bill and Joe shunned outside expertise. Advertising and promotion were handled by inside staff, and total expenditures averaged only one-quarter those of major competitors. Construction at the brewery was done by Coors' own construction crews. Company engineers designed machinery for the can plant. Management talent was developed and promoted from within the organization, rather than brought in from outside.

The guiding philosophy of the company since it was founded by a German orphan who stowed away on a U.S.-bound ship to avoid conscription into the German army—the first Adolph Coors, in 1873—was to refuse to go to a bank for a loan. Such fiscal conservatism led the company to reject some seemingly attractive expansion possibilities. For example, the company's can-manufacturing subsidiary, Coors Container Company, was instrumental in developing the technical process for making a two-piece aluminum can. Coors, however, sold the process to Continental Can Company and American Can Company: "We could have dominated the industry, but we would have had to borrow from the banks, and Coors doesn't do that."[3] Between 1970 and 1974, in order to keep up with the burgeoning demand for Coors beer, some $276 million was spent on plant expansion. And how was this financed? All of it from cash flow.

[3]"Colorado's Coors Family," p. 27.

How Come the Mystique?

What was the magic of Coors? How durable was this magic or mystique likely to be? Perhaps part of the mystique was accidental and fortuitous: being a Western-made brew at a time when the freedom and environmental purity of the West—emphasized by Coors' slogan, "Pure Rocky Mountain Spring Water"—was seen by many consumers as contrasting sharply with the degradation of the industrial centers of population. But was it a better beer—better tasting, higher quality? There were many who said it was. Whether real or imagined, Coors offered a "unique selling proposition" that distinguished it from other beers. One could claim that coming from a single brewery insured better quality control and uniformity of ingredients and flavor. The company liked to boast that Coors was the most expensively brewed beer in the world, even though it sold in the popular price range. A plant geneticist was employed full-time to develop improved strains of barley for malting. Most hops were imported from Germany. And, as noted before, great pains were taken to prevent any deterioration of the flavor in shipping and handling.

Undoubtedly, part of the mystique came from the contagion generated by the aficionados, those famous and not so famous. A Western image conveying the out-of-doors and environmental purity, a light-tasting beer—perhaps the timing would not have been better in the 1960s and early 1970s. (In the cigarette industry, Marlboro rose to become the top seller on a somewhat similar advertising and image thrust: the Marlboro man.)

It hardly seemed to Bill and Joe that the golden image of their beer could in the span of just a few years fade drastically. How could it help but be enduring?

Going Public

For 103 years, ever since the first Adolph Coors opened his brewery on the trail to the Colorado gold camps, the company stayed private—talks of having public or outside shareholders were anathema to the Coors family. And it seemed that the company could indeed finance large-scale capital expenditures internally. Throughout the decade of the 1960s its average rate of growth was over 10 percent, all this without turning to outside stock ownership or borrowing. In 1975, Coors had only $2 million in long-term debt on its books, against $375 million in equity.

But in 1975 the proud family tradition had to be abandoned. With the death of the parents of Bill and Joe, the Internal Revenue Service presented a bill for $50 million in inheritance taxes. While many companies would have solved such a problem by going into debt, Bill and Joe decided to go public as the lesser of two evils. In order not to risk relinquishing control of the company to outsiders, they would offer only nonvoting shares. Furthermore, to avoid diluting the equity, no more than 5 percent of net income would be paid as dividends.

The time for such a stock offering was not very propitious. The Dow Jones

Industrial Average was then moving between 620 and 690, and many were the investors who thought it would go still lower. Added to a sick stock market, the restrictions placed on this new stock venture were hardly likely to appeal to many investors. Since the shares would be nonvoting, this precluded listing on the New York Stock Exchange, as well as sale in many states, including California, where Coors' stock could otherwise have had a warm reception. The nonvoting feature would also make the stock offering unattractive to many large institutional investors.

In the end, Coors lucked out. When the offering finally reached the market, the stock market was beginning to rebound. Coors' investment bankers found so much interest in the stock in the last days before the offering that they raised the price to $31 a share. And it was a sellout the first afternoon. Not only was the $50 million raised to pay off the inheritance taxes, but an additional $77 million went into the company coffers. This $127 million offering was the first major new stock issue to come to market since 1973 and the fourth largest offering by industrial companies in the previous 10 years. The mystique of the company and its beer mitigated all the negative factors impinging on demand.

Geographical Expansion

Now Bill Coors turned his attention to geographical expansion. The first target was eastern and southern Texas. Prior to this the only Texas inroads were in the northern part of the state around Dallas, and the western part.

Eager to jump on a lucrative bandwagon, potential distributors lined up like beauty queen candidates, vying for selection by Coors. The contest, however, was hardly for the weak or poorly financed, since Coors' distributors had to build refrigerated warehouses so that Coors' unpasteurized beer could be kept under 40 degrees until opened by customers. From 4000 "panting" contestants, Coors selected 29 distributors for the eastern Texas expansion.

By 1976, Coors was also invading Montana, and looking closely at expanding into Washington state, Arkansas, Nebraska, and Missouri, the latter state being the home base of Anheuser–Busch, the largest brewer. Bill Coors was also laying plans for expanding to the heavily populated Eastern market: "I think we've got a good enough beer—the beer that won the West—to assure ourselves 20 percent to 25 percent of the nationwide market," he told *Forbes'* reporters in the summer of 1976.[4] A bold statement this, with Anheuser holding 24 percent of the total market, while Coors had only 8.2 percent, although admittedly on far less than national distribution, in fact on only 20 percent of the total national distribution.

The question of whether expansion could still be handled out of the one brewery in Golden seemed not particularly troublesome to Bill. While the Golden

4"Off Coors," *Forbes*, June 1, 1976, p. 60.

brewery was already at an annual capacity of 12.3 million barrels, about one million barrels of capacity was being added a year, and Bill was aiming for a total of 25 million. "Eventually we might build other breweries," he said. "But if you take a circle up around from where we already ship to in Northern California, you hit Atlanta, Georgia."[5]

The growth and profitability picture—and the highly successful public stock offering—should have been cause for heady optimism and great satisfaction for the Coors brothers. Sales for 1975 were $520 million, up from $350 million just four years before. Operating margin on net sales had reached 28 percent, the highest in the industry. Profit per barrel averaged almost $9, about double that of Anheuser. But there were some ominous portents on the horizon.

STORM SIGNALS FOR COORS, 1975–1976

While the successful public stock float spurred new ambitions, trouble was brewing in the California market—a key market that accounted for almost 40 percent of all Coors' sales. In a bitter dispute with Coors' Oakland distributor, the California Teamsters called for a statewide boycott of the beer. At the same time, Anheuser was bringing on line a new 3.75-million-barrel brewery in northern California. As a result, in this key market, Coors' sales dropped about 10 percent in 1975, while market share fell 4 percent to 36 percent. Anheuser picked up most of this, gaining 3 percent to a 23.2 percent share of the California market. Perhaps another contributor to the market share losses in California was a hefty price hike made in 1974 without first warning retailers.

Several other aggravations were also being encountered. The Federal Trade Commission in January 1975 was upheld by the Supreme Court in its efforts to loosen the tight grip Coors had held on its 167 distributors. Then the Equal Opportunities Commission filed a suit against Coors alleging discrimination against minorities in hiring and in promotions. And the Colorado Health Department charged Coors with polluting Clear Creek, in the very same valley where the "Rocky Mountain Spring Water" rises.

Finally, brother Joe was embarrassed as the Senate Commerce Committee vetoed his nomination to the board of the Corporation for Public Broadcasting, citing Coors' ownership of a right-wing television news service as a conflict of interest. Joe had long been known locally as an arch-conservative, but his political views came to national attention in 1975 when the *Washington Post* ran four lengthy stories about his right-wing efforts in allegedly using Television News, Inc., a broadcast news agency subsidiary of the Coors Company, to further his own political views. This publicity, as well as the fact that the news subsidiary was losing

[5]Ibid., p. 61.

money, induced the company to close down the TV news service. Whatever negative effect might have emanated from the hardly favorable publicity could not be gauged.

Some dangers could be seen in the decision to push East, even though such a move, if successful, would greatly increase the sales of Coors as well as lessen the risks inherent in relying on only a few markets—such as the California one—for maintenance of growth and even viability. To attempt to enter the Eastern markets would bring Coors face-to-face with entrenched major brewers: with Schlitz, Pabst, and Philip Morris's Miller, in addition to Anheuser–Busch. Miller, in particular, looked like a most formidable competitor: it had become the nation's fastest-growing major beer company, and by the beginning of 1976 had moved to third place in the U.S. beer market, moving ahead of Coors in the process. Undoubtedly Coors moving into the East would necessitate massive additional advertising expenditures. While sales might be increased by such expansion efforts, more questionable was what effect such would have on profits. Furthermore, despite optimism by Bill Coors about their one brewery being adequate to supply their entire national market, rather serious logistical problems could be expected.

THE BREWING INDUSTRY

Concentration has increasingly characterized the brewing industry. In the last several decades the number of beer firms dropped from 900 to 50. The smaller local and regional brewers just could not match the economies of scale of the big brewers, nor could they match their aggressive marketing efforts. In the span of only eight years, from 1970 to 1978, the combined market share of the five largest brewers increased from 49 percent to 74 percent of total industry sales.

The hottest product in the brewing industry by the mid-1970s had become light beer, or low-caloric beer. Almost 10 percent of industry sales were accounted for by lights, and 30 percent of Miller's, with the trend rising rapidly. Initial introductions of low-caloric beers had failed because they were marketed as diet drinks to consumers who did not drink much beer in the first place. Miller changed the thrust by positioning its Lite to heavy drinkers, with the theme that they could drink as much beer as before without feeling so filled (a subtle inference was that they thereby could consume more beer). Profitably speaking, the lights are good business: they sell for more than premium beers, and they cost less to make.

The other growth area is super premium beers, so called because they sell for higher prices. For years, Anheuser's Michelob had the market almost to itself, with its only real competition coming from imported beers. Miller was the first to intrude on Michelob's market niche by arranging first to import Lowenbrau from Germany, and then to produce a domestic version of Lowenbrau.

Table 4.1 Relative Sales of Top Five U.S. Brewers, 1973–1977

| | Sales (Millions of Dollars) | | | | |
	1973	1974	1975	1976	1977
Anheuser–Busch	1109.7	1413.1	1645.0	1441.2	1838.0
Miller	275.9	403.6	658.3	982.8	1327.6
Schlitz	703.0	814.5	923.0	1000.0	937.4
Pabst	355.4	431.3	525.0	600.5	582.9
Coors	378.8	467.8	520.0	593.6	593.1

Source: Company annual reports.

Table 4.1 shows the relative sales of the big five of the brewing industry from 1973 through 1977; Table 4.2 shows the relative profit performance for this period. Notice particularly the major burst of Miller both in sales and profits.

Anheuser–Busch, the industry leader, makes Budweiser, Budweiser malt liquor, Michelob, and Busch Bavarian. As Tables 4.1 and 4.2 show, its business has been booming. It has 10 breweries operating full blast, yet can hardly keep up with demand. However, the meteoric rise of Miller has to cause concern. Yet, Anheuser should have the marketing muscle and financial resources to more than match Miller's marketing efforts and building plans.

Miller Brewing Company makes Miller High Life, Miller malt liquor, Miller Lite, and Lowenbrau. Miller was a sickly company run by an aging management when it was acquired by Philip Morris, the tobacco company, in 1969. Philip Morris moved its tobacco executives in to run the brewing operations, and found that beer and cigarettes have a great deal in common, both being low-priced, pleasurable products processed and packaged on high-speed machinery, while they can be advertised and distributed similarly to many of the same end-use customers. With aggressive marketing efforts, Miller moved up from eighth to second place among U.S. brewers by 1977, and is trying hard to catch Anheuser. Its Lite beer, introduced in January 1975 with a blitz advertising campaign, was a marketing coup, and by 1978 Miller was selling 10 million barrels of Lite, equal to its entire beer sales only four years before.

Joseph Schlitz Brewing Company—maker of Schlitz, Schlitz malt liquor, Old Milwaukee, Promo, and Schlitz Light—has staggered badly, both in sales and especially in profits, as Table 4.2 shows. After 15 years of uninterrupted growth, it lost second place to Miller in 1977. The product mix has proven weak of late, with sales of premium and light beers—the more profitable items in the line—falling off more than its lower-priced beers. In addition, Schlitz has had problems coming up with a super premium beer to compete with Michelob and Lowenbrau.

Pabst makes Pabst Blue Ribbon, Pabst Extra Light, and Andeker of America. It has found it impossible to keep pace with Anheuser–Busch and Miller. Because of intense competition it has been forced to spend more and more for advertising,

Table 4.2   Relative Profits of Top Five U.S. Brewers, 1973–1977

	Net Profits (Millions of Dollars)				
	1973	*1974*	*1975*	*1976*	*1977*
Anheuser–Busch	65.6	64.0	84.7	55.4	91.9
Miller	(2.4)	6.3	28.6	76.1	106.5
Schlitz	55.2	49.0	30.9	50.0	17.8
Pabst	23.8	18.3	20.7	32.4	21.8
Coors	47.5	41.5	59.5	76.5	67.7

Source: Company annual reports.

but volume continues to slide. Pabst Blue Ribbon has lost considerable ground in certain major midwestern markets; Pabst's light beer and Andeker, its super premium beer, are both weak contenders.

TARNISH ON THE GOLDEN PROSPECTS, 1977–1978

In 1977 the boom lowered. While Tables 4.1 and 4.2 show Coors as faltering considerably less than Schlitz and Pabst in sales and profits, still, 1977 marked a serious trend reversal after the heady years of growth. Furthermore, the reversal appeared to be not short-lived, but rather symptomatic of serious underlying problems.

In 1977 Coors earned $1.92 a share, down 12 percent from 1976. It shipped 12.8 million barrels of beer, down 5 percent from 1976. It lost market share in many of the sixteen Western states where it had the bulk of its distribution. Its problems continued into 1978. For the first half of 1978, barrelage was down another 12 percent, per-share earnings were down from $1.02 the year before to 56 cents, and in California, which had accounted for 39 percent of its sales, it had been surpassed by Anheuser–Busch. Coors' stock, which had been subscribed for $31 in 1975, was now hovering around $16, a loss of about 50 percent for the first public stockholders. Only a few years before, Coors had been selling its beer by allocation only; now, suddenly it had to cut back production. Bill Coors was forced to admit: "Making the best beer we can make is no longer enough."[6]

The Eastern markets no longer beckoned, either. They were heavily saturated with strong, well-entrenched competitors. In fact, the big Eastern brewers were moving West because of this. Anheuser had built a new plant in California. Miller was building one. Schlitz had expanded its capacity in the West. Coors, with its single plant in the mountains of Colorado, faced exorbitant transportation costs in trying to reach the Eastern markets, all the more so because its beer had to be shipped under refrigeration to maintain quality. Unfortunately, the quality image of

[6]"A Test for the Coors Dynasty," *Business Week*, May 8, 1978, p. 69.

the beer had suffered from bootleggers bringing it East with careless handling and selling it at black market prices. Coors had even been forced to take out newspaper ads in some Eastern cities advising beer drinkers not to drink Coors. But a negative image had been created in the minds of many Eastern beer drinkers.

Labor Problems

Labor problems exacerbated a deteriorating situation. On April 5, 1977, the brewery workers at the Golden, Colorado plant walked out. A week after the walkout, the AFL–CIO approved a nationwide boycott of the company's beer.

The company was unyielding, and now raised the issue that all prospective employees take lie-detector tests. The idea of polygraph testing hearkens back to the kidnapping of Adolph Coors III and the family fears that this could happen again. Eventually more than 1000 of the 1472 workers who walked out returned, while the rest were replaced. The strike lasted 15 months, and eventually the union was rejected by the employees. But the wrath of labor was incurred in the process and Coors now ranked with J. P. Stevens Company on union hate lists.

Opinions differ as to the effects the union boycott had on Coors' sales and profits: how much of the decline was due to labor boycotting, and how much was due to intensified competition? Bill Coors blamed most on the union boycott: "It was a shock for us to find that, as far as the union is concerned, anything goes. No lie is too great to tell if it accomplishes their boycott objectives. We view the boycott as a monument to immorality and dishonesty."[7]

The mystique of Coors, the image it had gloried in and which seemed to give it a competitive edge over all other brews, was gone, abruptly, bewilderingly. Just perhaps, the ultraconservative policies spawned by the tragedy of a brother's kidnapping and murder, over a decade-and-a-half previously, had blinded the company to a changing environment.

Competition

As evident from Table 4.1, the aggressive marketing efforts of Anheuser and Miller were having detrimental effects on the other members of the big five, not to mention the smaller regional brewers. The erosion of Coors' market share in California, its biggest market, where previously it had a 40 percent market share, was particularly worrisome, especially as it hinted at a greater erosion to some. In the first six months of 1978, Anheuser took over first place with a 35 percent share, with Coors dropping to 25 percent. Even more threatening was the threat of the surging Miller. While number two nationally, Miller was still a poor third in California, with less

[7]"Coors Beer: What Hit Us?" *Forbes*, October 16, 1978, p. 71.

than 10 percent of the market. But Miller was building a brewery there and Coors certainly had to expect that once its production facilities were established at a sufficiently high level, Miller's aggressive marketing efforts would be leveled at California. Coors would be placed in the more vulnerable position in attempting to match the expenditures and the expertise of Miller and Anheuser in a hotly contested market.

DEFENSIVE REACTIONS

Bill and Joe turned to market research to determine where they had gone wrong. The answer was quite definitive. The beer industry was growing at only 3 percent a year, but almost all the growth was coming from two products: light or low-caloric beer, and super premium beer. Coors offered neither of these, relying still on its traditional one kind of beer. Furthermore, research revealed that four out of every ten new light-beer drinkers had switched from Coors. In addition to the lack of a responsive and aggressive product mix vis-a-vis competitors, Coors also had a hard-to-open press tab can that hardly met consumers' desire for convenience and ease of operation.

Coors finally moved to rectify the product deficiencies of a single-beer strategy, and in the spring of 1978 introduced its first new product in 20 years, Coors Light. The company also began developing a super premium beer, planning market tests in early 1980. It was considering naming this Herman Joseph's, after Coors founder Adolph Hermon Joseph Coors, thereby emphasizing family name and tradition.[8] Coors' reluctance in expanding the product line is understandable, if not recommendable: producing different kinds of beer in the same brewery poses serious production problems and results in sharply higher costs than where there is an infinitely long and unchanging production line.

Coors now began directing its geographical expansion to the central states and those parts of the West it had not previously served. In 1978 it began distribution in Missouri, Iowa, and in parts of Washington state. In early 1979 it announced plans to begin distribution in Arkansas, which would bring to 17 the number of states in which it was now marketing its beer. The Coors brothers were reaching some painful conclusions, among them that the company must abandon its comfortable regional brewer and emerge as a national power. "There'll be fewer than 10 breweries left in the United States in ten years," predicted Bill Coors. "I don't say we have to be number one, but we do have to stay in the top five to survive."[9]

Coors' promotional expenditures had been lagging far behind those of its major

[8]"New Coors Brand Nears Test Stage," *Advertising Age*, December 10, 1979, pp. 2 and 86.
[9]As quoted in "Men at Coors Beer Find the Old Ways Don't Work Anymore," *Wall Street Journal*, January 19, 1979, pp. 1 and 24.

Table 4.3   Relative Advertising Expenditures for Top Eight Brewers, 1973–1976*

	Expenditures (Millions of Dollars)			
	1973	*1974*	*1975*	*1976*
Anheuser–Busch	20.5	17.8	27.4	28.5
Jos. Schlitz	19.7	20.9	26.5	34.1
Miller	10.9	13.6	21.3	29.1
Pabst	7.2	8.4	9.6	9.7
Coors	1.4	1.6	1.2	2.0
Olympia	3.3	3.9	5.8	5.7
Stroh	4.5	4.4	4.0	5.0
F. & M. Schaefer	4.4	4.3	2.7	2.5

*These expenditures are understated since they do not include the large sums typically spent by brewers on point of purchase materials and other nonmeasured media.
Source: Advertising Age, September 26, 1977, p. 112.

competitors, and even of some of the much smaller regional brewers (see Table 4.3). Accordingly, in 1976 Coors had hired the J. Walter Thompson agency to enhance its corporate image, and in 1978 budgeted a whopping increase in the advertising budget to $15 million.

For the full year of 1978, Coors registered a small sales gain to $624.8 million. However, profits again declined to $54.8 million, almost 20 percent below 1977 profits and almost 29 percent under the peak year of 1976. Even back in 1975, profits had been higher. And Coors' stock had now declined to less than $14 a share by early 1978.

The question at this point is whether Coors waited far too long to awaken to a changing and much more aggressive marketplace. Deeply imbedded policies of conservatism, the misplaced confidence in the everlasting appeal of a beer and of an image that thereby dispelled the need for any aggressive or even conventional marketing efforts, and finally a confrontation philosophy with union employees— all these factors may have brought the venerable Coors brewery to a point of no return—not that the viability of the company is in jeopardy, but perhaps the golden glory years are over for all time.

WHAT CAN BE LEARNED?

The Coors case evinces a classical disregard for marketing techniques, at least until great damage had been down to a company's market share and future promise. It shows the consequences of de-emphasizing marketing in a production orientation. It is a prime example of "marketing myopia."[10]

[10]This famous phrase was coined by Theodore Levitt in "Marketing Myopia," *Harvard Business Review*, July–August, 1960, pp. 24–47.

The problem was not that the company was not growth minded; it was—if increasing the productive capacity of the single brewery and venturing into other geographical regions can be construed as growth minded. However, this philosophy or policy of growth gave no recognition to changes in the environment and especially in the competitive picture—changes that necessitated adjustments and modification in business and marketing strategy. But alas, it is so tempting when things are going well, when a product is receiving accolades not only of the common man but of the famous, to be lulled into a sense of unrelieved complacency, to envision nothing going wrong, to see a favorable image as insulating the company and its brand from all competition and adversity. Such a perception of the environment tends to provoke less than desirable consequences. It tends to make a firm arbitrary and dictatorial in its dealings with dealers, with employees, and even with customers—in other words, it promotes a "take it or leave it" attitude. It can also induce a company to regard its situation as a "cash cow"[11] from which the profits can be fully milked while investments in advertising, in new product planning, and other marketing activities are kept at a minimum. Certainly, as Table 4.3 reveals, Coors' expenditures for advertising were woefully below those of other brewers, even those much smaller than Coors.

We can also see from this Coors example the sad but nonetheless obvious fact of the impermanence of a good image. It is difficult to develop an image of quality and of great desirability; even more difficult and time-consuming is the cultivation of a mystique. While such an image can be a company's biggest asset while it is operational, it can be a fleeting thing. Coors' image of quality and great taste was lost in the Eastern markets because of difficulties in maintaining required refrigeration during transportation and far-flung distribution; as a result, a negative image was quickly incurred in these markets. But also we see that consumer wants can be fickle and can change drastically: the sought-after image of today may not necessarily be that of next year. The new sought-after image of beer became light or low-caloric beer, and super premium beer. The brand image of Coors was left in the dust—not completely, of course, but enough to mute the growth of the company.

A firm should not beguile itself into minimizing the threat of competition, both present and potential. Coors was guilty of this, under the illusion of the invincibility of their product vis-a-vis competing brands. Yet, we can see how easily such an entrapment could occur: during the heady days of the early 1970s, they dominated every market they were in. But the reality was soon to impose itself that without greatly increased marketing expenditures and probably the establishment of additional breweries closer to the market, there could be little chance of cracking the Eastern market against entrenched and powerful competitors. Furthermore, even Coors' captive and cherished Western markets—particularly the important California market—were vulnerable to the aggressive efforts of major competitors.

[11]The term "cash cow" was perhaps first used by the Boston Consulting Group.

A firm has to be adaptable; it cannot expect the status quo to endure. It has to be prepared to adjust to a changing environment. But ideally such a firm should anticipate changes, and should make needed adjustments before they are forced into it. Otherwise, an initial advantage can be lost, and never regained.

This suggests the need not to take an image for granted, but to continually monitor its standing in the marketplace, and how this may be changing. Clues of change can come from many sources: industry publications, dealer comments, attitude surveys of consumers, sales force feedback, and competitive activities and inroads.

Update

By 1981, Coors was budgeting some $87 million for advertising and promotion. This was nearly double what the company spent two years before, and compares with a bare $1.2 million spent back in 1975. Coors Light was running neck and neck with Miller's nationally dominant Lite in the 20 states in which Coors was now selling. But its problems were hardly solved.

Both barrelage and income were down. Coors' share of the California market had dropped to 20 percent in 1981. Anheuser was invading the Coors stronghold of Texas, and its Bud Light gained 3 percent of the total market in one month. And Coors was still undecided whether to begin total distribution of its Herman Joseph's 1868, which it had been test marketing for a year without making inroads against Anheuser's Michelob.

By 1984, however, Coors appeared to have honed its marketing strategy. It moved aggressively into the Southeast in 1983 and captured some 11 percent of the market, with a good coordination of advertising, point-of-sale materials, and wholesaler incentives. However, Coors was still struggling to combat market-share erosion in its original Western markets. In California, its market share had fallen to 16.1 percent by 1983; in this, the state with the highest beer consumption in the nation, it had had a 37.8 percent market share in 1972.

By 1984 Coors was in 26 states with its Coors Premium and Light brands. But it was still testing Herman Joseph's 1868, which had been in and out of test since May 1980, and was also testing another potential premium beer, Golden Lager, with the results not suggesting a strong "go." Coors was still clinging to its fifth place among all brewers, and had a 7.6 percent market share, exactly the same as it had had in 1978 with a much smaller geographic distribution.

Then, on August 19, 1987, the AFL–CIO ended its 10-year boycott against the company, satisfied that the major complaints had been addressed. In the next two months the company gained more than 1800 new accounts, and this spurred optimism. Advertising expenditures for 1987 were expected to total $200 million, with more planned for 1988. A massive campaign—with television, radio, print, and outdoor advertisements—was primarily aimed at young adults. Coors Light, dubbed the "Silver Bullet," was also being promoted to the large Hispanic market, with the beer described as part of the *pura vida,* the good life. For 1988, a major nationwide rollout of six products was planned: Coors, Coors Light, Coors Extra Gold, George Killian's Irish Red, Herman Joseph's Original Draft, and Herman Joseph's Light. Plans were to expand into Delaware and Pennsylvania in 1988 and Indiana in 1989, which would give Coors entry into all 50 states.

Looking ahead three to five years, Donald Shook, Jr., corporate communications specialist, foresaw Coors becoming the no. 3 brewer, behind only Anheuser–Busch and Miller.[12] While market share was still small, 8.4 percent at the beginning of 1987, the trend was encouraging. Now it remained for Coors, with no marketing department at all 10 years before, to show that it could market aggressively and well, that it was now a real turnaround company.

For Thought and Discussion

1. How do you account for the fact that Coors beer achieved such a success despite the company's lack of a marketing orientation?
2. Do you think the company's fortunes would have remained strong and growing if advertising expenditures had been doubled or tripled during the late 1960s and early 1970s?
3. Is it likely that Coors' labor disputes had any serious effect on its fortunes? Why or why not?
4. At this time (1986), should Coors plan to go national? Examine as many pros and cons as possible.

Invitation to Role Play

1. Place yourself in the role of Peter Coors, the 32-year-old, $94,000-a-year senior vice president for sales and marketing. How would you attempt now (as of 1980) to reverse the company's fading performance? Be as specific as you can; also consider and identify any constraints to a corporate strategy that should be recognized. You might also want to consider how a mystique might again be built up for the Coors brand.
2. Place yourself in the role of a staff analyst. You have been asked to evaluate the desirability of opening another brewery in the East—perhaps in Virginia. Consider as many pros and cons as you can (you will, of course, have to make some assumptions, especially regarding construction costs). Develop a recommendation for a go/no-go decision, and be prepared to defend it before a top management committee.

[12]"Coors Turns Focus to Market," *Cleveland Plain Dealer,* November 22, 1987, p. 4–E.

5

A. C. Gilbert
Company—Tearing
Down a Quality Image

A. C. Gilbert Company was not a youngster, having had some 58 years of toymaking experience at the time it failed. For years its products had filled a definite market niche. Its name was respected, well known, and signified quality.

In a few years all this was to end. Almost incredibly, bad marketing replaced the solid achievements of the past. Changing market conditions were ignored for too long. Then, rash, frantic decisions were substituted for a well-planned, corrective marketing strategy that would build on the strengths of the company. The result was self-destruction of the public image and, shortly, dissolution of the company.

BACKGROUND

The A. C. Gilbert Company was the product of one imaginative man's inventiveness and the willingness to back his ideas himself rather than selling out. Alfred Carlton Gilbert, after graduating from Yale, established the Mysto Manufacturing Company in 1909 to make the Erector set, which he had perfected. In 1916 this company became the A. C. Gilbert Company. In time, the son, A. C. Jr., joined the company as assistant to his father, and became president in 1943. In 1961 the senior Gilbert died, and the son became chairman of the board. Gilbert Jr. was a respected figure in the toy industry, serving as president of the Toys Manufacturers of the U.S.A. in 1962–1963.

While the company never became a large firm, it was firmly in the top ten of toy manufacturers in the 1950s, with sales reaching over $17 million. It was strong in science toys—chemistry sets, microscopes, and Erector "engineering" sets—at a time when science was becoming important as a national priority. Gilbert had the reputation of a quality toymaker, and its American Flyer trains and Erector sets were known by generations of children and their parents.

This was the situation as the company entered the 1960s. However, the environment of toy marketing was changing. The 1960s, with their attendant prosperity, brought a booming toy market. But it was different from what Gilbert was familiar with. A new promotional medium, television, had become important for toy marketing and was superseding catalogs and window displays. But television was expensive and made the break-even point on toy sales much higher. It also enabled many items, from hula hoops to Batmobiles, to attain quick popularity. The market was changing fast, and a firm had to be nimble to tap the sales potential and not be caught with too heavy an inventory when demand was superseded by another fad item.

The toy market was also changing in that the traditional toy stores, hobby shops, and department stores were being bypassed for self-service, high-volume supermarkets and discount stores. These new dealers were mainly interested in low-priced, heavily advertisted toys with attractive packages that could act as selling tools.

So the old, successful, well-entrenched company entered the 1960s, rather complacent and content with the status quo.

PROBLEMS

Anson Isaacson, president of Gilbert, had a desperate task before him. In April of 1966 he was searching frantically among financial circles to raise the money needed to operate another year, after suffering losses of $2.9 million in 1965.

Mr Isaacson had assumed the presidency in June 1964, after A. C. Gilbert, Jr. died. He was a former vice president of Ideal Toy Company, a larger toymaker, and had been brought into the company to straighten out serious sales and profit problems that had been getting worse since 1961.

After three weeks of scouring for financial aid, Anson Isaacson was successful. Pledging most of the remaining unpledged assets of the company, he was able to obtain a loan of $6.25 million, of which he himself put up $250,000 to show creditors his faith in the company and his confidence in his ability to straighten out the problems. There was one frightening stipulation in the loan agreement, however. The loan was contingent on the company's making a profit in 1966. If Gilbert failed to do so, the loan would be called and the assets liquidated to satisfy the indebtedness. Isaacson was not bargaining from a position of strength and had to accept the condition. Although he did feel that under his management the condition would not pose a particular problem, still it lurked in the background, ominous and threatening.

PRELUDE

Now let us examine how Gilbert got into this mess. The company did not really recognize a problem until the end of 1961, at which time sales dropped from $12.6 million in 1960 to $11.6 million. In 1961 the company counted a mere $20,011 in profits. Now the company was obviously facing serious problems, and a program was hastily devised to correct the situation.

In early 1962, with stock prices down, the company became attractive to Jack Wrather, president of a West Coast holding company that owned the "Lassie" and "Lone Ranger" television programs, the Disneyland Hotel, Muzak Corporation (piped-in music), and a boatyard. He acquired a 52 percent interest in the Gilbert Company for some $4 million. He then replaced Gilbert top executives with his own men. While A. C. Gilbert, Jr. remained as board chairman, his power was substantially lessened.

The 1961 sales drop was attributed to two factors: insufficient new products and insufficient advertising. Plans were formulated to boost sales to $20 million with the addition of new, "hot items." The sales staff was increased 50 percent, since more aggressive selling and more frequent contacts with retailers were assumed to be directly correlated with increasing sales. With an expanded sales staff, a new general sales manager and a new director of international sales were appointed.

But this marketing strategy proved of no avail. In 1962, sales dropped to $10.9 million, with a $281,000 loss. This loss was attributed to the cost of preparing the new, greatly expanded 1963 line and the scrapping of obsolete materials. The company was pinning its great expectations on the 1963 selling season. A major effort had been made to expand the line. For the first time, the company was offering toys for preschool children, and for girls in the six-to-fourteen-year-old bracket in addition to boys, who had been the traditional market segment. More than 50 new items boosted the line to 307 items, by far the largest in the company's history. The ambitious expansion program seemed fully justified and badly needed; now the market was 35 million boys and girls, instead of just 9 million boys.

Modern Packaging magazine hailed the package revitalization program in 1963.[1] Upwards of $1 million was spent to repackage the entire line. Packages for Erector sets and the other long-established toys had been virtually unchanged for many years; now they were given an "exciting" new full-color pictorial treatment illustrating the models in action.

The future looked bright at this time, and such an aggressive marketing approach was viewed as badly overdue in an old, conservatively managed family business. Officials confidently predicted record sales and earnings.

It must have been a bitter pill when sales results finally came in (in the toy

[1]"Saving a $500,000 Investment," *Modern Packaging*, August 1963, pp. 97–98.

business, the Christmas selling season is crucial for the year's performance; until the results of this business season are tabulated late in the year, no one really knows how successful a year has been). Incredibly, sales continued to slide in 1963, to $10.7 million; worse, instead of a profit, there was a whopping $5.7 million loss, stemming mostly from huge returns of low-priced toys shipped on a guaranteed sale basis to supermarkets. After Christmas, Gilbert had an inventory of almost $3.5 million of unsold toys.

Corrective Efforts

At this point, Jack Wrather decided that a toymaking company needed more expert toymaking experience. He fired most of the top management he had brought in nearly two years before. A. C. Gilbert, Jr. reassumed the presidency, but Anson Isaacson, former Ideal Toy Company vice president, was brought in as chief operating officer and chairman of the executive committee.

In two years, losses had reached almost $6 million. This was a terrible drain on a firm whose revenues were not much more than $10 million a year. But loans were renegotiated at higher interest rates, and major creditors agreed to a delay in payment over a three-year period. After the last several years of profligate expansion of sales staff and product lines, Isaacson began a strong economy drive.

He made a major change in the selling mechanism. In place of company salesmen, he fired the sales staff and switched to manufacturers' representatives. Manufacturers' representatives are independent sales representatives who handle a number of noncompeting lines of various manufacturers and charge a fixed commission, usually 5 or 6 percent on all sales made. They are somewhat less expensive than a company sales force and should be able to contact more dealers. Gilbert had less control over them, however, and their customer service for Gilbert could be erratic. In addition, major cuts were made in factory personnel, with the result that administrative and operating expenses were reduced from $10 million to $4.7 million for 1964. In June of 1964, A. C. Gilbert, Jr. died, and Mr. Wrather became chairman of the board and Mr. Isaacson president.

For the 1964 Christmas season, 20 new toys were added to the depleted line. Encouragingly, sales picked up almost 7 percent, to $11.4 million. The company would have registered a profit for the year, but Isaacson insisted on dumping excess inventory in order to enhance future years' profits, so a loss was registered of $1,900,000.

The expectations of Isaacson and the Gilbert Company now rested on the fall and Christmas selling season of 1965. This was to be the year the company turned around and reached for its new potential. To this end, the product line was again revamped and a heavy advertising and point-of-purchase display program budgeted. Television advertising centered on a 52-week schedule of Saturday morning Beatles cartoon shows, and $2 million was committed for this. In addition, the Gilbert

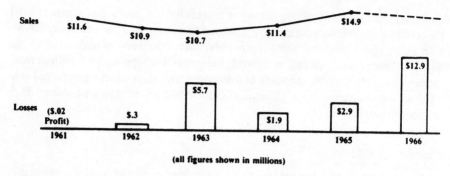

(all figures shown in millions)

Figure 5.1.

Company furnished some 65,000 animated displays free to dealers at a cost of $1 million.

Early indications for 1965 were favorable. By July, Isaacson predicted a net profit for the year. The order backlog was $12 million in July, and losses for the first six months of the year (toymakers characteristically incur losses through most of the year until the peak Christmas business is realized) were only half those for the same period in 1964.

Isaacson's optimistic prediction, however, proved wrong. The heavy promotional expenditures did bring sales of $14.9 million, the best since the early 1950s, and a 30 percent increase over the preceding year. However, losses were up to $2.9 million, mostly due to heavy returns on a 007 auto racing set, which was then handled exclusively by Sears, as well as other racing sets. These racing sets turned out to be poorly engineered and constructed, poorly packaged, and overpriced.

As the company's financial condition contined to worsen, Anson Isaacson began his rounds to find the financing necessary to keep the company alive. The multimillion dollar rescue loan that he finally obtained made virtually all the assets subject to liens to secure such indebtedness and was contingent on the company's making a profit in 1966.

It did not make a profit in 1966. Instead, the announced loss was $12,872,000. The once-proud A. C. Gilbert Company went out of business in February 1967. Gabriel Industries acquired certain of Gilbert's assets, including Erector sets and chemistry sets, for about $17 million. This was paid to the financial institutions holding Gilbert's indebtedness.

Figure 5.1 depicts Gilbert's last six years.

HOW DID IT HAPPEN?

We can group the mistakes that Gilbert made into two broad categories: lack of recognition of the problem until late, and frantic reactions once the problem was recognized, resulting in successive mistakes until the end. Each of these will be discussed in more detail, and the specific mistakes under these categories identified.

Gilbert failed to recognize that the toy environment was changing, and that the changes were causing an ever-worsening problem. Diminishing sales from the peak years of the 1950s apparently did not alert the company that there was a problem needing investigation and some adjustment in marketing strategy.

We have previously noted how major changes in advertising and distribution of toys were occurring and were only belatedly recognized by Gilbert. One change in toy demand that should have been quickly detected was that tabletop slot-car auto racing sets, almost unknown 10 years before, were now outselling toy trains. Gilbert should have been in this market near the outset. Instead, not until the mid-1960s were its racing sets introduced. And these were poorly engineered, fragile, and overpriced, and their returns in 1965 practically scuttled the company.

Apparently not until the end of the 1961 selling season, when the company barely made a profit, was there any awareness of a possible problem. At this point, frantic and poorly thought-out actions were commenced. With the serious loss of 1962, there was no longer any doubt that there was a problem.

Frantic actions took place with the product line. This had remained relatively unchanged for decades. Suddenly in one year the line was greatly expanded—more than 50 new toys were added, not only directed to the traditional target market of six-to-fourteen-year-old boys, but now also for girls and for preschool children. Furthermore, the toys were different from what the company had been used to making—lower priced, lower quality, and geared to large-volume sales. This placed great strains on the company's engineering and production capabilities. The almost inevitable result was poorly designed toys of not very good quality and of disappointing customer appeal. More than this, the company's unique niche as a quality toymaker of high-level educational toys was abandoned, and the company flung itself into the fiercely competitive marketplace against better experienced and mostly larger competitors.

Subsequent actions did nothing to restore the image of the reputable toymaker. A company and brand image is precious; a good image is not easily developed but can be torn down rather quickly.

Toy buyers were critical of the company's product changes and of its packaging:

> Gilbert had a natural in its Erector sets. Instead they neglected it. They used to offer sets up to $75 packaged in metal boxes. Now the most expensive is only $20, the parts are flimsy, and it's in an oversized cardboard box. They did the same thing to their chemistry sets. You can't store anything in those oversize see-through packages.[2]

---

[2] "Toymaker A. C. Gilbert Co., Poor Loser?" *Sales Management*, May 1, 1966, p. 27.

INFORMATION SIDELIGHT

USE OF MANUFACTURERS' REPRESENTATIVES vs.
A COMPANY SALES FORCE

While the switching of Gilbert to manufacturers' reps is cited as a drawback, we should recognize that such independent representatives pose some specific advantages to a firm over having its own sales force.

These independent reps are paid on a straight commission for sales, often 6 percent. This makes selling costs entirely variable, rising or falling with revenue. In contrast, a company-owned sales force has such fixed costs as sales managers' salaries, home and branch office overhead, and base salaries of salespeople, in addition to travel and entertainment expenses. These costs remain constant whether sales are up or down; commissions and bonuses would, of course, be variable.

Independent representatives also give a company considerable flexibility. During periods of rising sales, more reps can be used; during periods of falling sales, retrenchment is easier than with a company-owned sales force. Furthermore, when there are seasonal differences in demand for a firm's products, reps are a logical preference, since a company's sales force may not be effectively utilized during slack periods.

Some argue that independent sales reps can actually provide better sales production than company salespeople. Since they contact the same customers with products of a number of manufacturers, sales calls are more economical; the cost is spread over several products. These reps may also have more stature in the eyes of their customers because of the breadth of their lines and the fact that they may handle several important product lines for the customer. Generally, these reps tend to be experienced and competent salespeople. Of course, a firm has less control over such independent operators; but control is not altogether lacking, since the threat to take away a well-received line of merchandise unless performance improves is seldom taken lightly by the independent rep. However, if the product line or brand does not sell well, then such a threat would receive little attention.

Gilbert had high hopes for its new All Aboard series, consisting of landscaped panels that fit together to form a tabletop train layout. But:

> It's a real good idea, but the quality is poor. The locomotive and cars are cheap and lack detail.[3]

[3]Ibid., p. 28.

Gilbert's doll series was overpriced, poorly made, and incomplete because no changes in clothes were offered. This was at the time when additional wardrobes were the major appeal of many dolls, as well as a source of extra profits.

Incredibly poor timing was the lot of the company in attempting to compete with fad items. For example, in 1965, spy items were especially popular, with spy and secret agent movies and television series having high audience ratings. So Gilbert introduced such spy figures as Man from U.N.C.L.E., James Bond, and Honey West. The only trouble was that they did not reach the market until after Christmas Day in 1965, obviously too late for the selling season. While such timing was inexcusable and reflected drastic problems in the planning and operations of the company, the ground was laid for this situation in 1964.

Successive errors were piled on each other. After the ill-conceived product line expansion of 1963 that resulted in $5.7 million in losses, an austerity campaign was put in effect in 1964, with major cutbacks made in engineering and production—expenses were consequently reduced more than 50 percent for 1964. But such austerity hardly led to the planning and production efficiencies needed for the quick introduction of fad items.

Other aspects of this austerity were less obvious but consequential. The company switched from having its own sales force to contracting for independent manufacturers' representatives to handle its selling efforts. While this move was expected to increase dealer coverage while not adding to the cost of selling, dealers did not like the new arrangement: "It used to be that you could call a Gilbert salesman and get service on a problem. Now the reps just want to get the order," disgruntled dealers were saying.[4]

In attempting to widen its distribution to supermarkets, discount stores, and other aggressive promotional retailers, Gilbert made certain concessions that were to cost dearly, such as guaranteeing the sales of its products to some of these demanding outlets. By guaranteeing sales, the company assumed the burden of poor selling efforts, markdowns, and product write-offs of anything unsold after the Christmas season. Guaranteeing sales is usually a last-ditch effort by a new manufacturer trying to gain entry in the marketplace. Offering an unknown brand, such a supplier is totally dependent on retailers and may be forced to accept the conditions demanded by some. Gilbert was not a small unknown firm trying to crack the marketplace. In 1963, it still had a quality image, was widely known, and had good distribution, even though not as wide as desired.

A final dramatic mistake came in 1965. After the austerity of 1964, the spigots were reopened and with a vengeance. More new toys were added. Of more significance, a massive television advertising campaign and point-of-purchase display program were instituted. Here was a company with sales of just over $11 million facing the specter of insolvency; yet almost 30 percent of sales were budgeted for a

[4]Ibid.

massive promotion effort. The lack of success, due to poor judgment of products, of distribution, and of timing, laid the groundwork for the demise of the company. The image of a reliable producer of high-quality toys had been lost. The $6.25 million last-resort financing that Isaacson managed to come up with in 1966 could no longer support the company's efforts to regain a viable niche in the market.

WHAT CAN BE LEARNED?

Perhaps the first thing to be learned from the experience of Gilbert is that it does not take long for a supposedly healthy and long-experienced company to come to its end. A series of successive bad decisions coming in the space of a few years can destroy all the gains built up by decades of successful marketing. And the inexcusable self-destruction of the quality image paved the way. We are left to shudder at how quickly a good reputation can be lost, can be torn down, while we will learn from the Korvette case the difficulty of building up an image. These should be sobering thoughts for any organization.

Certainly the need for better attention to and monitoring of the marketplace is evident. While marketing research could have been of help to the Gilbert Company in better assessing changing conditions, both in consumer demand and in competitive actions, this probably was not essential. What was needed was alert and cognizant executives working with certain control or measuring tools such as market share analysis. The changes occurring were not difficult to detect; they were obvious to all, consumers, retailers, manufacturers alike. But Gilbert continued to operate as if the status quo could be maintained, as if the market were unchanging. If nothing else, this case should point out the need to be constantly alert and responsive to change.

But a firm must also beware of reacting too quickly, without careful analysis of alternatives. Problems need to be carefully identified, and probable solutions or adjustments to them weighed in view of the particular strengths and resources of the firm. In Gilbert's case, hasty actions only compounded past mistakes. To be specific, the major strength of the firm was its quality image; this should not have been sacrificed to hastily bring out a proliferation of "cheap" new products similar to competitors'. By expanding hastily with new products, the capabilities of the company were disregarded, and a flood of poorly made products resulted.

Mistakes on top of mistakes; frantic actions leading to more frantic actions and to disastrous decisions. Few company have made as many successive bad decisions as those evinced by Gilbert.

Update

While the Gilbert Company has folded, never to return to life, happily we can note that the Erector set has survived. As described earlier, Gabriel Industries, a large toy manufacturer that also makes Tinker Toys, acquired the Erector asset at the liquidation of Gilbert. In 1977, nearly 600,000 Erector sets, ranging in price from $1 for a 45-piece pocket set to $40 for a deluxe 450-piece set, were sold around the world.

In August of 1978, Gabriel and its Erector set subsidiary were purchased by CBS for $27.1 million. The senior vice president of Gabriel predicted: "A hundred years from now, I think you'll still be able to buy an Erector set . . . long after everyone here is gone."[5]

For Thought and Discussion

1. What controls should Gilbert have had to remain alert to changing market conditions? What research would have helped?
2. Do you think Gilbert was right in expanding its target market in 1963? Why or why not?
3. Evaluate the advertising efforts of 1965 and the point-of-purchase display expenditures.
4. Discuss the pros and cons of changing management quickly when adversity sets in.

Invitation to Role Play

1. As an assistant to the president, what would you have advised Gilbert to do at the end of 1961 when the first drastic decline in profit (to a $20,011 profit) occurred?
2. As a management consultant, what would you have advised at the end of 1963?

---

[5]"The Nuts and Bolts of Erector Set Firm," *Cleveland Plain Dealer*, September 10, 1978, Sec. 2-1.

PART TWO

CONTRASTS OF MISTAKES AND SUCCESSES (BLUNDERS AND BULLSEYES)

6

From Monumental Failure to Outstanding Success: The Edsel and the Mustang

In the annals of business history perhaps no greater turnaround was ever achieved by one company in the space of a few years than that of the Ford Motor Company in the late 1950s and early 1960s. In the late 1950s Ford hatched the blunder that to this day has become synonymous with fiascos of monumental proportions—the Edsel. A few years later, in 1962, it developed the most successful new car model ever introduced up to that time—the Mustang.

Did the Edsel mistake result in a tremendous learning experience at Ford? Or did the Mustang success result from simple luck? Or could the success of the Mustang reflect more the genius of one man, a man not involved with the Edsel but the key force behind the Mustang, a man we know today more for his success with another auto maker than with Ford—Lee Iacocca?

THE EDSEL: RESEARCH AND PLANNING GONE AWRY

An Earlier Blunder

Henry Ford introduced the Model T in 1909. It sold initially for $850 and was available in one color, black. The Model T quickly became a way of life. Ford conducted mass production on a scale never before seen, introducing and perfecting the moving assembly line so that the worker remained stationary while the work came to him. Ford sold half the new cars made in this country up to 1926 and produced more than double the output of his nearest competitor, General Motors.

By 1926 prices had fallen as low as $263. For 17 years the Model T had neither model changes nor significant improvements, except for a lower selling price as more production economies were realized.

But by the mid-1920s, millions of Americans wanted something fancier, and General Motors brought out the Chevrolet, featuring color, comfort, styling, safety, modernity, and—most of all—a showy appearance. The Model T was doomed.

In desperation, Henry Ford had painted the Model T attractive colors, rounded the fenders, lengthened and lowered the body, and slanted the windshield. Sales still declined. Finally, in May 1927, Ford stopped production altogether for nearly a year while 60,000 workers in Detroit were laid off, and a new car, the Model A, slowly took shape, with a changeover estimated to have cost Ford $100 million. While the Model A was successful, the lead lost to General Motors was never regained.

In the 1920s a failure in market assessment was devastating. To some extent the failure of the Edsel was also due to bad market assessment, but this time not for want of trying.

The Edsel

The Edsel, Ford's entry into the medium-priced field, was introduced for the 1958 model year in early September of 1957. This gave it a jump on competitors who traditionally introduced new models in October and November. Ford's board set the 1958 goal for the Edsel Division at 3.3 to 3.5 percent of the total auto market, or about 200,000 cars. However, the company executives considered this a very conservative estimate and expected to do much better. Ten years of planning, preparation, and research had gone into the Edsel. The need for such a car in the Ford product line appeared conclusive; $50 million was spent for advertising and promotion, and in late summer of 1957 the success of the massive venture seemed assured. The company did not expect to recover the $250 million of development costs until the third year, but expected the car to be operationally profitable in 1958.

Rationale for the Edsel. The rationale for the Edsel seemed inescapable. For some years there had been a growing trend toward medium-priced cars. Such cars as Pontiac, Oldsmobile, Buick, Dodge, DeSoto, and Mercury accounted for one-third of all car sales by the middle 1950s, whereas they had formerly contributed only one-fifth.

Economic projections confirmed this shift in emphasis from low-priced cars and suggested a continuing demand for higher-priced models in the 1960s. Disposable personal income (expressed in 1956 dollars) increased from $138 billion in 1939 to $287 billion in 1956, with forecasts of $400 billion by 1965. The percentage of this income spent for automobiles increased from around 3.5 percent in 1939 to 5.5 or 6.0 percent in the middle 1950s.

The Ford Motor Company was weakest in the sector where the company's economic forecasts indicated the greatest opportunity. General Motors had three makes—Pontiac, Oldsmobile, and Buick—in the medium-priced class; Chrysler had Dodge and DeSoto appealing to this market; but Ford had only Mercury, and Mercury accounted for a puny 20 percent of the company's business.

Studies revealed that in every year one out of five people who bought a new car traded up to a medium-priced model from a low-priced car. As Chevrolet owners traded up, 87 percent stayed with General Motors and one of its three makes of medium-priced cars. As Plymouth owners traded up, 47 percent bought a Dodge or DeSoto. But as Ford owners traded up, only 26 percent stayed with the Ford Motor Company and the Mercury, its one entry in this price line. Ford executives described this phenomenon as "one of the greatest philanthropies of modern business."[1] The entry of the Edsel seemed necessary, if not overdue.

Research Efforts. Marketing research studies on the Edsel covered a period of almost 10 years. Some studies dealt with owner likes and dislikes, other studies with market and sales analyses. Earlier research had determined that cars have definite personalities to the general public, and a person buys a car best thought to exemplify his or her own personality. Consequently, imagery studies were considered important to find the best personality for the car and to find the best name. The personality sought was one to make the greatest number of people want the car. Ford researchers thought they had a major advantage over the manufacturers of medium-priced cars because they did not have to change an existing personality; rather, they could create what they wanted from scratch.

Columbia University was engaged to interview 800 recent car buyers in Peoria, Illinois, and another 800 in San Bernardino, California (considered to be typical cities), about images of various makes. A personality portrait of each make was developed from these interviews. For example, the image of a Ford was that of a fast, masculine car with no particular social pretension. Chevrolet's image was a car for an older, wiser, slower person. Mercury, despite its higher price tag, was thought to be a hot-rod, best suited for a young racing driver.

Ford concluded that the personality of the new car (called the E-car initially) should be the smart car for the younger executive or professional family on its way up. Advertising and promotion would stress this theme, and the appointments of the car would offer status to the owner.

The name for the E-car should also fit the car's image and personality. Accordingly, some 2000 different names were gathered and several research firms sent interviewers with the list to canvass sidewalk crowds in New York City, Chicago,

---

[1]Henry G. Baker, "Sales and Marketing Planning of the Edsel," in *Marketing's Role in Scientific Management*, Proceedings of the 39th National Conference of the American Marketing Association, June 1957, pp. 128–129.

Willow Run, and Ann Arbor, Michigan. The interviewers asked what free associations each name brought to mind; they also asked what words were considered the opposite of each name since opposite associations might also be important. But the results were inconclusive.

Edsel, the name of Henry Ford's only son, was suggested for the E-car. However, the three Ford brothers in active management of the company, Henry II, Benson, and William Clay, were lukewarm to this idea of their father's name spinning "on a million hubcaps." And the free associations with the name Edsel were on the negative side, being pretzel, diesel, and hard sell.

At last, 10 names were sent to the executive committee. None of the 10 aroused any enthusiasm. Finally, the name Edsel was selected, although it was not one of the recommended names. Four of the ten names submitted were selected for the different series of Edsel: Corsair, Citation, Pacer, and Ranger.

Search for a Distinctive Style. Styling for the Edsel began in 1954. Designers were asked to be both distinctive and discreet, in itself a rather tall order. The stylists studied existing cars and even scanned the tops of cars from the roof of a 10-story building to determine any distinguishing characteristics that might be used for the Edsel. Consumer research provided some information about the desired image and personality, but furnished little guidance for the actual features and shape of the car. Groups of stylists considered various themes and boiled down hundreds of sketches to two dozen to show top management. Clay and plaster mock-ups were prepared so that three-dimensional highlights and flair could be observed. The final concept was satisfying to all 800 stylists.

The result was a unique vertical front grille—a horse-collar shape, set vertically in the center of a conventionally low, wide front end—push-button transmission, and luxury appointments. The vertical grille of the Edsel was compared by some executives to the classic cars of the 1930s, the LaSalle and Pierce Arrow. Push buttons were stressed as the epitome of engineering advancement and convenience. The hood and trunk lid were operated by push button, as were the parking brake lever and the transmission. Edsel salesmen could demonstrate the ease of operation by depressing the transmission buttons with a toothpick.

The Edsel was not a small car. The two largest series, the Corsair and the Citation, were two inches longer than the biggest Oldsmobile. It was a powerful car with a 345-horsepower engine. The high performance possible from such horsepower was thought to be a key element in the car's sporty, youthful image.

A Separate Division for Edsel. Instead of distributing the new Edsel through established Ford, Mercury, and Lincoln dealers, Ford created a separate dealer organization to be controlled by a separate headquarters division. The new dealers were carefully selected from over 4600 inquiries for dealer franchises in every part of the United States. Most of the 1200 dealers chosen were to handle only Edsel, with dual dealerships restricted to small towns. Consequently, there were now five separate divisions for the Ford Motor Company: Ford, Mercury, Lincoln, Continental, and Edsel.

While the establishment of Edsel as a separate division added to the fixed costs of operation, Ford took the step because it thought an independent division could stand alone as a profit center, and that this independence would encourage more aggressive performance than if Edsel were merely a second entry in some other division.

Dealer appointments were made after intensive market research to learn where to place dealers in the nation's 60 major metropolitan areas. Population shifts and trends were carefully considered, and the planned dealer points were matched with the 4600 inquiries for franchises. Applicants for dealerships were carefully screened for reputation, adequate finances, adequate facilities, demonstrated management ability, the ability to attract and direct good people, sales ability, proper attitude toward ethical and competitive matters, and likelihood to give proper consideration to customers in sales and service. The average dealer had at least $100,000 committed to his agency. Edsel Division was prepared to supply skilled assistance to dealers so that each could operate effectively and profitably and provide good service to customers.

Promotional Efforts. July 22, 1957 was the kickoff for the first consumer advertising. It was a two-page spread in *Life* magazine in plain black and white, and showed a car whooshing down a country highway at such high speed it was a blur. The copy read: "Lately some mysterious automobiles have been seen on the roads." It went on to say that the blur was an Edsel and was on its way. Other preannouncement ads showed only photographs of covered cars. Not until late August were pictures of the actual cars released.

The company looked beyond their regular advertising agencies to find a separate one for the Edsel. Foote, Cone and Belding, of the two agencies in the top ten without any other automobile clients, was selected. The campaign designed was a quiet, self-assured one avoiding the use of the adjective "new," since new was seen as commonplace and not distinctive. The advertising was intended to be calm, not to overshadow the car.

The general sales and marketing manager, J. C. Doyle, insisted on keeping Edsel's appearance one of the best-kept secrets of the auto industry. Never before had an auto manaufacturer gone to so much trouble. Advertising commercials were filmed behind closed doors, the cars were shipped with covers, and no press people were given any photographs of the car before its introduction. The intent was to build up an overwhelming public interest in the Edsel, causing its arrival to be anticipated and the car itself to be the object of great curiosity.

Some $50 million was allocated for the introductory period. Traditional automobile advertising media were used. Newspaper advertising was allocated 40 percent of all expenditures, magazines 20 percent; TV and radio 20 percent; outdoor billboards 10 percent; and a final 10 percent for miscellaneous media.

The advertising agency and the marketing executives at Edsel recognized that they faced a challenge in the effective promotion of the car. Because of the decision for secrecy, traditional advertising research was eliminated since, for example, copy tests could not be made without disclosing the features of the car. Furthermore, the introduction of the car and the promotion to accompany it had to be done at one time all over the country; there was no possibility of testing various alternatives and approaches.

The Results

Introduction Day was September 4, 1957, and 1200 Edsel dealers eagerly opened their doors. Most found potential customers streaming in, out of curiosity if nothing else. On the first day more than 6500 orders were taken. This was considered reasonably satisfying. But there were isolated signs of resistance. One dealer selling Edsels in one showroom and Buicks in an adjacent showroom reported that some prospects walked into the Edsel showroom, looked at the Edsel, and placed orders for Buicks on the spot.

In the next few days, sales dropped sharply. For the first 10 days of October there were only 2751 sales, an average of under 300 cars a day. In order to sell the 200,000 cars per year (the minimum expectation), between 600 and 700 would need to be sold each day.

On Sunday night, October 13th, Ford put on a mammoth television spectacular for Edsel. The show cost $400,000 and starred Bing Crosby and Frank Sinatra. Even this failed to cause any sharp spurt in sales. Things were not going well.

For all of 1958, only 34,381 Edsels were sold and registered with motor-vehicle bureaus. The picture looked a little brighter in November 1958 with the introduction of the second-year models. These Edsels were shorter, lighter, less powerful, with a price range $500 to $800 less than their predecessors.

Eventually the Edsel Division was merged into a Lincoln–Mercury–Edsel Division. In mid-October 1959, a third series of Edsel models was brought out. These aroused no particular excitement either, and on November 19, 1959, production was discontinued. The Edsel was dead.

Between 1957 and 1960, only 109,466 Edsels were sold. Ford was able to recover $150 million of its investment by using Edsel plants and tools in other Ford divisions, leaving a nonrecoverable loss of more than $100 million on the original investment plus an estimated $100 million in operating losses.

What Went Wrong?

So carefully planned. Such a major commitment of personnel and financial resources, supported by decades of experience in producing and marketing automobiles. How could this have happened? As with most problems, there is no one

Second, much of the research was conducted several years before introduction of the Edsel in 1957. While demand for medium-priced cars seemed strong at that time, it was wrong to assume such attitudes would be static and unchanging. The increasing demand for imported cars warranted further investigation and reexamination of plans in light of changing market conditions.

Third, marketing research efforts failed in selection of the name Edsel. Here the blame lies not so much with marketing research, which never recommended the name Edsel in the first place, as with management that disregarded marketing research conclusions. Perhaps the negative impact of the name has been overemphasized. Many successful cars today do not have what we would call winning names. For example, Buick, Oldsmobile, Chrysler, even Ford itself are hardly exciting names. A better name could have been chosen, and was a few years later with the Mustang and the Maverick, but it is doubtful that the Edsel's demise can justifiably be attributed to the name.

The Product. As mentioned earlier, changing consumer preferences for smaller cars came about the time the Edsel was introduced. However, other characteristics of the car also hurt. The styling, especially the vertical grille, aroused both positive and negative impressions. Some liked its distinctiveness, seeing it as a restrained classic look without extremes. But the horsecollar-shaped grille turned other people off.

The biggest product error had to do with quality control. There was a failure to adhere to quality standards; production was rushed to get the Edsel to market on schedule and as many Edsels as possible on the road so that people could see the car. But many bugs had not been cleared up. The array of models increased production difficulties, with 18 different models in four different series. As a result, the first Edsels had brakes that failed, oil leaks, rattles, and sometimes even the dealers could not start them. Before these problems could be cleared up, the car had the reputation of a lemon, and quickly became the butt of jokes.

The Separate Edsel Organization. In retrospect, the decision to go with a separate division and separate dealerships for Edsel was a mistake. The cost factors of additional personnel and facilities were underestimated. Furthermore, Ford did not have sufficient management personnel to staff all its division adequately.

Despite the care used in selecting the new Edsel dealers, some of these were underfinanced, and many were underskilled in running automobile dealerships in comparison with existing dealers selling regular Ford products. Other Edsel dealers were dropouts or less successful dealers of other car makers.

In addition, Edsel dealers had nothing to offer but Edsel sales and service. Dealers usually rely on the shop and maintenance sections of their businesses to cover some expenses. Edsel dealers had no other cars besides the Edsel to work on, and, since work on the Edsel was usually a result of factory deficiencies, the dealers could not charge for this work. The dealers quickly faced financial difficulties with sales below expectations and service businesses yielding little revenue.

Promotional Efforts. Contrary to what could be reasonably expected, the heavy promotional efforts preceding the unveiling of the Edsel may have produced a negative effect. The general public had been led to expect the Edsel to be a major step forward, a significant innovation. And many were disillusioned. They saw instead a newly styled, luxury Ford, uselessly overpowered, with gadgets and chrome, but nothing really different.

Furthermore, the Edsel came out early in the new car model year—in early September—and had to suffer the consequences of competing with 1957 cars going through clearance sales. Not only did people shy away from the price of the Edsel, but in many instances they did not know if it was a 1957 or 1958 model. *Business Week* reported dealer complaints: "We've been selling against the clean-up of 1957 models. We were too far ahead of the 1958 market. Our big job is getting the original lookers back in the showrooms."

While some dealers complained about over-advertising too early, they then complained about lack of promotion and advertising in October and November when the other cars were being introduced. At the very time the Edsel was competing against other new models, advertising was cut back as the Edsel executives saw little point in trying to steal attention normally focused on new models.

Finally, one of the more interesting explanations for the failure of the Edsel was:

> . . . oral symbolism . . . responsible for the failure of the Edsel. The physical appearance was displeasing from a psychological and emotional point of view because the front grille looked like a huge open mouth . . . Men do not want to associate oral qualities with their cars, for it does not fit their self-image of being strong and virile.[5]

THE MUSTANG: THE GREAT REVERSAL

The Mustang was introduced April 17, 1964, a little over four years after the Edsel was discontinued. In the first four months that the Mustang was on the market, more Mustangs were sold than Edsels had been sold in its 26-month history. The Mustang ranks as one of the automotive industry's most successful new model introductions, and demand continued to flourish.

Lee Iacocca

Lee Iacocca played a primary role in the success of the Mustang, becoming Ford Division's general manager in 1960. He embodied the great American success story. The son of an Italian immigrant, he saw education as the route to success. He

---

[5]Gene Rosemblum, *Is Your VW a Sex Symbol?* (New York: Hawthorne, 1972), p. 39.

went to Lehigh University and later to Princeton for a master's degree in engineering. "In my day you went to college, not to go into government or to be a lawyer, but to embark on a career that paid you more money than the guy who didn't go. For 32 years I was motivated by money," Iacocca was to say some years later.[6]

He started with the Ford Motor Company as an engineer trainee in 1946 at $125 a week. As he moved upward through the Ford organization, he transferred to sales, later becoming sales manager and then vice president and general manager of the Ford Division. By 1977 he was president of the entire Ford Motor Company, earning $978,000. But in July 1978 Henry Ford abruptly fired him. The falling-out was attributed to basic disagreement between Ford and Iacocca over the pace of downsizing cars: Iacocca wanted to move fast, whereas Ford was worried about the impact of such additional investment on short-term profits and wanted to move more slowly. Today, Iacocca is better known for being the savior of Chrysler.

In addition to being a natural salesman, Iacocca has a genius for assessing the general public's desires for cars. While still a sales manager he noticed that many people were pleading for Ford to bring back the old two-seat Thunderbird. The youth market appeared to Iacocca to show increasing potential, and as his voice began to be heard more in the organization he was able to push his ideas of a personal car directed to the youth market. He wanted such a car to be inexpensive, but peppy and sporty-looking.

The Environment for the Automobile in 1964

The decade 1954 to 1964 brought big changes to the auto industry. In 1954, Nash and Kelvinator merged with Hudson Motor Company to form American Motors, and Studebaker merged with Packard to form the Studebaker Corporation. The Packard line was discontinued in 1958, and Hudson was dropped in 1959. The Edsel was introduced in late 1957 and dropped in 1959. Import cars were trickling into the United States around 1955 and gaining popularity. By the late 1950s, both Studebaker and American Motors were successfully producing small cars.

In 1960 Kennedy was elected President. His popularity brought with it a new emphasis on youth. Kennedy also inherited a sluggish economy, and this he tried to remedy with tax cuts that increased disposable income. In 1963 he dropped the excise tax on automobiles. The ground was now laid for a greatly stimulated demand for cars.

In 1961 some 23 auto makers were fighting for a market that had been 7,920,000 cars in 1955 (1955 is used as a base comparison year since it was the industry's best year, not exceeded until 1964). The number of makes of cars had been steadily declining since

---

[6]"Off to the Races Again," *Fortune*, December 4, 1978, p. 15.

1921, when 61 competitors were vying for a much smaller market. Some of the well-known makes that failed were:

- Packard, after 59 years
- Hudson, after 49 years
- Nash, after 40 years
- Auburn, after 38 years
- Pierce Arrow, after 37 years
- Franklin, after 33 years
- Hupmobile, after 32 years
- Reo, after 32 years
- Stutz, after 24 years

In the early 1960s, the remaining car makers began introducing many new models: some 350 different ones were brought to market in 1961 and another 400 in 1962. Consumer preferences appeared to be changing, and the auto makers were offering a great assortment trying to find which would gain acceptance. But the sheer number of choices was leading to customer confusion. Adding to the confusion was the introduction of luxury series of Chevrolets, Fords, and Plymouths, while additional models of Pontiacs, Buicks, and Dodges were being brought out at both the high and low end of their markets. There was severe price overlapping. The top three auto makers were also now producing compacts to counter the inroads being made by imports as well as by American Motors' Rambler compact.

The economy was sluggish in 1961, the economic uncertainties about the Kennedy administration appeared to throttle demand. Many consumers delayed their purchases during the 1961 and 1962 model years, but confidence began building. Dealer stocks at the beginning of the 1963 model year were the lowest since 1957. The year 1963 proved to be a good sales year, with about 7 million cars sold.

The overall economy looked good in 1964. Disposable income was increasing about 5 percent over 1962. Consumer use of credit was burgeoning, and this always augured well for car sales. The growth of two-car families was a particularly optimistic factor, with well over 700,000 expected in 1964. More sobering was the gain made by imports to about 8 percent of the U.S. market. Other lower-priced sports cars were also gaining in popularity.

For the most part, car makers virtually ignored the fascination of youth with autos. Cars play an important role both as a symbol and as an instrument of maturity, although such insights had only begun to be recognized in the early 1960s. But now the realization was growing that the 15- to 24-year-old group constituted a vibrant and growing market segment. Demographic studies showed that the number of 20- to 24-year-olds would increase by 54 percent by 1970. In the same period, the 15- to 19-year-old group would grow 41 percent. Both increases were far greater than anticipated gains in total population.

The Mustang

Marketing Research Efforts. After the prodigious marketing research efforts that preceded the Edsel disaster, it would not have been surprising for Ford to give short shrift to marketing research in the succeeding years. But research was used, though on a smaller scale than in the 1950s.

The statistics on demographics, and particularly on the growing youth market, were widely circulated throughout the company. The company received strong indications that older Americans were acquiring more youthful tastes and becoming involved in activities considered youthful for the time, such as golf and tennis. Thus it seemed that the right car might appeal not only to youth but to older people looking for symbols of youth. Additional research revealed that more people were buying sports cars and their accouterments: bucket seats, zippy engines, and four-speed stick shifts.

It was decided to make the Mustang a sports car. Since many of the individuals in the youth market were just getting started in their careers, the new car had to be versatile. It needed to be priced low enough to meet the needs of the young, low-income earner in addition to middle-income groups; it had to have a back seat and a trunk to accommodate small families, and, if possible, it should appeal to the growing number of two-car families. Thus it should be a family car. In sum, the Mustang ought to be all things to all people. These were the conclusions of the research studies. Now these had to be turned into specifications for the styling and engineering departments.

After designs were drawn up, the results from showing the designs to panels of consumers were fed back to product planning where reevaluations were made of the designated desirable and undesirable design features. After a model of the car was developed, there was further research into how well the design met consumer preferences. An interesting situation developed. In trying to determine the best price for the Mustang, Ford invited 52 couples to view a model of the car. When they thought it was to be priced at $3500 they found a lot of things wrong with the car, but when they were given a price less than $2500, the consumers thought it had great styling and plenty of backseat room.

At this point, with the car now developed and favorable consumer research feedback at hand, Mustang sales were projected at 200,000 units for 1964. Before the official launch date, Ford test-marketed the car with strongly positive results.

The Product. The Edsel fiasco was still a sharp and painful memory: the $200 million loss and nine years of "wasted" research soured upper management on any similarly ambitious undertaking. Recognizing managerial prejudices, Iacocca developed the Mustang for only $65 million, and did so in three years. The car was pieced together from the Falcon, a compact car, and the Fairlane, a midsize car. It was "cross-sourced," that is, built from existing stock. The six-cylinder engine and transmission to power the car were taken from the Falcon. Beyond the costs of new body styling, the only other major expense was in designing a suspension system. Iacocca in an interview described the people involved with it as basically "lunching off the rest of the corporation."[7]

The long hood and short deck style of the Mustang was to fascinate buyers through the 1960s and early 1970s. In fact, the styling hardly changed during those years. The car came in three basic forms: a hardtop, a convertible, and a semi-fastback coupe. Convertible sales started at the 100,000 unit annual level but dropped to 15,000 a year by 1969. The notchback hardtop was the sales leader. The coupe, also known as the 2+2, soon overtook the convertible in sales and averaged about 50,000 units annually through 1970.

The standard Mustang engines during the first six months of production were the 170-cubic-inch six-cylinder, and the 260-cubic-inch V-8 small block. By Fall of 1964 these engines had been bored and stroked to 200 CID and 289 CID respectively. More powerful engines were added, including large-block V-8s by 1970.

Part of the Mustang's appeal lay in its many options, which enabled a customer to personalize the car. Careful use of the order form could result in anything from a cute economy car to a thundering fast drag racer or a deceptively nimble sports car. Transmission choices included automatics, four-speeds, three-speeds, and stick-overdrive units. Handling packages, power steering, disc brakes, air conditioning, and tachometer and clock packages were also available. A special GT package offered front disc brakes, a full-gauge instrument panel, and special gadgets. Several interiors were available, along with accent stripes and special exterior moldings.

To position the Mustang in the marketplace and to make it affordable by youth, the base sticker price was set at $2368 for a six-cylinder hardtop. The price was advertised nationally in virtually all announcement material.

Choosing a name for this new car presented the expected problems: ". . . the name is often the toughest part of a car to get right. It's easier to design doors and roofs than to come up with a name," as Iacocca reminisced in his autobiography.[8] Finalists from thousands of suggestions were Bronco, Puma, Cheetah, Colt, Mustang, and Cougar. Finally Mustang was chosen, not named for the horse but for the famous World War II fighter plane. But it was thought to have "the excitement of wide-open spaces and was American as all hell."

The Promotional Blitz. Ford launched a massive campaign in print and television to promote the Mustang. The intent was to cover as many potential markets as possible in a short period of time. Families, women, and youth were target audiences for Ford's bold introduction of the new model.

On April 2, 1964, barely two weeks before Mustang's debut, Ford began the

---

[7]"Ford's Mustang: The Edsel Avenged," *Forbes*, September 1, 1964, pp. 13–14.
[8]Lee Iacocca, *Iacocca* (New York: Bantam, 1984), p. 69.

TV onslaught. Simultaneous programs were purchased on all three networks. During the next month, Mustang commercials were run on 25 different programs on all three networks. The TV coverage placed Mustang commercials in 95 percent of all homes with TV, with an average frequency of 11 messages per home. Color pages were bought in 191 newspapers in 63 markets. Black and white ads were placed in other newspapers, for a total of 2612 newspapers in 2200 markets. Four-page color inserts appeared in *Life, Look, Reader's Digest, Saturday Evening Post,* and 20 other national magazines.

There were also additional promotional efforts that were more innovative. Ford joined with Alberto-Culver to run a national contest for Command hair dressing: the Command Sports Car Sweepstakes. This brought mention of Mustang on radio in 60 to 70 commercials per week in 31 major markets for almost two months. Mustang was also pictured on display material, on two million Command packages, and in Alberto-Culver national advertisements.

Ford worked out similar arrangements with other companies, such as AMT Toy Company, Holiday Inn, Sea & Ski Company, Jantzen, and the Indianapolis Motor Speedway. A model Mustang could be purchased for $1 from AMT Toys. Mustangs were displayed in lobbies of 200 Holiday Inn motels and were featured in their directories and in their national advertising. They were displayed in 15 of the country's busiest airports. At University of Michigan football games several acres of space were rented, with huge signs proclaiming, ''Mustang Corral.'' Sea & Ski introduced a new style of sunglasses called Mustang, and the company's national advertising featured the sports car with the glasses. Major department stores used actual Mustangs as props for some of their displays. Jantzen conducted a Miss Smile contest with the Mustang as its grand prize. The Indianapolis 500-mile race had a Mustang convertible as its pace car for 1964.

Among other things, Ford set up a traffic-building registration contest that offered 1000 prizes, including 25 Mustangs. A three-million-piece mailing inaugurated the contest.

Four days before the official launching, a hundred reporters participated in a 70-car Mustang rally from New York City to Dearborn, Michigan, some 700 miles. Enthusiastic commentaries in hundreds of magazines and newspapers added to the growing excitement about this new car. A coup of no small moment was the simultaneous featuring of the Mustang on the covers of both *Time* and *Newsweek.*

Results. The Mustang took off. On April 17, Ford dealers were mobbed with customers; one dealer even had to lock his doors against a huge crowd outside. During the first weekend it was on sale, four million people visited dealer showrooms.

Initial expectations were that 75,000 Mustangs would sell during its first year. But optimism was growing, and by the introduction sales projections were 200,000. A second plant was converted to Mustang production, bringing annual capacity up to 360,000. And still it was not enough: a third plant had to be converted. While people were buying Mustangs in record numbers, most were also ordering from a long list of profitable options, spending an additional $1000. And in the first two years alone, the Mustang generated net profits of $1.1 billion.

The first 100,000 units sold in only 92 days. Over 400,000 were sold in the first 12 months. The success of the Mustang brought some production economies. There was no complete assembly-line shutdown for model changes between 1964 and 1965: the 1964 models were still rolling off the line while the 1965 models were being tooled for the next production line.

How long would it last? Ford expected General Motors and Chrysler to enter the market with a competitive model, although it was thought it would take several years to develop a new model. It was not until Fall, 1966 that Chevrolet introduced a competitor, the Camaro, with styling similar to the Mustang: long hood, short deck, and same length wheelbase. Chrysler followed soon after with the Barracuda. But the Mustang more than held its own, maintaining more than half of the market for lower-priced sports cars.

Keys to Success

External. The economic cards were better stacked for the Mustang than for the Edsel. Productivity was increasing by 1964 and, as a result, so was the standard of living. Since wage increases did not outpace changes in productivity, inflation was not a problem. By the mid-1960s there was a build-up of demand for new cars. Table 6.2 shows total U.S. car sales for the period between 1960 and 1970. Up to that time, 1965 was the largest sales year in automotive history. With the luck of perfect timing, the Spring introduction in April 1964 enabled the Mustang to take full advantage of the situation. There was less competition from new model introductions since these had taken place in the Fall.

There were also social changes taking place that benefited the Mustang. A national preoccupation with youth and physical fitness, just beginning to emerge, accelerated by the late 1960s.[9] The Mustang was a car that portrayed youth and vitality, even in its name. A sports car or a sporty car was a natural product for this changing environment.

Marketing Research. In contrast to the Edsel experience, marketing research was kept current. Several methods were used by the company to monitor the youth market, including hot-rod shows and sponsorship of college campus activities. The hot-rod shows gave Ford ideas about car styling, handling, and performance. The

---

[9]Indicative of this was a running boom that was to bring millions of runners to the streets by the late 1960s and throughout the 1970s and beyond. We will discuss another contrasting "bullseye and blunder" relating to the running shoe market in Chapter 10.

Table 6.2   U.S. Motor Vehicle Sales, 1960–1970

Year	Units Sold
1960	7,905,117
1961	6,652,938
1962	8,197,311
1963	9,108,776
1964	9,307,860
1965	11,137,830
1966	10,396,299
1967	9,023,736
1968	10,820,410
1969	10,205,911
1970	8,283,949

Source: Automotive News 1978 Market Data Book Issues, p. 10.

youth market was creating its own type of automobiles, which the researchers saw as supporting the need for a personal car. By being on college campuses, Ford could see that students bought foreign cars as a display of independence, individualism, and personal taste. Ford researchers concluded that this was the age when buyer preferences form. Consequently Ford made a major effort to capture this growing market.

The Product. The unique body style—long hood and short deck—appealed to many. Quality control was high. This emphasis on quality became a companywide policy for all models (although quality never seemed to match that of foreign cars in many person's minds). The Mustang also filled a need in the market for a personal car: it could be tailored to the individual through the wide choices of models and options. The more options a customer bought, the greater the profit margin since options typically carry higher markups than basic cars. Furthermore, since production costs were low, there was a large profit margin on the basic car. Therefore, record sales were accompanied with above-average profit margins.

Promotion. Virtually every medium was used effectively. The various creative promotional contests helped gain additional attention as well as conveying desirable image associations, particularly that of the youthful sports car. Drawings or raffles helped increase traffic flow through dealer showrooms. Promotional efforts had continuity and timing. Information flowed constantly from television to radio, to print, and finally to personal selling. Before long, almost everywhere one looked, the Mustang could be seen. Knowledge of the Mustang was pervasive throughout the country.

Distribution. This time Ford decided to use its regular dealers to sell Mustangs. By using its existing 6400 dealers, the substantial added costs of a new division were avoided, and the breakeven point for reaching profitability was kept moderate. See the boxed information on the breakeven point for a more specific discussion of these issues.

INFORMATION SIDELIGHT

THE BREAKEVEN POINT

A breakeven analysis is a vital tool in making go/no-go decisions about new ventures. This can be shown graphically as follows: Below the breakeven point, the venture suffers losses (as Edsel did); above it, the venture becomes profitable.

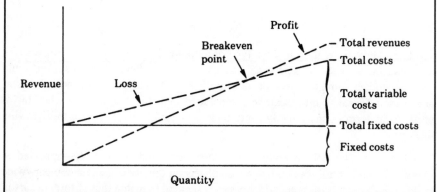

Hypothetical comparison of Edsel (with separate dealer organization) and Mustang (without separate dealer organization):

For this example, let us assume that promotional expenses and other basic operating expenses for the first year are $50,000,000 for both cars. These are fixed costs or overhead that the two ventures will incur regardless of sales. Assume that the average profit contribution beyond production costs and the other variable costs is $400 per car (actually, for the Mustang the profit contribution was considerably higher because of lower production costs and increased sales of more profitable optional equipment). The sales needed to break even are:

$$\text{Breakeven} = \frac{\text{Total fixed costs}}{\text{Contribution to overhead}}$$

$$= \frac{\$50,000,000}{\$400} = 125,000 \text{ units}$$

But the Edsel had substantial additional fixed costs because of its separate dealer organization. We can estimate these additional costs as:

Salary and expenses for 100 field representatives for liaison with 1200 dealers	$ 6,000,000
Salary and expenses for Edsel organizational staff— management and back-up personnel and facilities	4,000,000
Additional operating expenses—overhead, telephone, postage, etc.	2,000,000
Total additional costs	12,000,000

Therefore, the Edsel breakeven point is:

$$\frac{\$12,000,000 + \$50,000,000}{\$400} = 155,000 \text{ units}$$

But the actual sales of the Edsel were 54,607 units the first year, 26,563 the second, year, and 29,667 the last year, far below the breakeven point. The higher fixed costs of the separate dealer organization only exacerbated the situation.

In making go/no-go decisions, these costs can be estimated quite closely. What cannot be determined as surely are the sales figures. Certain things can be done to affect the breakeven point. Obviously it can be lowered if the overhead is reduced, say, from $50,000,000 to $30,000,000. Higher sales prices also result in a lower breakeven because of higher per unit profit (but would probably affect total sales quite adversely). Promotional expenses can be either increased or decreased and affect the breakeven point; but they probably also have an impact on sales. But the drain of a costly separate dealer organization had a major negative impact on the breakeven point, and does not appear to have made any positive contribution to sales.

In addition, the increased traffic that Mustang created brought potential buyers for other Ford models. Many of the operational expenses normally incurred by a new model can be spread over the older models. Dealer reputations were already established with adequate financing and sales and service-center staffing. With a product in great demand, there is no concern about having a sufficiently motivated sales force. Once the sales potential of the Mustang could be seen, any sales force would be highly motivated and enthusiastic. Success feeds on success.

THE EDSEL AND THE MUSTANG: WHAT CAN BE LEARNED?

Few pairs of successes and failures can match the learning insights provided by analysis of the Edsel and the Mustang.

Learning Insight. For new products, the calculation of sales potential is risky, but crucial.

A major contributor to the Edsel disaster was an imprudent estimate of sales potential: the expectation was way too high. Sales forecasting for a new product is hazardous at best. Sometimes sales greatly exceed expectations, as with the Mustang; at other times they may not even come close to achieving expectations. This is one of the calculated risks of decision making in an uncertain environment. If one is too optimistic, product and other resource allocations will be too high, and heavy costs will be incurred. Yet, as we see in other cases presented in this book, forecasting too low is also fraught with danger. The sales potential is untapped, and a significant opportunity is likely to be handed to competitors.

The prudent way of dealing with uncertainties, such as sale forecasting, is to maintain the greatest possible flexibility, to prepare the organization for expansion

---

INFORMATION SIDELIGHT

CONTINGENCY PLANS

Planning involves resource deployment through the use of budgets. Resources include both personnel and facilities. Resource deployment is based on assumptions made about both the external and the internal environment. When plans are made for major projects, such as the Edsel, and resources are committed based on long-range predictions of as much as five years and more, success of the commitment depends greatly on the accuracy of the assumptions. As events unfold and it is seen that certain assumptions are either overly optimistic or overly pessimistic, plans and resource deployment need to be revised; otherwise breakeven points are unrealistic or unattainable.

Contingency plans are helpful when dealing with a new product or project and an uncertain future. Plan A may assume a certain level of acceptance of the product, and a particular volume and cost of production; Plan B may be developed for better-than-expected circumstances; and Plan C may be ready to implement if early results are discouraging. When these plans are drawn up in advance, a firm is better able to cope with varied outcomes and can either marshall additional resources or cut back to more realistic expectations.

Edsel could have made better use of contingency planning for different levels of competition, different economic conditions, and varying consumer acceptances. Lesser expectations and a lower breakeven point might have sustained the Edsel until its product could be better tuned to the marketplace and better economic conditions prevailed.

while not allowing the commitment of resources to bring on disaster if expectations are not realized. Contingency planning plays a vital role in making decisions under conditions of uncertainty.

> *Learning Insight. The breakeven point should be kept as low as possible, especially on new and untried ventures.*

Edsel's separate dealer organization had a devastating effect on profitability because of the high breakeven point it required. The Edsel could have been sold through existing Ford and Mercury dealers without greatly increasing distribution costs of the new car and without subjecting the dealers to high risks, because they would have had their other makes of cars on which to fall back. The 18 models of Edsel further increased the breakeven point. While the optimistic sales forecast led to decisions that increased the breakeven point, this need not have been the case, as was shown by the Mustang. Less ambitious organizational and product planning would have lowered the breakeven point.

What can be learned? Optimistic forecasting is bad? Confidently going ahead with an ambitious project is folly? No, not at all. But the decision maker must weigh carefully the risk and reward factors of costly and ambitious decisions. Mistakes *will* be made. The future is never certain, despite research and careful planning. The environment is always changing, whether we consider customer attitudes and preferences, competitive efforts, or such unpredictable factors as OPEC-created petroleum shortages and skyrocketing energy prices, or the reverse—petroleum gluts and plummeting prices.

When a decision involves high stakes and an uncertain future—which translates into high risks—is it not wiser to approach the venture somewhat conservatively, not spurning the opportunity, but also not committing all resources and efforts until success appears more certain?

It can be argued that with a new model of car—whether the Edsel, or K-cars, or X-cars—the huge start-up investment militates against halfway measures. But separate dealerships need not be established; an array of models can be reduced; even advertising can be more conservatively placed. And the compelling example of the Mustang shows that not all new model introductions need involve gigantic tooling and production costs.

> *Learning Insight. The external economic and social environment is important, and so is luck.*

Some maintain that luck confounds careful planning and analysis and rewards the intuitive and impulsive. Some even rail against the injustice of raw luck and its rewarding of the unworthy. But let's face it. Luck, opportunism, providential timing—these can be powerful factors in the success of firms and individual careers; and they can also be handmaidens of disaster.

The Edsel could hardly have been introduced at a worse economic time, with a recession in full force and demand for all cars dropping. The Mustang caught the other swing of the pendulum, with an upward-looking economy and pent-up demand leading to the largest sales volume year in automotive history in 1965. This raises the intriguing question: Would the Edsel have been a success if it had been introduced later, say, in the early 1960s? We would still have to answer in the negative, however. Despite a more favorable economy, something else in the environment was against the Edsel. Consumer tastes and interests had shifted from the type of car the Edsel represented to smaller, sportier models that the Mustang heralded.

Learning Insight. Organizations need to monitor and react to a changing environment.

To monitor is to seek feedback and keep alert to subtle and not-so-subtle changes taking place in the environment. Formal marketing research may help, although this is not always the case, but simple executive alertness can often suffice. Changing environmental factors, such as consumer tastes, or the demographic profile of consumers, are not arcane or difficult to read and interpret. They are not abrupt and cataclysmic, but occur gradually. We will see many instances in this book where management has failed to recognize such changes. Edsel planners failed to recognize shifting consumer sentiment; Iacocca correctly assessed the environment and rode the trend to the industry's greatest success.

Learning Insight. Marketing research does not guarantee success.

Despite being regarded as the mark of sophisticated management, marketing research by no means guarantees a correct decision. Marketing research provided the Mustang planners with insights that aided the success of the car with respect to design acceptability and optimal pricing, but marketing research is not a panacea. Consumer statements regarding preferences often can be difficult to interpret and translate into design characteristics of a finished product. And when research is done incorrectly, or research conclusions are biased or self-serving, it may be worse than useless since it may allay reasonable cautions by prudent executives. The millions of dollars spent on marketing research for the Edsel was wasted since research efforts were terminated two years before the car was introduced, at a time when consumer preferences were changing. Dated research is worse than stale news, since it may lead to costly decisions that are far off the mark.

Learning Insight. Planning and long lead-time preparations do not assure success.

This caveat flies in the face of the common belief—even the gut feel—that better planning is the key to personal and all other kinds of success. The stark reality, we are forced to concede, is that heavy planning efforts have the same relationship to success as heavy marketing research efforts—they should help improve the decision-making process, but they by no means guarantee correct decisions. Circumstances and opportunities can drastically change between the planning and the realization.

The Edsel case brings reality to the rosy veneer associated with exacting planning. The planning of the Mustang, on the other hand, was done with far less specificity, with years less lead time, and while it erred on the side of conservatism, there was sufficient flexibility built into the production planning to cope with success. Does this excoriate extensive planning? Have executives deluded themselves about the benefits of finely honed planning? We hardly want to condemn planning as worthless and a waste of time. Rather, planning ought to be relegated to a more realistic role—along with other popular tools of "sophisticated" management—and concede that it can err. Perhaps moderation in relying on planning and other sophisticated managerial tools is best—even though in some circles this smacks of heresy.

Learning Insight. Poor quality control creates a lasting stigma.

The first Edsels had many defects, worse than most new car introductions. The reputation for poorly constructed cars soon spread and became pervasive—long after the worst flaws had been corrected. Any firm flirts with danger when it allows lax quality control to permit many defective products to reach the market. Reputations are long lasting. And this can be a significant impediment, or a powerful advantage. For example, consider Maytag.

The Maytag Company is located in a small town, Newton Iowa. Compared to its competitors, General Electric and Whirlpool, it is a small company. But Maytag makes what many people, including *Consumer Reports,* consider to be the best equipment. The company has not directed its efforts to the new-home market and builders who demand price concessions. Instead, it has chosen as its major market the customer seeking a replacement for a cheaper washing machine that has given trouble. Such a customer often is willing to pay a premium for a trouble-free machine. And this Maytag achieves. Unlike other companies in the industry, the company makes no periodic model changes. Instead, it seeks to simplify its products and make them reliable. And Maytag's advertising of the "lonesome repairman" effectively reinforces the deserved reputation for trouble-free quality.

Learning Insight. There is no assured correlation between expenditures for advertising and promotion and sales success.

Ford spent millions of dollars to promote both the Edsel and the Mustang. We might surmise that the Mustang promotional efforts were more effective than the Edsel, especially in attracting a particular segment of consumers, the youth market. In fact, neither promotional campaign can be seriously criticized. There was, however, one key difference. While Edsel advertising brought people into dealer showrooms, what they saw there did not meet their expectations as the Edsel car itself had little appeal when seen close up. The Mustang, on the other hand, was appealing both in ads and in physical presence.

Creative advertising, if backed with sufficient expenditures, can induce people to try the product—or at least to examine it more closely. But if the product does not meet expectations, there will be no repeat buying or, in the case of cars, no purchase.

For Thought and Discussion

1. How would you have designed marketing research to have provided more useful information for the Edsel marketing decisions?
2. Should the Edsel have been test-marketed? Why or why not?
3. How would you respond to the comment that the failure of the Edsel despite extensive planning (starting 10 years before the product finally was introduced) means that planning too far in advance is futile?
4. List as many pros and cons as possible for having Edsel as a separate division (with separate dealers) rather than as part of an existing division (and dealer organization) such as Lincoln–Mercury. On balance, which direction does the weight of pros and cons seem to point?
5. Was the success of the Mustang more attributable to lucky timing than to any inspired planning?

Invitation to Role Play

1. Assume the role of the Ford executive responsible for the Edsel operation. What strategy would you have used both in the introductory period and in the subsequent several years to enable it to attain both viability and success? Be as specific and complete as you can and be prepared to defend your proposals against other alternatives. Be sure your recommendations are reasonable and practical.
2. As a staff planner for Ford, you have been asked to evaluate the desirability of a luxury addition of the Mustang line. How would you research the market potential, and what other factors do you think ought to be considered in this $100 million decision?

7

Harley Davidson
Versus Honda

In the early 1960s, a staid and unexciting market was shaken up, was rocked to its core, by the most unlikely invader. This intruder was a smallish Japanese firm that had risen out of the ashes of World War II, and was now trying to encroach on the territory of a major U.S. firm that had in the space of 60 years destroyed all of its U.S. competitors, and now had a firm 70 percent of the motorcycle market.

Yet, almost inconceivably, in half a decade this market share was to fall to 5 percent, and the total market was to expand many times over what it had been for decades. A foreign invader had furnished a textbook example of the awesome effectiveness of carefully crafted marketing efforts. In the process, this confrontation between Honda and Harley Davidson was a harbinger of the Japanese invasion of the auto industry.

HARLEY DAVIDSON: THE OPPORTUNITY UNNOTICED

Historical Background

Harley Davidson motorcycles date back to 1903 when the Harley and Davidson families, in a 10-by-15-foot wooden shed in the Davidson backyard, built motorcycles in evenings and weekends. Members of both families participated in the endeavor, aided by a few other people, notably Ole Evinrude, who became a well-known manufacturer of outboard motors. The first year they sold four motorcycles, the next year eight. Production continued to increase, aided by a demand that was greater than could be filled, as motorcycles began replacing horses. By 1915, Harley Davidson was producing 18,000 machines a year, and another brand, Indian, joined it in dominating the U.S. two-wheel machine industry. With America's entry into World War I, practically all of Harley Davidson's production went to the military.

However, the boom collapsed with peacetime. The horseless carriage, particularly Ford's Model T, was tough competition. A motorcycle with a sidecar could never provide the comfort and convenience of the Model T. And Ford priced his cars so low that they cost little more than Harley Davidson motorcycles, and sometimes even less. The situation did not improve during the depression years of the 1930s. Rather than making motorcycles inexpensive to appeal to consumers' reduced incomes during the 1930s, Harley Davidson and its major competitors, Indian and Henderson, made motorcycles more luxurious and more powerful—and, of course, more expensive. A deluxe model with a sidecar in 1930 sold for as much as $2000—all the Spartan comfort of two wheels at more than the price of most automobiles.

World War II again buttressed the motorcycle industry, with Harley Davidson selling 90,000 machines alone. But motorcycles played only a minor role in this war, where the emphasis was on other types of motorized equipment. The peacetime booming economy still found the motorcycle industry on the sidelines. Sales increased much less in proportion than did the sales of automobiles. And now motorcycles were being purchased by some of the wrong people—drifters, gangs of hoodlums, and other undesirables.

In 1953 the Indian Motorcycle Company folded. This was the largest motorcycle manufacturer to fail; others, such as Henderson, Yale, Merkel, Minnesota, Pope, and Thor, preceded Indian. Now only Harley Davidson was left to make motorcycles in the United States, where once there had been 114 makers of motorcycles.

The Public's Perception of the Motorcyclist. Over the decades, the motorcycle became synonymous with blackleather jackets and deviant and even violent behavior. This perception dates back to the late 1920s and the 1930s, years of hard times and high unemployment, when a gypsy lifestyle was embraced by some as they roamed over the country untethered by job or responsibilities, often dirty, sometimes drunken, always noisy as their machines roared through city streets. Regardless of the number of motorcyclists who actually fit that description, and regardless of the general invalidity of it, the idea stuck.

The years after World War II reinforced the idea. In 1947 in Hollister, California, a town of 4800 people, a gang on big, black Harley Davidsons rolled into town, converging on the open taverns, and by evening had torn up the town. The outnumbered police, gathering volunteer deputies and aided by vigilante bands of outraged citizens, met them in a pitched battle that left 50 people injured. The episode led to a widely screened movie, *The Wild One*, starring Marlon Brando, in which a gang of hoodlum motorcyclists roam the country, contemptuous of law and order, and take over a small town. As *The New York Times* reported:

> A little bit of the surface of contemporary American life is scratched in Stanley Kramer's "The Wild One" . . . and underneath is opened an ugly, debauched and frightening view of a small, but particularly significant and menacing element of modern youth.[1]

In subsequent years, the antics of motorcycle gangs, particularly Hell's Angels, increased the public's negative image of motorcyclists. In 1966 a Florida police official was quoted:

> These punks with their cycles and their Nazi trappings have it in for the world—and for everyone in it. They're a menace, a damned serious menace, that's growing bigger every year.[2]

The Invasion Sales in the United States were around 50,000 per year during the 1950s, with Harley Davidson, Britain's Norton and Triumph, and Germany's BMW accounting for most of the market. By the turn of the decade, the Japanese firm Honda began to penetrate the U.S. market. In 1960 less than 400,000 motorcycles were registered in the United States. While this was an increase of almost 200,000 from the end of World War II 15 years before, it was far below the increase in other motor vehicles. But by 1964, only four years later, the number had risen to 960,000; two years later it was 1.4 million; and by 1971 it was almost 4 million.

As we examine in depth in the next section, Honda instituted a distinctly different strategy to expand the demand for motorcycles. The major elements of this strategy were lightweight cycles and an advertising approach directed toward a new customer. Few firms have ever experienced such a shattering of market share as did Harley Davidson in the 1960s. (Although its market share declined drastically, its total sales remained nearly constant, indicating that it was getting none of the new customers for motorcycles.)

Reaction of Harley Davidson to the Honda Threat

Faced with an invasion of its staid and static U.S. market, how did Harley Davidson react to the intruder? They did not react! At least not until far too late. Harley Davidson considered themselves the leader in full-size motorcycles. While the company might shudder at the image tied in with their product's usage by the leather

---

[1]Bosley Crowther, *The New York Times*, December 31, 1953, p. 9:2.
[2]Lee Gutkind, *Bike Fever* (Chicago: Follet Publishing, 1973), pp. 38–39.

jacket types, it took solace in the fact that almost every U.S. police department used its machines. Perhaps this is what led Harley Davidson to stand aside and complacently watch Honda make deep inroads into the American motorcycle market. The management saw no threat in Honda's thrust into the market with lightweight motorcycles. Their attitude was exemplified in this statement by William H. Davidson, the president of the company and son of the founder:

> Basically, we don't believe in the lightweight market. We believe that motorcycles are sport vehicles, not transportation vehicles. Even if a man says he bought a motorcycle for transportation, it's generally for leisure-time use. The lightweight motorcycle is only supplemental. Back around World War I, a number of companies came out with lightweight bikes. We came out with one ourselves. They never got anywhere. We've seen what happens to these small sizes.[3]

Eventually Harley recognized that the Honda phenomenon was not an aberration, and that there was a new factor in the market. The company attempted to retaliate by offering an Italian-made lightweight in the mid-1960s. But it was far too late; Honda was firmly entrenched. The Italian bikes were regarded in the industry to be of lower quality than the Japanese. Honda, and toward the end of the 1960s other Japanese manufacturers, continued to dominate what had become a much larger market than ever dreamed.

What Went Wrong for Harley Davidson?

Harley Davidson's error was one of omission. It took no action, made no commitment—an approach that was to turn out rash and costly. Its problems did not come from misguided expansion. Its problems came from a null decision, the lack of aggressiveness, an unwillingness to change anything. We can identify Harley's problems under what we might term the "three C's" syndrome of failure.

The "Three C's" Syndrome of Failure. Firms that have been well entrenched in their industry and that have dominated it for years often fall into a particular syndrome that leaves them vulnerable to aggressive and innovative competitors.
The "three C's" that are detrimental to a front-runner's continued success are:

Complacency

Conservatism

Conceit

We can define *complacency* as smugness; a self-satisfied firm, content with the status quo, is no longer hungry and eager for grwoth. This term describes Harley in

---

[3]"Harley Sets New Drive to Boost Market Share," *Advertising AGe*, January 29, 1973, pp. 34–35.

the 1950s and into the 1960s, even while Honda was intensifying its American invasion. The last major U.S. competitor, Indian, had closed its doors in 1953. There was no competitor within sight who might contest Harley's share of the market for large motorcycles; Harley was the lone survivor, and it had a comfortable captive market, the police. Even the bad image continuing to plague the civilian motorcycle user could not dent the complacency of Harley.

Conservatism characterizes a management that is wedded to the past, to the traditional, the way things have always been done. There is no need to change because nothing is different today. And to a complacent management the environment seemed static, with little growth potential. There was no need for any strategy changes from the satisfactory ways of the past: big machines, expensive options— profitable—all aimed at the hard-core motorcyclist. The possibility that the market might be far greater than the hard-core user of big, expensive machines was never even considered.

Finally, *conceit* can further reinforce the myopia of the managerial perspective: conceit for present and potential competitors. A belief that ''we are the best,'' and ''no one else can touch us'' can easily permeate an organization when everything has been going quietly for years. It must have given Harley management great satisfaction to think of themselves as the best of the 100-plus former manufacturers of motorcycles. A feeling of self-confidence and a disdain for potential competitors is easy to come by, especially back in the 1950s and early 1960s when the potential competitor was a small Japanese upstart.

With the three C's syndrome of failure, there is no incentive to undertake aggressive and innovative actions. There is disinterest in some important facets of the business, particularly in quality control, customer relations, and servicing. Further, there is no incentive to develop new products, and an aversion to sharp promotional activities. With such a syndrome, a firm sets itself up for a fall to an aggressive and hungry competitor, no matter how small and unknown the competitor might be at first.

Harley, in defense of its conviction that there was no market for lightweight cycles, was quick to cite how it had attempted to introduce them twice, and failed badly both times. It tried once in 1925, and again in 1949. ''Therefore, how could the market want these now?''

In retrospect, a major reason for the failures was that it had priced the light-weights only a little below the heavier motorcycles, and most people consequently saw the heavier machines as the better values. But, more than this, Harley should have recognized that no market is static and unchanging. America's tastes were changing by the late 1950s. A greater interest was being shown in smaller cars and in economy of operation. The Edsel also failed in the late 1950s as consumers spurned its high horsepower and size and turned to the smaller and more economical imported cars. The way was paved for an aggressive and ingenious David to confront Goliath and leave him sprawled in the dust.

THE HONDA MOTORCYCLE INVASION

Soichiro Honda was the son of a blacksmith. When he was three years old, his father gave him a pair of pliers. It remained his favorite possession. He only went to the tenth grade in school, but he had great mechanical ability and received his first patent when he was 14. He became an auto mechanic and by the time he was 21 had opened a garage where he became known as the man who could fix anything. By the time he was 27, his garage had grown to the point where he had 50 employees.

Honda was not only a fixer, he was also a creator. He bolted an old Curtis airplane engine into an auto chassis and had a racing car that nobody could beat. He designed his own piston rings and by World War II had developed the finest piston rings in Japan. His entire output was taken for military vehicles. Near the end of the war, a bomb demolished his factory. He was then 41, with almost all his money gone.

Honda began looking for other ventures. He purchased 500 small war-surplus gasoline engines that had been used to power communications equipment. He mounted these on standard bicycles. While crude and difficult to start, they sold rapidly in a country with little transportation. After the engines were gone, Honda designed and built his own engine, and later also began producing frames and wheels. By 1949 his plant was manufacturing all the basic components and was assembling Honda motorcycles. These early cycles could go 45 miles per hour, getting up to 200 miles per gallon of gas. In 1950 Honda produced 3600 motorcycles. In only two years he employed 1000 men in a plant 100 times larger than he had before. In 1959, Soichiro Honda decided to invade the American motorcycle market.

The Japanese Invasion

Honda's introduction of the lightweight motorbike in the United States did not have a very auspicious beginning: only 167 units were sold during the first year. Motorcycle experts laughed at the puny Japanese machines. But such derision and skepticism were to change quickly. In 1960 sales were 22,100 units, increasing in only five years more than tenfold to 270,000 units in 1965. By 1965 Honda had 80 percent of the expanding U.S. market, and Harley Davidson was still selling about 35,000 units per year.

While Honda enjoyed steady growth after 1965, it was not as dramatic as during the real growth years from 1963 to 1965. Sales increased to 650,000 units by 1974, but market share steadily declined from 80 percent in 1965 to 45.6 percent in 1977. However, this was still the major share of the U.S. market, which Honda now was contesting with other Japanese firms. Market shares for the leading motorcycle makers in 1977 were:

Honda	45.6%
Yamaha	18.9
Suzuki	10.7
Kawasaki	14.4
Harley Davidson	5.7

In few annals of business history had an invader come into an entrenched market and so quickly gained mastery. How could this have happened?

The Invasion Strategy. Soichiro Honda's philosophy has been widely stated:

> If you turn out a superior product, it will be patronized by the public. Our policy is not simply to turn out a product because there is demand, but to turn out a superior product and create a demand.[4]

To move beyond Japan and open up the export market, Honda thought that his machines would need an international reputation, and that this could best be gained on the international racing circuit. In June 1954 he went to the Isle of Man to enter his machines in the oldest of the international racing classics. He was shocked to learn that the European competition was fielding models with three times the horsepower of the Hondas. By 1961, however, Honda won world championships in the 125-cc. (cubic centimeter) and 150-cc. engine classes.

But it took more than racing trophies to open the U.S. market. At best only a limited number of bikes would have been sold to motorcycle buffs. So Honda moved his attack on the United States and international markets to a different level, a level never before achieved in the industry, and advertising was given the key role in this.

Promotional Strategy. The Grey Advertising Agency was commissioned to handle the U.S. promotion. The task assigned was to win social acceptance for the motorcycle and its rider. The basic thrust of the communications strategy was to create a fresh image for the Honda motorcycle and to educate the general public to a new mode of transportation.

Honda wanted to promote the idea that riding a motorcycle is fun. A basic theme of advertising in the early 1960s was "Holidays and Honda days," and "Go happy, go Honda." To promote this theme, Honda had to buck the negative perceptions of motorcyclists as the black-leather-jacketed characters widely publicized in a continuing negative press. Most Americans had never ridden on or driven a motorcycle, and the negative image of motorcyclists stood in the way of Honda, who wanted to attract a large new market.

[4]*Journal of Commerce*, November 6, 1965, p. 23.

Social acceptance was finally achieved by heavy promotion of the theme, "You meet the nicest people on a Honda." Early advertisements showed nine totally different kinds of people—old, young, casual, formal, but they all had in common the fact that they were nice, acceptable people, and they were all riding a Honda. One ad read:

> You meet the nicest people on a Honda. It's largely a question of personality. A Honda is easygoing, dependable. Makes few demands. Prices start at around $215. And it runs all day on a nickel's worth of gas. That's the kind of friend to have. Frugal. How about one in your family? World's biggest seller.

Despite the quiet tone of this ad, it puts over the Honda story through words like "nice," "easygoing," "friend," "family," and "frugal."

Ads with this theme were placed in magazines, network TV, spot radio, newspapers, outdoor farm publications, and direct mail. The media chosen were designed to reach nontraditional bike owners, people who might never have thought of owning any vehicle with less than four wheels. Ads were placed in magazines such as *Life, Look, Saturday Evening Post,* and *Sports Illustrated.*

People already sold on motorcycles were not overlooked either, as many ads were also placed in magazines for cycle enthusiasts. Commercials were run on the top 40 radio stations favored by young people. Newspapers were used in key markets as well as large space advertising in more than 225 college newspapers where the message was stressed that Honda had the answer to campus parking problems. Even billboards were used in a unified program to give Honda maximum public exposure.

The major target of the promotional efforts was the young. Honda and Grey Agency believed that with the increasing number of World War II babies growing up, products that would assert their individuality could become popular. The new lightweight bikes of Honda were introduced as such a product (the Mustang was also introduced about this time, riding the youth crest). While it was expected that many parents would oppose the purchase of a motorcycle, it was thought that their resistance could be overcome by the advertising.

The buyers were primarily young males between 16 and 26: college students, young professionals, and others getting started in their white-collar careers. Studies showed that teenagers were becoming the largest group of owners, with 32 percent of the first-time purchasers under 20.

While there were other factors in the strategy that contributed to the success of Honda, the importance of the advertising campaign can hardly be overemphasized. Honda succeeded in selling the idea that it was smart and sophisticated to ride a motorcycle through their "nice people" advertising. American and European makers alike credited this advertising campaign with sparking the enormous growth of the entire industry. Indeed, in the annals of advertising there are few such examples of the effectiveness of the mass media in radically changing mores and social acceptability in such a short period of time.

The Product Strategy. Honda invaded the U.S. market with small (50 cc.), light-weight bikes that could go miles on a thimbleful of gasoline, and that could be purchased for less than $300 when most of the other motorcycles cost $1500 and more. Furthermore, a customer had six snappy colors to choose from in three different models, at a time when most other motorcycle makers offered no more than two or three models and color choices. The little Hondas could go 55 miles per hour for 180 miles on 30 cents worth of regular gas. And the product quality was impressive. A top executive of a British motorcycle firm examined a Honda machine in 1961 and made a widely quoted statement: "When we stripped the machine, frankly, it was so good it frightened us. It was made like a watch, and it wasn't a copy of anything."[5]

As Honda began to dominate the U.S. market, it expanded the product line, aiming to have a model for every potential rider. By 1965, 14 different motorcycles were available, ranging from a light 50 cc. to a fast 305 cc. In 1966 a larger 450-cc. bike was added to compete with the Harley Davidson models, but the bulk of Honda sales in 1965 was in the 150-cc. and smaller models.

But the potential for trade-up sales spurred Honda to offer larger models, and a few years later there were models available up to 1100 cc., fully as large as any Harley Davidson. As people traded up to get bikes with more horsepower, they looked to Honda for the larger motorcycles, not Harley Davidson. One study found that 40 percent of those with light machines were buying heavier ones.

Production Advantage. Honda had certain inherent advantages in its effective strategy to invade the U.S. market. Japanese labor was much less expensive than American, contributing to competitively lower production costs. In addition, the size of the Japanese home market afforded a substantial advantage over any American producer. The demand for motorcycles in Japan was in the neighborhood of two million machines a year. This large sales base made it possible to keep production high and unit costs low. Consequently, motorcycles could be exported at prices unmatchable by foreign producers.

Handling Service Problems. A servicing problem emerged as sales began to mushroom. Growth was so rapid that not enough trained mechanics were available. Parts warehouses encountered severe shortages. The problem for a time became so bad that the growth of Honda was jeopardized, and there was the potential for a long-term image problem and loss of customer loyalty. To Honda's credit, once the

[5]Gutkind, op. cit., p. 160.

problem was recognized, immediate corrective actions were taken. More mechanics were quickly trained, more parts warehouses were opened, existing warehouses were enlarged, and dealer inventories were maintained at more adequate levels. There was no serious long-term harm to Honda.

Distribution Strategy. Honda continued its innovative approach to the U.S. market in its distribution strategy and choice of dealers. Previously, most motorcycle dealers were located on the outskirts of cities, often in seedy neighborhoods where the leather-jacketed crowd felt more comfortable. Dealerships tended to be dirty and noisy places and rather undesirable neighbors. Honda spurned this approach and often located its dealers in the center of town. New York City for some time had a dealer on Madison Avenue, only three blocks from Grand Central Station and its concentration of commuter traffic. By 1965 more than 1500 Honda dealers were located in every state, making the product readily available. Most of these locations were where the traditional motorcyclist would hardly feel at ease. This was 19 percent of a national total of 8000 dealers, and it compared with Harley Davidson's 880 dealers, or 11 percent.

In addition to selling and servicing Hondas, another plum was offered dealers as Honda sought to tap a different customer—the person who preferred to rent—at least at first—rather than buying. By 1965 rentals amounted to some $40 million. In addition to providing extra income, many of those who rented eventually bought. Rentals provided a good way to try out a new form of transportation and to determine how easy it was to handle, and how economical and convenient these vehicles really were. The general public would never rent the large, expensive Harley Davidsons, but many were keen to rent the light and easy-to-handle Hondas.

Reactions to Looming Problems. In 1966 total sales of motorcycles slumped. Although Honda sales increased, they were less than projected, and Honda was concerned. The cause was not difficult to pinpoint. Activity in the Vietnam War was increasing and more 18–25 year olds were being drafted. This was the group that comprised 50 percent of the Honda market. Adding to the problem, banks were becoming more reluctant to finance purchases for draft-age buyers.

Such problems, of course, were external factors in the environment, presumably conditions that Honda or any other motorcycle maker could do little about. But Honda did. Amid a slumping market, Honda actually increased advertising expenditures from $6 million to $7 million. They mapped out a campaign aimed primarily at the undraftables. One such target was women.

And such a natural this was. The inexpensive, light, easy-to-manage motorbike was attractive for women. They could buy or rent at convenient and comfortable dealerships, where service was no problem. The image had changed so that housewives, students, young professionals all could feel compatible. And more and more women were induced to turn to this new mode of transportation.

Ingredients of Success

The successful incursion of an unknown foreign invader into a long-established traditional market appeared easy. It took only a few years to accomplish. This experience should be sobering for many firms—competitive entry can be easy for the innovative outsider with a wider perspective who is willing to accept some risks.

Practically everything that Honda did during the 1960s has escaped criticism. All the elements of the strategy seemed to mesh beautifully. There were a few servicing problems during a period of the most rapid growth, but these were quickly identified and corrected. We might question the dogged perseverance of Honda in gearing itself to winning international racing competitions, and doing so successfully. How relevant were such trophies to the consumer Honda was hoping to woo?

Let us examine what appear to be the key ingredients to the Honda success.

Willingness to Beard the Lion. For any upstart firm to try to beard an entrenched competitor is perilous indeed. When the newcomer is an unknown foreign firm attempting to gain entry to the home ground of its formidable foe, and when the foe has been well entrenched for decades, and when the entrenched firm has driven out all the other domestic competitors over the years, the chances of any kind of success appear quite small. In this situation a willingness to beard the lion is a key ingredient of success.

While the attack could have failed, there was sufficient confidence in the planned strategy that the risks were considered worthwhile. This was no reckless and foolish charge; it was carefully crafted, and while the premises that guided it—namely that the market for motorcycles could be greatly expanded to nontraditional users—were unproven as yet, they were reasonable and worth testing.

Identifying the Potential for Expanding the Market. How did Soichiro Honda arrive at his vision of a widely expanded potential market? While we cannot know for sure, we can make some reasonable assumptions. He did not use an extensive marketing research study. Though such might have confirmed what was already known about the characteristics of the present market, it probably would not have uncovered the widened perspective. It might even have discouraged any such efforts to expand the market because of the negative impressions that motorcycles had with the general public and the sheer audaciousness of the idea that the average person could enjoy two-wheel transportation.

Most likely Soichiro Honda recognized that the light motorcycles he had been manufacturing should be adaptable to commuter traveling in the United States, just as they were being used in Japan. While America was a far different country, with less traffic and more affluence, should not economy and ease of transportation and parking also be desirable there? The product was available, and it was far different from existing competitive products.

Such reasoning seems to violate a solid marketing principle that customer needs and wants should be firmly ascertained, and then products developed to best serve these needs and wants. But sometimes there are exceptions to cherished principles.

Effective Use of Advertising. The negative image of the black-leather-jacketed cyclists was erased and a positive image of upwardly mobile youth and common folk substituted. Mass-media advertising was the main force in changing the image, and in doing so highlights one of the best examples we can ever find of the effectiveness of advertising. While the budget used to achieve such results was unheard of for the industry, the $6 or $7 million spent per year was certainly modest by today's perspectives—when a single-minute commercial during the 1986 Super Bowl game cost more than $1 million for the air time, not counting the production costs.

Complementing and reinforcing the effective advertising campaign was the coordination of all facets of the strategy and operations. The product was light, pretty, comfortable, nonthreatening to ride, and inexpensive; dealers were recruited who were far removed from the dirty and noisy establishments on the outskirts of towns; product quality was emphasized; and servicing was convenient and more hassle-free than generally encountered with automobiles.

Honda was even careful to shy away from words that had a negative connotation. For example, headgear were not called "crash helmets," which conveyed something negative and rather fearful, but were called "safetywear." And the word "motorcycle" was never used in an advertisement because it was still thought to have a negative image; instead, the Hondas were described as "two-wheeled motoring sport."

Honda was the precursor or trailblazer for the Japanese cars that were soon to flood the U.S. market, capitalizing on a growing public image of quality and economy.

HARLEY DAVIDSON VERSUS HONDA: WHAT CAN BE LEARNED?

In the space of a few years a long-standing U.S. industry came to be dominated by the Japanese. This phenomenon was to occur in other industries as well in later years. The skill of the Honda takeover should have warned other smug American industries; but, alas, most of them, if they paid any attention to this struggle, would have considered the results a fluke. After all, in the 1950s people associated most Japanese goods, as well as products made in other Far Eastern countries, to be poorly made with cheap labor and far below the level of American or European-made goods. Honda blazed the trail that changed that misperception.

Learning Insight. Never underestimate a competitor.

It is possible for the most unlikely firm to rise and become an aggressive and major factor in an industry. The inclination of a firm in an industry, however, is to underestimate, belittle, or disdain the competition, and not even deign to react or respond to the initial puny efforts of the competitor. (Remember that Honda in its first year in the U.S. market sold only 167 motorbikes.) Later in this book we will see another example where an entrenched firm underestimated an upstart competitor, where the upstart American firm, Nike, grasped market share dominance from Adidas. But there are few examples as dramatic as that of Harley Davidson.

Earlier in this chapter, we noted the "three C's" syndrome of failure: complacency, conservatism, and conceit. These attitudes, which originate from top management, can permeate an entire organization—from production workers to sales staff to those who service customers. The consequences are a reduced commitment to consistency of quality, an aloofness to customer needs and concerns, and a lack of innovativeness in seeking new markets and improved products. There is decreased emphasis on pricing for good value and more on maximizing per-unit profits. And the foundation is laid for vulnerability against the aggressive competitor foolish enough to invade a seemingly static market and its entrenched firm.

What can an organization do to guard against this dangerous syndrome? In general, these are the best tools for guarding against the insidious syndrome:

1. **Bring fresh blood into the organization.** This step is applicable to all levels of staff and managerial personnel. New people bring with them diverse experiences that result in new ideas and different perspectives from those who have long been with the organization. However, these new people must be listened to if their presence is to have any impact on the three C's syndrome.
2. **Monitor the environment and be alert to any changes.** Such monitoring can be formal (perhaps through the systematic use of marketing research) or informal. Every executive can do his or her own monitoring. Generally, monitoring takes three directions:
    a. Keep abreast of the latest statistics and other information in industry and general business publications.
    b. Obtain feedback from customers, dealers, and sales staff about environmental changes and any unmet needs and possible opportunities and dangers.
    c. Be receptive to new ideas from wherever they may come.
    In general, the executive needs to cast a wide net, to pull in information and ideas from as many diverse sources as possible. Customer feedback is an important source of such monitoring, but it will not often provide the forward-looking insights that may be critical. For example, a survey of Harley Davidson customers, their dealers, and their shops probably would not have yielded much value since most of these customers would not have realized the attractiveness of light-weight motorbikes. Perhaps a better monitoring of dealers, however, might have led Harley Davidson more quickly to recognize the seriousness of the Honda threat.

Receptivity to new ideas is the most important ingredient if desirable changes are to be made. Where an organization has grown accustomed to a certain way of doing business, any changes can be traumatic and unwelcome.

3. **Always keep a strong commitment to customer service and satisfaction.** The successful and dominant firm must especially beware of slipping here. A systematic survey of customers to measure their satisfaction can be a useful tool. The boxed information describes how customer feedback can be obtained.

4. **Maintain continuing corporate self-analysis.** It is difficult to sell healthy firms on the need for such an analysis; with sick firms the need is more obvious. Such self-analysis should be particularly directed to the marketing efforts of the firm and should be comprehensive. In particular, answers should be sought for these questions:

What are we doing right?

What could we do better?

Self-analysis needs to be objective. Care must be taken to minimize defensiveness and obstructionism from involved executives. While no one relishes having his or her performance evaluated and scrutinized more closely than before, it is in the best interest of the firm, and of all involved, to detect promptly any deficiencies or any unmet opportunities. A ''marketing audit'' is the term most often used for such self-analysis. The boxed information describes a marketing audit in more detail.

INFORMATION SIDELIGHT

USE OF CUSTOMER SURVEYS FOR MEASURING SATISFACTION

For a retail firm, attitude surveys can be made by interviewing customers leaving the store or department, perhaps those without a package, under the assumption that such people did not find what they wanted or were in some other way not satisfied. Brief questionnaires inviting customer opinions may be inserted in packages or in monthly statements. The samples need not be large. They should, however, be systematic and continuous; otherwise, trends in attitudes go unnoticed and danger areas may not be spotted until serious erosion of old customers occurs.

More ingenuity may be required by manufacturers to obtain feedback on customer attitudes, but this is not usually difficult. Customers can always be invited to express their opinions and their satisfaction or dissatisfaction. The more serious complaints or the strongest customer feelings will be brought to light.

Direct measures of customer satisfaction have these particular advantages:

1. Trends can be established for customer attitudes, and problems can be detected before they become serious.
2. Goodwill can be gained by continuing efforts of this kind (the company will gain the reputation of "the firm that cares").
3. Time and expense need not be great.
4. Unfilled customer needs and wants may be revealed, and these may suggest opportunities to be tapped.

Customer panels can be useful in obtaining clues for various facets of customer satisfaction. Where the panel is used systematically, the firm may detect changes in its customer-satisfaction effectiveness before they become serious. However, these panels of customers suffer from the flaw of not always being representative of customers in general.

A firm can better maintain and improve competitive position if it closely monitors customer satisfaction. Direct measures, as in the surveys described, are far superior to any indirect estimates, such as from profits, sales, and market share. The latter lack sensitivity because many other determinants, such as environmental elements, quality of competition, and economic factors affect sales, profits, and market share.

Learning Insight. *Any industry or market may have untapped potential—but only an innovative approach can harvest it.*

The notion of untapped potential may appear unlikely in supposedly mature industries where sales have been on a plateau for years. Such an industry not only appears to offer no growth potential, but it also appears unlikely to attract new competition. How could any industry offer less growth and be less likely to attract competition than the old motorcycle industry?

Not only stagnant industries may find untapped potential—it can lie anywhere. A growing industry may find new customers other than those presently cultivated, and thereby improve its growth rate. Of course, not all companies and industries can discover untapped potential. Perhaps it is out there, but no one recognizes it or is able to develop it. Sometimes unsuspected opportunities can be found in even stranger places than motorcycles.

Church and Dwight was a small, family-owned firm that made Arm & Hammer baking soda. It had the dubious distinction of being a 125-year-old one-product company. Though its baking soda had almost 100 percent market dominance, sales

---

INFORMATION SIDELIGHT

THE MARKETING AUDIT

An audit implies an objective and critical review. A marketing audit is an objective evaluation of marketing efforts. To ensure objectivity, a separate department in the firm or, preferably, outside consultants, should conduct the audit. The marketing audit goes beyond other analyses to evaluate the objectives, policies, and even the management of the firm. To gain the possible benefits that come from a comprehensive audit, management must admit their efforts can be improved and that their performance is not as good as it might be.

Most audits fall into the realm of "fire fighting," a last desperate device to save a company or a division. But this is not the way the audit can best be used. It should be used for prognosis as well as diagnosis. It can be used to evaluate various alternatives before a decision is reached. It can be used to single out strong points so that these can be exploited. If certain parts of the operation are weak, an informed management is better able to take corrective action. If used to its fullest potential, a marketing audit can lead to new perspectives and innovative thinking.

---

were declining. In 1970 the company conceived the idea of using Arm & Hammer to eliminate foul odors, and it really did absorb them. Church and Dwight began a TV campaign touting the benefits of using Arm & Hammer inside refrigerators. The results of this innovation? In four years, sales doubled and profits tripled.

There is also the classic example of Listerine. An old product, it was originally sold as a mild external antiseptic. Sales were static until in the 1920s someone came up with the idea of promoting Listerine as a mouthwash.

As these examples illustrate, new potential may lie in two areas:

1. Finding new customers
2. Finding new uses

Honda essentially used the first approach. It modified the conventional motorcycle to make it attractive to entirely different customers. Arm & Hammer and Listerine found success with the second approach: they promoted new ways for old customers to make greater use of the products.

A more recent example of success in finding new customers involves not a product but a service—legal service. Hyatt Legal Clinics has grown in less than a decade to one of the nation's largest law firms. After a Supreme Court ruling in 1977 giving lawyers the right to advertise, Joel Hyatt opened his first clinic in Cleveland, Ohio. He wanted to offer low-cost legal services targeted to the great majority of Americans who were not rich enough to afford the high lawyer fees customarily charged for such routine procedures as wills, uncontested divorces, and bankruptcy proceedings. It was acknowledged that "if you're rich, you can afford a good lawyer and if you're poor, there's free legal aid, but if you're in the middle, you're stuck."[6]

Hyatt quickly realized the importance of television advertising in promoting a low-cost clinic that could survive only with a high client volume. He himself appeared in the commercials, and his low-key, personable, and sincere manner was a powerful inducement to hundreds of viewers who previously had viewed all lawyers with suspicion.

Learning Insight. Mass-media advertising can be a powerful tool. It can even change an image for the better.

It is easy to tear down a good public image: an episode of defective products, poor servicing, noncompetitive prices, or a bad press. But it is extremely difficult to build up an image. We have already seen an example of the difficulty in upgrading an image. The poor reputation of Edsel's initial quality control continued to haunt it. But Honda proved that an image can be improved with the right advertising and a coordinated strategy. And Joel Hyatt improved the public perception of lawyers with his low-key, sincere personal appearances in commercials.

Usually the effectiveness of mass-media advertising is difficult to measure. We can determine the attention-value of certain ads, but their real impact on sales is more difficult, often impossible, to measure since so many factors affect sales other than advertising. Competitive efforts and prices, dealer displays and in-stock conditions, customer attitudes, the economy, and even the weather play major roles. Furthermore, there are thousands of commercial messages competing for the average person's attention. Many of these are screened out and do not even consciously register. Consequently, greater and greater expenditures are necessary for advertising to have any impact. In the United States advertising expenditures are approaching $100 billion a year. One firm, Procter & Gamble Company, alone spends almost $1 billion a year. How much of this huge expenditure is wasted? Do the firms that spend over a million dollars for a single minute of Super Bowl time get their money's worth?

Yet Honda—and Hyatt—with only modest expenditures for advertising achieved extraordinary impact and effectiveness. The keys, of course, were the uniqueness of the messages, their tapping of latent consumer needs, and their adroit presentation of clean-cut images for the person who rides a Honda and the head of the Hyatt Legal Clinics. These are two great examples of the effective role that advertising can play—but practically never does. The coordination of the other elements of the strategy with the advertising reinforced the effective image change.

[6]Craig Waters, "The Selling of the Law," *Inc.*, March 1982, p. 58.

For Thought and Discussion

1. We have suggested that complacency, conceit, and conservatism led to Harley's vulnerability. How could such an organizational flaw have been prevented?
2. Could Honda have successfully entered the market with big motorcycles in 1960?
3. How could Harley have anticipated the competitive incursion of Honda, or some similar firm?

Invitation to Role Play

It is 1962. As one of the senior executives of Harley Davidson, you have been given the assignment of developing plans to counter the competitive thrust of Honda. What marketing strategy would you recommend, and why?

8

Korvette, Woolworth, W. T. Grant—And Then There Was K mart

In this chapter we examine four different retail organizations competing to become the dominant firm in the discounting or lower-priced sector. Three of these firms had a run at it, and then faltered. One of these, W. T. Grant Company, so aggressively went after the trophy of "biggest" that it overextended itself fatally. The most unlikely firm of the four made it to the top, becoming the world's largest discounter and second only to Sears in total retail sales. S. S. Kresge Company, with its K mart stores, triumphed in one of the great success stories. What was the secret—the magic ingredient(s)—that spelled success for K mart and failure for its major competitors? The answer is an intriguing story with sad overtones: the unfulfilled promise of Korvette and the extinction of the 70-year steady growth of Grant.

THE DREAM THAT WAS KORVETTE

Gene Ferkauf was the classic American success story. He began his retail career in his father's luggage store. Visionary and eager to grasp opportunities, he disagreed with his father's traditional philosophy of merchandising, which was to sell goods at prices to maximize per-unit profits. He believed that pricing that achieved a small profit per unit of sale would yield greater total profits, *if sales volume could be greatly increased by so doing.* Accordingly, Ferkauf struck out on his own, opening a luggage shop in a second-floor loft on an offstreet in Manhattan. The name of the business he chose arbitrarily: E. J. Korvette.

While the basic stock was luggage, as an accommodation to his customers Ferkauf began selling appliances at close to cost. Soon he branched out into fountain pens and photography equipment. In the early days, Ferkauf sold all appliances for $10 over the wholesale cost. And people began lining up on the sidewalk outside and down the block to get into the store to purchase such bargains. Ferkauf found he was making money with the appliance sales and was operating at a $1 million a year rate. By the end of 1951 he had moved his store to street level and opened a branch in Westchester. Sales climbed to $9.7 million in 1953.

Gene Ferkauf was a quiet man who shunned public limelight. At stockholder meetings he liked to sit mute. He believed in casual clothes, was contemptuous of formality, and spurned an office and other executive amenities. But he believed in friends.

In the early 1950s, a group of 38 men, almost all Brooklyn high school pals of Ferkauf, ran the company. They were called the "open-shirt crowd" or "the boys." Korvette's management operated from a dingy old building with Ferkauf presiding at a beat-up desk in one corner. The company grew, incredibly, from $55 million to $750 million in sales within 10 years, thereby becoming one of the fastest growing companies in the history of retailing. In the early 1960s, the company was opening huge new stores on the average of one every seven weeks.

In the 1950s and early 1960s Korvette led the discount revolution sweeping the country. The American consumer relished the idea of low prices, some of which were 40 percent less than department store prices. Korvette profits and stock seemed headed for the stratosphere. To achieve profitability with low markup requires low overhead. To achieve the latter, Korvette and the other discounters operated in austere surroundings. Stores and fixtures were simple, even pipe racks were used for hanging garments; no credit or delivery were offered at first; and self-service was the rule in order to cut down on salary expense. Just as important as paring costs, lean stocks of merchandise were offered—a narrow selection of best-selling sizes and styles—to maximize merchandise turnover and thereby increase the return on investment. (See the following boxed information.)

As the company continued its discounting policies, it encountered state fair-trade laws, which permitted manufacturers to set the minimum prices for which their goods could be sold by retailers. Some of the major manufacturers, including General Electric, wanted to maintain an image of quality and protect their regular dealers from price cutting. Korvette, by selling below the fair-trade prices, was vulnerable to lawsuits by such manufacturers. At the time the company went public in 1955, 34 fair-trade lawsuits were pending against it. This was not as bad as it might seem, however. Enforcement of fair trade rested with the manufacturer who wanted it for his products. In 1956 Korvette received a legal boost when a New York court threw out a suit brought by the Parker Pen Company on the grounds that Parker was not sufficiently enforcing its fair-trade program. Many manufacturers found enforcement difficult amid the spate of discount stores, and the lack of severe

INFORMATION SIDELIGHT

IMPORTANCE OF TURNOVER IN PROFITABILITY

For an example of the effect of higher turnover on profitability, compare the operations of a department store and a similar size discount store.

Department store sales	$12,000,000
Net profit percent	5
Net profit dollars	$600,000
Stock turnover	4

$$\text{Average stock} = \frac{12,000,000}{4} \qquad \$3,000,000*$$

Return on investment (without considering investment in store and fixtures) =

$$\frac{600,000}{3,000,000} = 20\%$$

A similar size discount store might have a turnover of 8 with a net profit percentage of only 3%:

Discount store	
Sales	$12,000,000
Net profit percent	3
Net profit dollars	$360,000
Stock turnover	8

$$\text{Average stock} = \frac{12,000,000}{8} \qquad \$1,500,000*$$

Return on investment =

$$\frac{360,000}{1,500,000} = 24\%$$

Thus, the discount store can be more profitable than the comparable department store (as measured by the true measure of profitability, the return on investment), even though the net profit is less. Furthermore, the discount store not only has a lower investment in inventory to produce the same amount of sales, but also has less invested in store and fixtures.

*To simplify this example, inventory investment is figured at retail price, rather than cost, which would technically be more correct. However, the significance of increasing turnover is more easily seen here.

penalties limited its effectiveness as a deterrent. Actually, fair trade and list prices aided discount stores since customers could readily see the base price from which the item was discounted.

Trouble!

In the four years between 1962 and 1966, store space and sales volume more than tripled. But "genius though Ferkauf might be at minding the store, he had neither the temperament nor the desire to mind the office."[1] With no more than a dozen outlets, Ferkauf, on "foot patrol," could give on-the-scene guidance. But his organization failed to provide any serious substitute for the diminishing face-to-face supervision of Ferkauf and his home-office executives. The constant addition of stores placed enormous pressures on management. There was enough work and problems in running existing stores without having simultaneously to bring on the additional operations. Buyers, busy filling the needs of the old stores, had somehow to provide for the new stores as well. Advancement, of course, was fast. Section and department managers moved quickly into jobs as store managers, and less experienced people took their places. But there was little time either to develop top-notch management people or to screen for the best.

Along with the sheer number of new stores opening, the doubling and tripling of floor space, and merchandise and management problems, there were several other factors destined to create trouble by the mid-1960s. One was geographical. As long as new stores were added in the East, and particularly around metropolitan New York City, close contact of the stores with the home office was maintained, but this close personal guidance and control was lost with the expansion to Detroit, Chicago, and St. Louis.

There were difficulties in lining up good management people to run operations out of New York City, and profits were lower. Invading a new market area often induced strong competitive reaction from established merchants. In Chicago, for example, Sears and other retailers reacted to Korvette's entry with heavy price reductions and promotional efforts, making it difficult for Korvette to gain a solid market position.

Further strains were caused by Korvette's switch to soft goods and fashion merchandising. Ferkauf, as most discounters, started out discounting hard goods: refrigerators, washing machines, TV and stereo equipment, small appliances such as irons, toasters, blenders, etc., and photo equipment. But the route to a general merchandising operation brought Korvette into clothing and other soft goods, which offered higher profit margins. However, the risks were high from markdowns and unsalable inventories brought about by fashion and seasonal obsolescence, and the demands on management were greater than for the more stable hard goods.

[1]Lawrence A. Mayer, "How Confusion Caught Up with Korvette," *Fortune*, February 1966, p. 154.

Food merchandising presented Ferkauf with new difficulties. There was a good rationale for expanding with supermarkets—consumers generally stock up with groceries weekly; by building supermarkets adjacent to discount stores, heavier and more constant customer traffic can be realized. In 1961 Korvette had two supermarkets. Then the firm started adding supermarkets, winding up with 22, six of these in Detroit and Chicago, unfamiliar territory to an Eastern retailer inexperienced in the local purchase of meat and produce.

Unfortunately, the basic tenet of discount merchandising—high turnover—was disregarded with the food operation. The food stores were opened without warehousing, which meant they had to stock more goods to minimize out-of-stocks. But a heavy inventory is not compatible with lean, fast-moving stocks and high turnover. Furthermore, competition in the supermarket industry was increasing about this time.

Losses from food operations reached $12 million by 1964, and Ferkauf was forced to turn to the outside for help. A merger with Hill Supermarkets, a 42-store chain on Long Island, seemed the answer. But the merger did not solve the problems, and in 1968, after several years of frustration, the food division was finally abandoned.

The final problem plaguing Korvette was its furniture department which was, in fact, a leased operation. The lessee's operations were undercapitalized, and serious management and inventory problems were emerging by 1963, the time of Korvette's greatest expansion efforts. Since customers were not aware that the furniture operation was leased, Korvette bore the brunt of complaints about service and deliveries, and its reputation was being badly affected. Finally, Korvette took over the operation, but it continued to be a profit drain.

1966, The Year of Decision

The strains on Korvette were beginning to show clearly by 1966. Although net sales for the last six months of fiscal 1965 were more than 10 percent higher than for the same period the year before, earnings declined from $16.6 million to $13.9 million. Then, for the generally unprofitable first quarter of the year, Korvette saw the deficit grow from $1.12 million in 1965 to $4.45 million in 1966. There were other indications of trouble. Inventory turnover was down by one-third from 1961; sales per square foot also fell by one-third. And Korvette stock had dropped from a peak of 50½ in May 1965 to 13 by the beginning of 1966.

Finally, the expansion policies were toned down. Only three new stores were opened in 1966, and attention was turned to the existing stores and efforts to increase customer traffic.

Rather unexpectedly, on September 25, 1966, Korvette was merged with Spartans Industries, a smaller discount chain with only $375 million in sales in 1965 compared with $719 million for Korvette. Ferkauf, eased out of active management, left Spartans in 1968 to develop his own boutique chain and faded from the limelight. Charles Bassine, the chairman, turned his attention to developing tighter controls for the Korvette operation: controls over merchandise, costs, markups, markdowns, shrinkage, and expenses.

After 1966

Despite the stronger management that Spartans provided, the Korvette operation could not regain its previous strength. An attempt was made to raise Korvette's profit margins by upgrading the merchandise with higher-price lines, but this served to drive away many of the old bargain-hunting customers. While sales of Spartans Industries were now over a billion dollars, there was a continual fight to generate profits. Bassine tried to unload the unprofitable parts of his operation, such as the supermarkets, but profits were little improved. In 1970, the apparel business was hit by a flood of cheaper foreign imports, and a recession hurt retail sales. In 1970, the Korvette division lost $3.7 million.

In 1971, Spartans merged with Arlen Realty & Development Corporation, a big real estate developer, and younger blood was brought into top management. To no avail—Korvette continued either to lose money or barely break even. In early 1979, Korvette experienced a third transfer of control. Arlen was able to sell a majority 51 percent interest in the Korvette 50-unit chain to a French retail and manufacturing group, Agache-Willot, for $30 million.

Continued losses and cash crises plagued the retailer, and bankruptcy was threatened in 1980 before the French parent agreed to restructure $55 million of debt to institutional lenders. The decision was made to liquidate the company gradually, and by the middle of 1981 the remaining 12 stores were in the process of being sold. Korvette, the pioneer discounter, is little more than a memory.

WOOLWORTH'S WOOLCO: DISCOUNTING PROVES INCOMPATIBLE

Woolworth has a long and successful history. It was the first variety store chain, and it became the largest—with Kresge a distant second. With the growing popularity of discount stores by the early 1960s, the decision to move into discounting with a Woolco subsidiary seemed unquestionably right. Kresge was attempting this with its K mart venture, and Woolworth had greater size and resources than Kresge. But by 1982 Woolworth had had enough and called quits to the money-draining discount operation. How could Woolworth have failed so mightily—when K mart's success was so great that the venerable name of Kresge was changed to K mart?

The Beginnings of Woolworth

Frank W. Woolworth conceived an exciting idea during the 1870s when the country was still recovering from the Civil War: a one-price retail store. He conceived the idea while working as a clerk in a retail store in Watertown, New York where he helped introduce the "5¢ counter." The success of this counter convinced him that a five-cent store would also thrive.

He opened his pioneering store in 1879 in Utica, New York. His first sale was a five-cent fire shovel. However, the location proved to be bad, and the enterprise failed in less than four months. Not deterred, Frank Woolworth opened another store in Lancaster, Pennsylvania, and by the end of the first day knew he had a success and began thinking of other stores.

The five-cent price proved somewhat limiting, and a year later he added a ten-cent line. The ten-cent limit held for 52 years. The idea of offering a great variety of merchandise at one low fixed price, and of keeping goods on open display was adopted by other pioneer merchants including Sebastian Kresge in the late 1800s and W. T. Grant in 1906. The concept was revolutionary for the time since in most retail outlets counters were kept bare, with merchandise on high selves or under the counter and brought out only at the customer's request.

Woolworth continued opening new stores and acquiring other smaller chain operations. In 1909 Woolworth opened his first dime store in Liverpool, England, and within five years had 44 stores in England. By 1955, at the threshold of the discount movement, Woolworth had 2064 stores with sales of almost $800 million; Kresge had 673 stores and sales of $354 million; and W. T. Grant had 572 stores and sales of $350 million.

Woolworth Moves Into Discounting

By 1962 discounting was at its height. Traditional retailers were running scared, and the movement was attracting dozens of brash interlopers. Many of these firms failed in the next decade as competition became keener and retailers with greater resources and merchandising acumen began to diversify into discounting.

Discounting seemed a natural diversification for such major variety chains as Woolworth and Kresge. Larger stores and a wider range of merchandise would be needed, but the customers would be the same and the merchandising strategy would not be that different. Both Kresge and Woolworth opened their first discount stores in the same year, 1962.

While Kresge dedicated itself to discounting, Woolworth moved far more slowly. Resources for expansion were divided among development of the Woolco stores, upgrading and enlarging the regular variety stores, and expansion of certain specialty operations, notably the Kinney shoe stores and Richman clothing outlets. In 1970 Kresge overtook Woolworth in sales, and by 1973 Kresge was the country's largest discounter.

Some Worrisome Portents

By 1974 the Woolworth Company was a giant complex of 2058 variety stores, 283 Woolco stores, 1481 Kinney shoe stores, and 266 Richman outlets. In 1973 sales

Table 8.1   Profit Margins of Major Retailers, 1973

Company	Net Profit Percent of Sales
Sears	5.5%
Penney	3.0
Kresge	2.9
Woolworth	1.8

Source: Company public records.

were $3.7 billion, more than twice the volume of 10 years before, but profits were only half the level of 10 years before. Woolworth's position was particularly worrisome because it compared poorly with that of other leading retailers as shown in Table 8.1.

The retail environment had become tougher than ever, and while the discounting field had grown to a $30 billion annual business, it was going through a massive shakeout. Woolworth's profit margins were too low to generate the capital needed for expansion, and even with borrowing, start-up plans had to be scaled down. To reduce short-term debt, Woolworth floated a $125 million issue of debentures in 1974, the second time in three years that the company had to resort to debt financing.

Still, the outlook did not appear too bad for Woolworth in the mid-1970s. Chief executive officer Lester A. Burcham could tell shareholders that 1974 sales had comfortably passed the $4 billion milestone, just two years after breaking the $3 billion level. However, in a more somber note, company executives worried: "We can get the sales. But we have to get the profitability."[2]

But even sales of individual Woolco stores did not meet expectations. Sales for the large units were conservatively expected to be at least $5 million a year, and such sales were achieved by a disappointingly few stores. Meanwhile, foreign operations, especially in the British subsidiary, showed a similar pattern—increasing sales and languishing profits. All the while, K mart was achieving new heights of sales and profits.

Edward Gibbons Faces a Worsening Situation

Edward G. Gibbons joined Woolworth in 1973 as vice president for finance. At the time, Gibbons worked hard to improve the company's serious debt problems. In 1975 he was made president, and later became the company's first outside chief

---

[2]"The Problems That are Upsetting Woolworth," *Business Week,* June 28, 1974, p. 72.

executive officer (CEO). It had been traditional for all the top executives to have come up through the ranks of the Woolworth organization. (This policy or practice has certain advantges and limitations as discussed in the boxed material.) Gibbons was respected by both the retailing and financial communities as a sound and objective analyst and corporate executive. He was a deeply private man, a nononsense type of manager. And his performance as president seemed impressive as he took the company from sales of $4.7 billion in 1975 to $7.2 billion in 1981.

But the Woolco operation continued to bedevil Gibbons and Woolworth. It was not profitable and, worse than that, was a serious drain on financial resources. In December 1981 both Standard & Poor's and Moody's downgraded the company's senior debt. Belatedly, Gibbons tried shrinking the stores' size by renting space to outside retailers. But more drastic measures appeared needed if Woolco was to be salvaged. Gibbons recruited Bruce G. Allbright, a discounting expert, to

---

INFORMATION SIDELIGHT

THE ISSUE OF PROMOTION FROM WITHIN

When it comes to promoting its personnel, an organization has two options: it can promote from within, or it can fill important management positions from outside the organization.

Promotion from within was the policy traditionally followed by a number of major retailers, including Woolworth, Penney, and Kresge, for virtually all their line management positions. For some specialized staff jobs, such as law and research, outsiders were sought if such expertise could not be found in the existing organization.

A rigid policy of promoting from within—some call this inbreeding—has several advantages. It develops intense motivation, loyalty, and dedication to the traditions of the company. The rungs upward in the ladder can be seen by many aspiring trainees and executives as entirely possible and within reach, and this can be a powerful spur.

But the policy of promoting from within can be carried too far. Policies can become self-perpetuating. Innovation can be stymied without the fresh ideas—even disruptive influences—of outsiders. In such an environment a narrow perspective and traditional ways of doing things almost invariably prevail.

A middle ground usually is more desirable: filling many executive positions from within the organization in order to motivate present executives and help in recruiting trainees, while at the same time bringing strong outsiders into the organization where their strengths and particular experiences can be most valuable. As with most things, moderation is more desirable than relying predominantly on either promotion from within or from without.

engineer Woolco's recovery. Gibbons noted, "We feel that the discount-store business has a very bright future but only for those who do it very well. Anyone else won't survive."[3]

Allbright had impressive credentials. He was president of the Target Stores discount division of Dayton-Hudson Corporation. Target was one of the most successful discount chains, with sales of $2.4 billion and profits of $150 million from 167 stores in 1982. Gibbons gave Allbright virtually a free hand to solve Woolco's problems.

But the woes intensified during 1982. In the first six months Woolco lost more money than in all of 1981, and it was now losing in excess of $1 million a week. Standard & Poor's placed the company on credit watch, and major lenders were pressuring Woolworth to do something about its short-term debt, which had reached $788 million by October 31.

In August, Allbright persuaded Harold Smith to leave his post as executive vice president of the Magic Mart discount store chain to help him revive Woolco. Meantime, Woolworth's other businesses were not doing well enough to help Woolco's cash position, and even though Gibbons had confidence in Allbright, there seemed little doubt that it would take at least three years before Woolco could hope to turn a profit.

The Decision

On September 24, 1982, Chairman Gibbons announced at a board meeting the termination of the company's largest division, Woolco. Pressure had been building throughout the year to shutter all 336 of the Woolco stores, despite their contributing $2.1 billion or almost 30 percent of all Woolworth sales. Jobs of 35,000 to 40,000 people were eliminated, and a $325 million after-tax write-off was taken.

Two days after this announcement, Gibbons, a troubled man at age 63, entered the hospital for a routine operation. Thirty days later he was dead from kidney failure. Allbright was the hoped-for savior but in his nine months with the company, he did not have enough time to resurrect the division. Apparently not informed beforehand of the closing, Allbright was publicly outlining his plans for reviving Woolco less than two weeks before the closing announcement. He was asked to stay on with the company but declined to do so.

Postmortem

Problems of Growth. Vigorous expansion creates problems and stresses for any organization. In Korvette's case, the expansion came from a small base of nine stores; suddenly there were 25. Supervision and control formerly handled on a face-

[3]"Finally, Woolworth Wields the Ax," *Business Week*, October 11, 1982, p. 119.

to-face basis proved insufficient. The company did not have enough trained executives at all levels. While promotion was necessarily fast, ill-trained and marginal people were thrust into responsible positions. Recruiting top-notch people was a problem, partly because discount stores lacked the prestige of more conventional retailers. Organizational policies did not help either, since Korvette was highly centralized with all merchandising and other policies dictated from the home office. If rapid growth was to be achieved in an absence of tight controls, decentralization, giving more authority and responsibility to store executives, would have helped, but decentralization would have been possible only with higher-paid and more carefully selected store executives.

Korvette started from a hard goods base. Before Ferkauf and his associates could gain experience in merchandising the riskier soft lines and fashion goods or recruit people with this experience, the go-ahead was given for rapid expansion. A delay until soft goods merchandising was better understood would have helped.

With Woolworth, the problem was not one of too rapid and unassimilated expansion, but rather too conservative growth. Kresge was opening an average of 45 to 50 K mart stores a year up to the 1970s when it began opening much larger numbers, but Woolworth was not opening even 30 stores in one year until 1980. Furthermore, these openings were scattered rather than geographically concentrated: "Woolco would open one store in Columbus, Ohio and move on to another market, while K mart opened up three, four, and five stores in Columbus and got economies of distribution and, more important, advertising."[4]

A crucial flaw in the Woolco venture dated back to the beginning in 1962. Woolworth management was ambivalent about the move to discounting, not committing itself fully to either variety stores or discounting—at a time when Kresge shifted its whole emphasis to discounting. The ingrained variety store management just could not let go and give priority to the discount operation.

Woolworth management believed that their cautious attitudes were fully justified. They felt that the "Woolworth Company was too valuable an asset to just go in one direction."[5] Although a conservative approach and a multifaceted strategy may be prudent under many circumstances, it made Woolworth vulnerable to aggressive competitors.

Image Problems. Image was a troublesome factor for both Korvette and Woolworth. At first, in the golden days of Korvette, the discount image—bare-bones prices—had great customer appeal. However, as Korvette expanded with more stores and into soft goods and fashion lines, Ferkauf's conception of the company changed. He saw it no longer as a discount store, but rather as a promotional department store. He opened a store on Fifth Avenue of Manhattan, only a few

[4]"We're Moving! We're Alive!" *Forbes*, November 21, 1983, pp. 66–71.
[5]"How Kresge Became the Top Discounter," *Business Week*, October 24, 1970, p. 63.

blocks from some of the most fashionable stores in the world, such as Bonwit Teller and Lord & Taylor. A massive chandelier was placed in the lobby; the discount image was disavowed. "We have Cadillacs that pull up to the store, and women get out and enjoy, as everybody enjoys, being able to buy something a little bit cheaper than they normally would. We have some of the most famous people come into our stores."[6]

But with upgrading of the merchandise, markups rose from less than 8 percent in 1950 to 33 percent in 1965. If Korvette was to escape the discount image, how could it do so and keep its old customers? Korvette became similar to the basement operations of departments stores—it carried standard markup items supplemented by loss leaders used for promotional purposes. As merchandise was upgraded, as new stores became more elaborate, as services such as credit were offered, there was an increase in overhead. The uniqueness was lost. Gradually Korvette acquired the expense structure of traditional retailers, but without the level of expertise of department and specialty stores in the way of quality and fashion merchandising.

A hazy or imprecise image plagued Woolco right from the beginning. Woolworth management could not decide what they wanted Woolco to be—an expanded variety store, a discount store, or a medium-priced department store. Advertising featured Woolco stores as "promotional department stores," implying something of a cross between a discount and a department store. The company failed to establish a clear identity, either for its variety or discount outlets. Indeed, the variety stores and the Woolco stores tended to blur together. The bigger variety stores began to rival the Woolco stores in size, while the Woolco discount prices were often no lower than those of the variety stores.

Organizationally, confusion existed also. Initially, the Woolco division was established as an autonomous unit, completely independent of the variety store division. While this seemed to signify a major commitment to discounting, it increased fixed costs, fragmented the efforts of the total company, and certainly involved less total commitment to discounting than that of Kresge where the whole organization, and not just a separate division, was geared to discounting. More than this, Woolworth faced inherent problems with inexperienced managers and the plodding efforts of a new organizational structure.

By 1971, faced with a heavy overhead that seemed to destroy any hope of profits, the buying and distribution for both Woolco and the variety stores were consolidated. While this lowered the breakeven point, it led to further blurring of the Woolco and Woolworth images. Despite efforts to vary brands and merchandise selections between the two, there was considerable overlap, and prices continued to run higher than those of discount-store rivals. Consolidation did not bring the needed profits.

---

[6]Robert Drew-Bear, *Mass Merchandise: Revolution and Evolution* (New York: Fairchild Publications, 1970), p. 124.

External Factors. With Korvette leading the way, the onslaught of discounters in the 1950s and early 1960s was traumatic; some called it the revolution in retailing. However, by the mid-1960s, other retailers were beginning to act aggressively against discounters. Department stores and appliance retailers blunted the initial competitive advantage of discounters either by matching them price for price on identical goods, or else by stocking their own private brand appliances and other items that prevented price comparisons. Many retailers shifted parts of their operations to self-service and eliminated some of the frills that made their operations high cost. And the major advantage discounters got from using high merchandise turnover to yield a good return on investment despite low markups was copied by other retailers. Meanwhile, average costs and markups were rising for all discounters. The result, predictably, was that customers no longer streamed in to just any discount store. Those stores that expanded too rapidly or those less efficient than competitors were ousted from the market.

With the maturing of the discount-store industry in the 1960s, other kinds of discounters came on the scene; they were well-financed, well-managed, and they swept away marginal competitors. K mart was one of these. Major department-store corporations, such as Dayton-Hudson, L. S. Ayres, and Allied Stores, opened discount subsidiaries, carefully run with well-trained, high-caliber personnel, and with definitive policies. These latter discount stores had the advantage of drawing on years of experience with fashion merchandising of their mother firms.

Woolco seemingly should have been one of these survivors. Instead, it found itself beset on all sides. In the middle of the road, it faced the vigorously expanding K mart with more attractive prices and a much more efficient operation. Away from the middle of the road it faced other discounters moving in two directions: (1) toward plusher atmospheres while still keeping low prices (such as the Target Stores of Dayton-Hudson), and (2) toward specialization in limited merchandise areas (such as Toys "Я" Us) offering tremendous assortments in narrow lines at low prices. Despite its huge stores and heavy quantities of goods, Woolco compared poorly with many of its competitors, while its prices were turning off bargain-conscious consumers.

Update

Did getting rid of Woolco improve the operating results of Woolworth? The answer is yes, but one wonders what might have been achieved several years down the road if Woolworth had persevered with Woolco and brought it into the black. The immediate result was that sales dropped from over $7 billion in fiscal 1981 to $5 billion the next year while profits remained virtually the same at $82 million. In the following years, sales gradually rose toward the $6 billion level, although not achieving this level by 1986, while profits showed a nice rise, reaching $177 million for fiscal 1985.

Woolworth concentrated its efforts on specialty retailing. Its Kinney Shoe division became one of the country's largest shoe retailers with some 3282 stores, including Foot Locker, a subsidiary specializing in athletic shoes. Kinney, accounting for 25 percent of Woolworth sales in fiscal 1985, contributed 44 percent of all corporate profits. Other speciality store divisions, such as Richman Stores and Anderson-Little were less significant factors in the operating performance but were considered to have good growth potential. Efforts were also made to refurbish the regular Woolworth stores both domestically and abroad.

W. T. GRANT COMPANY: THE FATAL EXPANSION

In June of 1975, James Kendrick, 62-year-old chief executive of W. T. Grant Company, had his back to the wall. He was in charge of a retail giant of almost 1200 stores with sales of nearly $2 billion. But the company was on the verge of bankruptcy. Grant owed $600 million in short-term loans and $100 million in long-term debt to 143 banks. It had incurred a staggering $175 million loss for 1974. And the losses were continuing: $54 million in the first quarter of 1975. Dividends, which had been paid for 69 years, were suspended. On June 1, Grant was to pay $57 million to retire its debt to 116 of the banks. Failure to do so might well induce some of the creditors to push Grant into bankruptcy.

Prelude

The blame for this situation was not Kendrick's. The previous management had been deposed in a director's revolt in August 1974. Kendrick was a long-time Grant employee who had been running a subsidiary, Zeller's, Ltd., in Canada. Seven years before, he had been a candidate for president of Grant. But he had been passed over and exiled to Canada because he had questioned policies of the Board. Now Edward Staley, chairman of the board, and the other top executives had been ousted and Kendrick had been tapped for the company's greatest trial.

Staley was founder William T. Grant's brother-in-law. As the aged Grant became less active, he turned increasingly to Staley to run the company. Staley was president from 1952 to 1959, but he remained in active control under various titles until 1974. He supported Richard C. Mayer, the president of Grant from 1968 to 1974, who led Grant into an expansion course that was both heady and disastrous.

Before Richard Mayer became Grant's president in 1968, he had set up the company's credit operation so successfully that it contributed 25 percent of sales in 1972. Mayer was interested in vigorous expansion. Shortly after he assumed the presidency, the company broke out of a three-year earnings rut and joined the ranks of $1 billion plus retail firms. Encouraged by this progress, Mayer set a goal of $2 billion in sales by 1972, one of the most ambitious expansion programs ever plotted by a retailer.

History

"Looking back to the earliest days I can remember, it seems to me that I always wanted a store," wrote William T. Grant. He sold shoes in his hometown of Malden, Massachusetts, and headed the shoe department of a Boston department store when he was only 19. In 1906, taking his life savings of $1000, he opened his first store in Lynn, Massachusetts. A second store was opened within two years, and the firm continued its steady growth.

While his stores were similar to the five-and-tens of Woolworth and Kresge, William Grant saw an opportunity for stores with prices above those of the five-and-tens and below the more expensive department stores. His first stores carried the 25-cent price theme. As the company expanded through the years, it was thought of primarily as a variety store. In the late 1960s, Grant's went heavily into high-ticket durables such as TV sets, furniture, and appliances.

Grant retired from active management of the company at age 48, but continued as chairman of the board until his ninetieth birthday in 1966. On his fiftieth anniversary with the company in 1956, Grant reiterated his childhood conviction about the thrill of retailing:

> I know of no other business which could give a man so much action, so much challange, so much satisfaction and so rich a reward for good service to the community than this wonderful business of ours. I have enjoyed every minute of it.[7]

The Go-Go Expansion Years

As 1972 drew to a close, Richard Mayer looked back with satisfaction at the company's growth in the previous 10 years, and he ordered the record of this growth distributed to the financial community, company employees, interested vendors, and stockholders. The statistics were indeed impressive. Some of the more important ones are shown here:

	1962	*1972*	*Percentage Increase in Ten Years*
Total number of stores	1,032	1,208	17
Total sales	$686,263,000	$1,644,747,000	140
Credit sales	$ 97,478,000	$ 406,763,000	317
Net earnings	$ 9,004,000	$ 37,787,000	320
Net worth	$141,381,000	$ 334,339,000	137

[7]Adapted from a publication of the W. T. Grant Company commemorating the decease of William T. Grant.

Percentage earned on net worth	6.4	11.3	
Dividends paid on common stock	$ 6,997,000	$ 20,807,000	197

Mayer was particularly proud of the statistics on store growth since he had assumed the presidency in 1968:

	1963–1967	1968	1969	1970	1971	1972
New stores opened	202	41	52	65	83	92
Stores enlarged	55	11	3	8	5	5
Stores closed	148	35	49	44	31	52
Store space in thousands of square feet:						
Opened during period	10,933	3,205	3,950	5,360	7,254	7,070
Closed during period	(2,962)	(759)	(1,277)	(1,058)	(693)	(1,198)
At end of period	28,736	31,182	33,855	38,157	44,718	50,618

Source: T. Grant Company, *Facts and Highlights, Ten Fiscal Years Ended January 31, 1973*, p. 5.

These statistics made Grant look like a winner, a growth company attractive both to investor and creditor. However, one aspect of the operational performance nagged Mayer a bit and gained some attention from the investment community. Earnings were in a three-year decline from a high of $41,809,000 in 1969, despite sales increases of over $500 million. However, Mayer had a ready explanation. He figured three to five years were necessary for a new store to mature before customer acceptance allowed a store's sales and profits to reach an acceptable level. Mayer assured his critics that he expected a couple of years of flat earnings as multiple openings caused start-up expenses to balloon while recently opened stores were still in the maturing period.

There were other statistics that should have given him concern. Long-term debt had risen from $35 million to $126 million in the 10-year period, an increase of 377 percent. The stock-to-sales ratio had risen sharply. Sales per square foot between 1968 and 1972 dropped from $35.13 to $32.50. At this level it was less than half those of its major competitors. During this same period the company had closed over six million of its least productive square feet. This, along with the worsening ratios, suggested that the new stores were not generating strong sales.

The expansion efforts of Grant during 1971 and 1972, as measured by square feet of space added, were a close second to Penney in 1971 and third in 1972 behind

Penney and Kresge. The expansion policies are the more amazing considering how much bigger Penney and Kresge were than Grant:

	Sales	
	1971	*1972*
Penney	$4,812,000,000	$5,530,000,000
Kresge	3,140,000,000	3,875,000,000
Grant	1,375,000,000	1,645,000,000

Furthermore, Grant far exceeded the expansion efforts of Sears, the largest retailer, with sales about ten times greater than Grant's.

The new stores Grant opened were more than twice the size of the average store of 1964, and some 75 percent were in suburban shopping centers. (The smaller stores that were being phased out were often located in deteriorating downtown locations.) Average sales per store had risen to about $1 million compared to $646,000 in 1964.

Grant's expansion was highlighted by their superstores, stores of 180,000 square feet, although the size of other new stores ranged down to 60,000 square feet. There were two separate location strategies. The big stores, 120,000 to 180,000 square feet, were placed in medium-sized enclosed malls, with a Sears, Ward, or even a major discounter as a co-anchor. On the other hand, smaller stores being built in neighborhood and convenience centers were aimed at dominating a small market where there was no nearby competition from major general merchandisers.

The larger stores were required by Grant's effort to expand and upgrade the product lines to include big-ticket items such as television sets, major appliances, power tools, automobile accessories, sporting goods, and camera equipment. The superstores even carried garden equipment, furniture, and auto servicing. By 1971 the product line was made up of about 25 percent family fashions, 50 percent hard goods, and 25 percent small wares and services. This was a distinct change from the product line of a variety chain that once had 50 percent of its products in family fashions and very little in hard goods. The average store now stocked over 21,000 items in all price ranges. About 70 percent of the merchandise carried the Grant private label, permitting Grant to offer somewhat lower prices than if nationally advertised brands were handled.

A program to facilitate all-out expansion was implemented that cut down the development time for new stores from 90 days to 60 days. The developer's architect was no longer required to submit working drawings to the chain for final approval provided he would certify that the plans conformed to Grant's specifications. Under the old method, plans were submitted to Grant and usually many changes were made before final approval. Eliminating the review procedure resulted in widely fluctuating costs. But with an objective of pell-mell expansion, shortcuts had to be taken.

Approaching Disaster, 1973 and 1974

Mayer's expansion plans continued unabated for most of 1973. Only Kresge's K mart added more square feet of space. Operations were deep in the red for the first nine months of 1973. But since the last quarter of the year is the most crucial one for retail operations because of the peak Christmas business, management waited until December to make any further decisions regarding the expansion program. In December, Grant had gains of 3.7 percent, the smallest of any major retailer. The expansion program was a disaster. Management belatedly became aware that more stores do not necessarily mean profitable sales. While remaining chief executive, Richard Mayer gave up the presidency to operations man Harry Pierson. The expansion program was over.

For the full year of 1973 sales rose to $1.8 billion. But profits dropped 78 percent to $8.4 million, the lowest profits since 1967 when sales were only $575 million. And 1973 was a year in which Sears, Penney, Kresge, and Woolworth all showed record earnings. Grant's return on equity, once 15 percent, dropped to less than 5 percent. More ominous, however, long-term debt increased to $222 million from only 35 million in 1970, and short-term debt increased to $450 million.

Grant's troubles were only beginning. In 1974 sales fell to $1.7 billion, and the firm suffered a gargantuan loss of $175 million. Dividends were suspended for the first time in Grant's 69-year history. And James Kendrick was engaged in an eleventh-hour effort to save the nation's seventeenth-largest retailer from extinction.

To cut costs, Kendrick planned to close 126 stores in 1975, trim the payroll from 82,500 to 69,000, and pare the company's credit unit, which accounted for 62 percent of the 1974 losses. Contributing to the problems facing Kendrick was a loss of $24 million for store closing costs, heavy interest charges, and massive markdowns of slow-moving goods.

June 1975

Finally, Kendrick was sweating out the June 2, 1975 payment of $57 million required to retire the company's debt to 116 of the 143 banks that provided the financing for the ill-fated expansion. Failure to pay these smaller creditors might well force bankruptcy. The bigger banks had more at stake and would not be inclined to sink the company in an effort to get a faster settlement. The financial and investment community waited. The news finally hit the press and the market tape that Grant had somehow managed to come up with the $57 million. Kendrick now had a little breathing room.

Causes of the Dilemma

Ill-conceived and too-vigorous expansion certainly must take the blame for many of the Grant problems. Kendrick said:

> The expansion program placed a great strain on the physical and human capability of the company to cope with the program. These were all large stores we were opening, and the expansion of our management organization just did not match the expansion of our stores.[8]

A former operations executive noted: "Our training program couldn't keep up with the explosion of stores, and it didn't take long for the mediocrity to begin to show."

There was another underlying factor that played a major role in the Grant dilemma. After all, other firms have expanded rapidly in the past, such as the Penney Company and most of the other major chains in the 1920s. Kresge and their K mart stores vigorously expanded for over a decade, and were the epitome of success. But Grant's expansion was hindered by a lack of a definable and distinctive image. Was Grant a variety chain? A discounter? A general merchandise chain? What should Grant be? Or more realistically, what should it strive to be?

The company assumed a mid-position between a discounter and a general merchandise firm—neither fowl nor ass. As merchandise lines were expanded and prices upgraded, Grant veered strongly away from the variety-store image, but in some ways still retained it. (For example, certain typical variety-store departments, such as candy, were still kept near the front of stores.) On the other hand, Grant did not try to keep up with K mart in discounting prices although its prices were competitive enough to be called promotional. Mayer coined the phrase "one-stop family shopping stores," suggesting a general merchandiser such as Sears and Penney. However, Grant lacked the punch of either of these and was unable to offer the service or the established brands of Sears or Penney. For example, Grant's major brand, Bradford, was practically unknown, and many people were reluctant to buy appliances and similar goods where quality and service were questionable. Given time, Grant could have established acceptance of its own brand, but problems were emerging too fast under its expansion policies.

The vigorous expansion, which led to inefficiencies and mediocre performance, added to an uncertain and murky image, and resulted in inventory problems as some merchandise from the broadened product line—especially appliances—did

---

[8]"How W. T. Grant Lost $175 Million Last Year," *Business Week*, February 24, 1975, p. 75.

not sell. Store buyers, in their eagerness to stock huge stores, often bought larger quantities than could be moved as seasons, styles, and tastes changed. But there was a reluctance to mark down and clear out this inventory. One merchandising executive recalled "mounds of goods that just sat year to year collecting dust; they had so much stuff just sitting there they couldn't free up the dollars to do a good seasonal merchandising job."[9]

Many of the new stores were not living up to expectations and with some merchandise categories stagnant, Grant began a heavy credit promotion in an effort to move these goods. But too much leniency in granting credit led to disastrous uncollectible accounts and credit write-offs.

The mix of stores added to Grant's difficulties. The new stores were never really standardized. They came in sizes from 54,000 square feet to 180,000, with different interiors and exteriors and different merchandise assortments. Some stores were free-standing, without other stores nearby; others were in malls; still others in strip centers.

Since many Grant stores had low sales productivity, developers often refused to give them choice locations. Consequently, many of the new stores were in poor sites. On top of these problems, Grant filed a suit in February 1975 against three former employees charged with taking "hundreds of thousands of dollars in bribes in connection with store leases," which relegated Grant to many poor store locations. Lawsuits were pressed against the former real estate vice president, the Southern real estate manager, and the Midwest real estate manager, alleging kickbacks and bribery: "some store sites and rental terms may not have been in our best interest and may have contributed to some of our problems."[10]

Climax, 1975

The $57 million payment toward the debt reduction was made. Slender breathing room was gained, but could Kendrick bring the company back to viability? Kendrick sought to undo the damages and move ahead. He proposed going after the same mass market as K mart and Woolco and to be competitive in price. He decided to de-emphasize big-ticket items, and strengthen infants' and children's wear, white goods, and curtains and draperies. He planned to spend $6 million on television spots in 35 major markets. Mayer had been a credit man, little versed in merchandising and operations. Now Kendrick proposed to stress basic merchandising, such as keeping stocks fresh and clean and taking prompt markdowns. "We failed to stock staples, which in turn led to an overabundance of slow-selling items," Kendrick pointed out. He also recognized that Grant's merchandising program may

[9]Ibid., pp. 75–76.
[10]Ibid.

INFORMATION SIDELIGHT

IMPORTANCE OF MAINTAINING STAPLE GOODS

Staple items sell day by day in steady, if unspectacular, amounts. In many departments, such as stationery, notions, hosiery, housewares, hardware, sporting goods, candy, toilet goods, and domestics and linens, staples account for most of the total sales. But because such goods sell steadily without fanfare, there is the temptation to pay little attention to them. Special purchases, new items, interesting styles—these tend to get the attention and enthusiasm.

But a serious error is made in minimizing the importance of staple goods. Out-of-stocks here result not only in a lost sale, but, since many staple items do not have ready substitutes, customers are forced to go to competitors to purchase the items. Sending a customer away may have these undesirable consequences:

The store loses customer goodwill because of the extra shopping effort required.

A customer perceives the store as inefficient and poorly merchandised, and decides to shift business permanently.

A customer may decide to satisfy other buying needs in the competing store where the staple item is available.

---

have been too promotional-minded, and that not enough reliance was placed on national brands.[11]

In the next few years, Kendrick hoped to pare the system to a core group of 900 stores, and stabilize sales volume at about $1.5 billion. He intended to increase the use of brand-name goods and increase the dollar volume per square foot. Complicating the problem of streamlining, however, were the many long-term leases running anywhere from 10 to 20 years for some stores due to be closed because of poor locations. Unless these could be subleased, their expense drain would continue for some time.

As a further merchandising tool, Grant planned to accept BankAmericard and MasterCharge sales, thereby playing down its own dismal credit operation. While recognizing the expenses involved in these bank cards, the company hoped to attract more customers.

Despite the efforts of Kendrick and the sharp reversal of previous policies, the picture steadily worsened during 1975. For the six months ended July 31, 1975, the chain lost $111.3 million. Landlords were asked to roll their store rents back 25 percent; some complied. Loan agreements were renegotiated with 27 banks headed

[11]"It's Get Tough Time at W. T. Grant," *Business Week,* October 19, 1974, p. 46.

by Morgan Guaranty, in which $300 million of the $640 million owed to the banks was subordinated (that is, given lower priority for repayment) to bills owing suppliers, and, in general, the loan provisions were moderated. Subordinating the bank loans was vital, since Grant had some $500 million worth of goods on order, but many suppliers were holding up deliveries for fear they would not be paid.

Grant was losing money faster than anticipated and was forced to announce that it was operating with a negative net worth; that is, its debts exceeded its assets. This was the beginning of the end. On October 2, 1975, Grant entered bankruptcy proceedings, filing a petition under Chapter 11 of the federal Bankruptcy Act. W. T. Grant Company thus became the second biggest U.S. company to enter bankruptcy proceedings (the biggest was Penn Central Transportation Company in 1970), and the largest retailer ever to do so.

Under Chapter 11 bankruptcy, a company continues to operate, but has court protection against creditors' lawsuits while working out a plan for paying its debts. Some shareholders, in a separate action, filed to have the proceedings converted to Chapter 10 bankruptcy. This is a more drastic move in which control of the company passes to a court-appointed trustee whose interests are more with the creditors and who will try for a complete financial reorganization and, if necessary, may liquidate some or all of the company's assets to raise money to pay creditors.

In the fall of 1975, the company squeaked past the threat of complete liquidation, retrenching with hundreds of store closings, including most of those west of the Mississippi. If there was to be any chance for survival and eventual payment of creditors, strong Christmas sales were needed. However, with suppliers fearful of providing goods because of the bankruptcy proceedings, the chance of the company's being adequately stocked for Christmas business was jeopardized.

Update

W. T. Grant Company did not make it. On February 9, 1976, six banks and one vendor on the creditors' committee that had been formed after Grant went into Chapter 11 bankruptcy proceedings voted for liquidation (four other creditors on the committee voted against liquidation). On February 11, the federal Bankruptcy Court in New York ordered the liquidation to begin. Some 1073 retail stores were closed and 80,000 persons put out of work. Furthermore, Grant's banks had to write off approximately $234 million in bad loans, and its suppliers some $110 million in unpaid bills.

K MART: THE DISCOUNT LEADER

K mart was a latecomer to the discount scene. Kresge brought to its K mart operation proven management and merchandising techniques and resources, with which it was able to convert the operations of a neighborhood variety store to the operations of a giant discount store. And one man brought about the change.

Harry B. Cunningham

In 1957 Harry Cunningham left a meeting with Frank Williams, the president. Cunningham was in a state of shock, tinged with euphoria. He had just been informed of his appointment as a vice president of the Kresge Company. This did not completely surprise him, since he had had a feeling a promotion was imminent. But his assignment—that was the surprise, and what a wonderful challenge— perhaps.

Harry's thoughts went back to his early years with Kresge, the only firm for which he had ever worked. He remembered his beginnings—a stockroom trainee in the Lynchburg, Virginia, store back in 1928, almost 30 years before. After attending Miami University (Ohio) for two years, his money ran out and he could not return to school. The stockroom job was uninteresting and unchallenging compared to the intellectual stimulation of college, but he stuck it out and gradually worked up in the ranks of store management. In 1953 he was promoted to the home office as sales director of the company. There, top management was impressed with his ideas; he was even invited to some of the board meetings. And now this.

His thoughts swung from his career path to the company and its deteriorating prospects. The S. S. Kresge Company, founded as a five-and-dime in 1897 by Sebastian Spring Kresge and second only to Woolworth among variety store chains, now faced greatly worsening prospects. Part of the problem appeared social: the company's traditional customers' needs and wants were changing. At the same time, discounters were invading the market with a strong price appeal. Part of the problem, Kresge management admitted, was that Kresge had moved away from the founding philosophy of "quality at the lowest possible price" to a larger concentration on specialty items with low turnover rates and higher prices. But regardless of the causes, the situation seemed clear: Kresge had a serious long-term problem, and the solution was uncertain.

Back in his office, with an effort Harry focused his mind on the present and the promise or disappointments lurking in the future. His new assignment as vice president was bewilderingly different and completely unstructured. He was freed of operating responsibilities for two years to study the changing competitive environment, with particular attention to the discount stores threatening the variety stores. At the end of the two years, Frank Williams told him, he was to return with his recommendations for the Kresge Company, and to prepare himself for the presidency of the company.

The Turning Point

In those two years, Harry Cunningham logged more than 200,000 air miles studying competition all over the country. In Garden City, Long Island, he observed in great detail a major unit of Korvette. He concluded that the concept was great, with the key element being the tremendous rate of turnover. But he also recognized shortcomings in the Korvette operation, namely that Ferkauf was running the business singlehandedly and that it lacked the organizational expertise to handle the growth Cunningham hoped to achieve. He came to believe that Kresge was "overstored" with variety stores, and was competing with itself in the shopping centers, whereas other units were tied to long-term leases in deteriorating neighborhoods. Meanwhile, the discounters were cutting deeper into sales; only a minuscule sales gain was recorded from 1955 to 1960, and profits were slipping.

Cunningham came back convinced that discounting was the way to go. In May 1959 he was made president and chairman of the executive committee and began laying the groundwork for the expansion he saw ahead. He was determined that Kresge would build the needed organization within the company. His executives were instructed to study intently the discount industry. He wanted to take Kresge into discounting full scale, with no room for second thoughts, but he had to sell the idea to his organization:

> Discounting at the time had a terrible odor. . . . If I had announced my intentions ahead of time I never would have made president. . . . I had the authority, but if you haven't sold the people in your organization, you'll fall flat on your face. I had to convince them that they were an important part of an exciting venture.[12]

He first had to sell the board, and this was not easy. His initial presentation was met by reservations such as "We have been in the variety business for sixty years—we know everything there is to know about it, and we're not doing very well in that; and you want to get us into a business we don't know anything about."[13]

Part of the persuasive argument that Cunningham used to convince the board was that the basic concepts of discounting—low gross margin, high turnover, concentration on return on investment—merely represented a return to the basics of the original variety-store concept, except that the discount format meant much broader merchandise assortments. Looked at this way, the proposed venture into discounting was less daunting, a less extreme diversification than appeared at first glance.

In March 1961 the official decision was made to move into discounting. But Cunningham found that some of the older executives at all levels were incapable of making the adjustment and had to be replaced. By the fall of 1961, every operating vice president, regional manager, assistant regional manager, and regional merchandise manager was fresh on the job. But these new executives were all insiders who had proven themselves in various aspects of Kresge management, were receptive to new ideas, and eager for the challenges Cunningham envisioned.

---

[12]"K mart Has to Open Some New Doors on the Future," *Fortune*, July 1977, p. 144.

[13]"Kresge Company and the Retail Revolution," *University of Michigan Business Review*, July 1975, p. 2.

A vice president, C. Lloyd Yohe, was sent out in the field to study exactly how Kresge should enter this market; Yohe was subsequently made general manager of the discount operation. On his return, he set up guidelines for the new operation, including facilities and layout, siting, salaries, operating ratios, and productivity.

In October 1961, Cunningham ordered his real estate department to obtain signed leases for no less than 60 stores, with 40 to be opened in 1963. This was a rental commitment of $30 million—and certainly millions more in fixtures, merchandise, and other needs—before the first prototype store even opened. It was an audacious move, but it was supported by the firm confidence of Cunningham in the viability of the discount concept and the strength of his organization.

To staff the stores, the vice president of personnel was assigned the job of working out a work-force formula for recruiting, training, and executive development. One of the big questions at that time was whether or not the present Kresge buyers were competent to buy for the new discount operation. The buyers were emphatic in declaring that they were, and the decision was made not to establish a separate buying staff.

Staffing such a vast expansion program was challenging; but it was also highly motivating for the rank and file management personnel, who could readily see the vastly expanded promotional opportunities in the months and years ahead. Over 400 new employees were hired after recruiting teams visited more than 100 colleges and universities. Work-force development was considered indispensable to a rapidly growing, far-flung operation.

In the beginning, certain of the new departments—cameras, sporting goods, jewelry, men's and boy's furnishing, and food—were so unfamiliar it was decided to lease them to experienced operators. Gradually as the organization gained more experience with the diverse lines, these departments were taken over by K mart people. By 1980, of the nonfood departments only footwear was still leased.

Action

In the first two years of his presidency, Cunningham was faced with the problem that an increasing number of variety stores were in poorer, decaying neighborhoods where Kresge had long-term leases. Instead of closing these stores, even though their rent would continue, it was decided to experiment and convert some of them to small discount stores called Jupiter Stores. These were a far cry from the much larger K marts, but they were successful enough that many were again able to turn a profit. The Jupiter Stores sold basic staple products at low prices in austere surroundings. But they were profitable, gave the company an additional taste of discount strategy, and provided a training ground for future K mart managers.

In March 1962, in Garden City, Michigan, the first K mart was opened. It was an immediate success, as customers thronged to the attractive store with the low prices. Cunningham's bold gamble appeared vindicated. Company executives observing the milling crowds and the many busy checkout stands had to believe this was the way of the future for Kresge.

At the time, the company had 803 variety stores and a few Jupiter Stores. The company had experienced a 34 percent decrease in profits between 1958 and 1962. Before the end of the decade, S. S. Kresge Company owned the nation's largest discount store chain. Table 8.2 shows the rapid growth of K mart during the 11 years from 1968 to 1978. The number of new stores added each year is almost incredible, particularly in 1976. In that year, Kresge took over 145 former W. T. Grant stores and in addition established 126 new units for a total of 271 new stores. To do so, K mart promoted 310 assistant store managers to store managers and hired 27,000 people to support one of the greatest yearly expansions ever achieved by a retailer—one that experts believed could never be topped.

The growth of Kresge's sales volume is compared to its major competitors in Table 8.3. Starting from a much lower base, in 1976 Kresge became the second largest general merchandise retailer, passing J. C. Penney Company and trailing only Sears, with almost twice the sales volume of Woolworth.

With such rapid expansion, was Kresge in danger of overcommitment and even bankruptcy with its bold expansion? The answer is a resounding "No!" If we examine the long-term debt as a percentage of sales of Kresge and its major competitors, we find Kresge's is the lowest. For example, in 1974 long-term debt of Kresge was 3.8 percent of sales; Sears was 8.4 percent; Penney 5.3 percent; Woolworth, 9.9; and (soon-to-be-bankrupt) Grant at 12.1 percent. Kresge financed its expansion for the most part with internally generated funds.

During the early and mid-1970s, nearly a dozen discount chains were in bankruptcy, reorganization, or receivership. In addition to Grant, some of the better known firms with severe problems were Arlan's (which had acquired the faltering

Table 8.2   The Growth of K mart, 1968–1978

Year (as of January 31)	Number of K marts in Operation	Stores Added Each Year
1968	216	54
1969	273	57
1970	338	65
1971	411	73
1972	486	75
1973	580	94
1974	673	93
1975	803	130
1976	935	132
1977	1206	271
1978	1366	160

Source: S. S. Kresge published reports.

Table 8.3   Sales Volume and Percentage Change for K mart and Major Competitors, 1961–1976 (Millions of Dollars)

	Kresge		Sears		Penney		Woolworth	
Year	Sales Volume	Percent Change	Sales Volume	Percent Change	Sales Volume	Percent Change	Sales Volume	Percent Change
1961	$ 450		$ 4,267		$1,554		$1,061	
1966	1,090	142	6,805	59	2,549	64	1,574	48
1971	3,100	184	10,006	47	4,812	89	2,801	78
1976	8,380	170	14,900	49	8,354	74	5,152	84

Source: Moody's Industrial Manual and company annual reports.

Korvette in 1971), Mammoth Stores, and Spartan. Penney's Treasure Island stores and Woolworth's Woolco followed a few years later. K mart, however, emerged strong, profitable, and dominant in most metropolitan areas. Indeed, up to 1980 only one K mart store was ever closed, and five new K marts were opened in the same market area at the same time.

On March 17, 1977, shareholders of S. S. Kresge Company voted to change the corporate name to K mart Corporation in recognition of the success of the discount operation, which by 1976 was producing 94 percent of the corporation's annual domestic sales.

Ingredients of Success

Observers have cited a number of factors behind the success of K mart:

- Emphasis on high turnover
- Emphasis on low markups, low prices, and heavy sales volume
- Emphasis on first-quality goods and national brands—no seconds or distress goods
- Across the board discounting rather than selected specials
- One-stop shopping format
- Clustering

What these observers fail to appreciate is that these factors are not unique to K mart: these same policies and practices are common to almost all discount operations.

High turnover is the key ingredient of discounting strategy for all discounters. It is the kingpin that enables firms to emphasize low prices and yet prosper on low markups. (Review the boxed information in the Korvette case, which demonstrates with numbers the impact of turnover on profitability.) High turnover is achieved by carrying only the most popular sizes and items—there is no room for slow sellers or fringe sizes.

The policy of carrying only first-quality goods with an emphasis on national brands was a policy of the early discounters. This was in contrast with the policy of bargain basements of department stores and some promotional-type stores that sought closeouts, distress goods, and seconds that could be sold at low prices and still yield a good markup. Discounters believed the only way they could gain customer acceptance was to offer regular quality merchandise, preferably well-known national brands that were presold by the manufacturers' advertising.

The one-stop shopping format adopted in the early planning for K mart was a practice followed by Korvette and many of the early discounters. A wide range of departments, including food and furniture, was common. Actually, K mart did not go as far with the one-stop format as stores like Korvette, since it did not try to maintain a full furniture and carpeting department.

The idea of clustering—opening a number of stores in a metropolitan area at the same or nearly the same time—was also a strategy practiced by Korvette. The advertising impact of a number of stores sharing the expense was more powerful than that of competing firms with fewer units to share the advertising burden, and the technique also increased the effectiveness of management and control.

Consequently, we have to look further to identify the factors unique to K mart's success at a time when many discount firms were faltering and some areas were becoming oversaturated with stores. The following are characteristics we can identify as the unique ingredients of the success of K mart:

- *Rapid but controlled growth.* The line is thin between overly ambitious expansion and overconservative caution. The first can leave a firm vulnerable to financial overextension, and the latter can result in lost opportunity and competitive inroads.

  Kresge may have walked the thin line in its ambitious expansion plans. But it had several trumps. Most of the organizational requirements were already in place. Management personnel and training programs were well established and tested. Store location and planning research and analyses were also well seasoned. Controls for far-flung units had been operational for decades. All of these important factors for a mighty expansion drive already existed.

- *Organizational simplicity.* Unlike other established firms, such as Penney and Woolworth who ventured into discounting with a separate subsidiary, K mart kept its variety store organization—the same buyers, store planners, and management personnel. And this worked. Their skills were transferable and could be shared. In return, there is organizational simplicity. And this brought the advantages of better communication, coordination, and cooperation by all sectors of the corporation than normally could be expected when such functions and activities are divided. It also brought lower overhead.

- *Simplicity of store planning and layout.* According to the size of the market area, five different sizes and models of K marts were constructed:

1. 40,000 square feet (for cities 8000 to 15,000 in population)
2. 65,000 square feet (for up to about 50,000 population)
3. 70,000 square feet (for the 75,000 population target)
4. 84,000 square feet (for the large metropolitan markets)
5. 95,000 square feet (for still larger metropolitan markets)

Thus, K mart was able to enter a market with the most effective competitive size for the market. Stores and layouts were standardized to maximize the effectiveness and speed of planning, stocking, and opening.

- *High-quality store management.* The key factor of high-grade management differentiated K mart from most of its competitors, including the ill-fated Korvette. Kresge had long had one of the strongest college recruiting and management development programs of any chain, and this commitment was intensified with the heavy labor requirements brought about by the K mart expansion. Each manager was given considerable autonomy—far more than is customarily given to chain store managers—and responsibilities, including hiring and training personnel, ordering merchandise, and controlling expenditures and inventory. To ensure their preparation for such responsibilities, store managers were given top salaries and intensive training. A 21-week orientation program began their training, followed by on-the-job experience as a manager of either a Jupiter or Kresge variety store. The next step was co-manager of a K mart unit. After approximately nine years of management experience, the successful candidates were given a K mart to manage. Compensation and further promotion were based on how well the manager handled the profit-center responsibilities and his or her ability to generate a proper return on investment.
- *Adaptability.* K mart exhibited an adaptability to changing circumstances unusual in a large organization that had been successful following a different strategy. At least four strategy modifications can be identified:

1. The early strategy of all discounters was a bare minimum of service, to keep costs and prices rock-bottom. Consequently, they offered no credit, nor did K mart in its early years. However, by 1970 the company sensed the need for credit service and began accepting bank credit cards as well as issuing its own credit card. The latter was dropped four years later because of costs, but the bank credit cards are still accepted.
2. Early discounters were located in free-standing sites or abandoned warehouses and the like, and K mart found great success in building its own free-standing stores isolated from other stores and from the restrictions of shopping centers. But the company was flexible enough to enter its first regional mall in 1978 and now uses both types of locations.
3. By the mid-1970s Kresge determined that stores could be located much

closer together than had earlier been thought. This strategy change paved the way for greater expansion and more density of market coverage.

4. When the first K mart store was opened, leased departments accounted for half of total sales volume. But K mart began taking over the leased departments as it acquired more experience with the unfamiliar lines of merchandise, allowing it to exercise greater control and to obtain greater profits over a wide-ranging array of products.

Update

During the early and mid-1980s, K mart continued to move ahead. By 1985 it had 2178 K mart stores and 227 old Kresge and Jupiter outlets. It began diversifying, particularly into discount specialty stores, with a Designer Depot off-price apparel chain and Builders Square home improvement centers. However, these were not yet contributing much to earnings. A major acquisition was the 898-unit Waldenbooks chain.

The growth of K mart continues unabated. Between 1983 and 1987, K mart's annaul sales jumped 37 percent, to $25.6 billion; during this time, Sears' volume increased only 12 percent to $28.1 billion. At this rate, K mart would overtake Sears' merchandise operation within two years. It would then be the biggest retailer of all.

K MART AND THE FAILURES: WHAT CAN BE LEARNED?

The success of K mart contrasts sharply with the failures of other what-should-have-been major forces in the discount arena. Intuitively we know that powerful learning experiences exist here for all firms faced with powerful competitors—this includes practically all firms.

Learning Insight. Success can come simply, merely doing the ordinary better than competitors.

K mart in many ways followed the traditional discount store format, the same format and policies followed by Korvette, Woolco, Topps, Spartan, Zayre's, and a host of others. But it did it better: a better job of planning operations and selecting locations; a better job of training and developing people, both managerial and nonmanagerial.

Not surprisingly, we find a similar situation with McDonald's in the fast foods industry: McDonald's, at least in its great growth years toward market dominance, simply did things better and more consistently than its competitors.

Learning Insight. One individual can exert a profound influence—for good or bad—on an organization's fortunes.

In less than a decade, Harry Cunningham transformed the slipping and mediocre Kresge into an industry leader. At about the same time, another chief executive, Richard Mayer of W. T. Grant Company, led his firm to disaster and liquidation. And Eugene Ferkauf, the pioneer, the one with the vision and head-start, saw Korvette crumbling around him.

Suppose Harry Cunningham had been mistaken in his assessment of the opportunity for Kresge in discounting. The Kresge Company might have become another Grant if it had attempted uncontrolled expansion. The line can be thin between aggressiveness and rashness. Vigorous growth can lead a firm to great success or total failure.

Learning Insight. Rapid growth is possible without jeopardizing viability, but it must be controlled growth. Beware of a growth-at-any-cost mentality.

K mart showed that rapid growth is possible without jeopardizing viability, whereas Korvette and Grant show the perils of overextension. But rapid growth should only be attempted when it can be controlled, when it does not outstrip the workforce, research and planning, and financial resources. Objectives, policies, and management and financial controls should be well defined, and lines of authority and performance measures should be specified. It must be clear who is responsible for what, and how performance is to be measured.

Only when growth is controlled is it likely that a seasoned and strong management team can be available so that merchandising, operating, and staff departments can function smoothly. (The boxed information discusses the important role of management development for an organization aspiring to rapid growth.) In building the most effective operation, testing is necessary in order to make adjustments and modifications where needed. Without time to sit back and analyze past successes and failures, faults are undetected and uncorrected, and strengths are not pinpointed and acted upon. For example, a well-run discount operation needs strong and well-designated policies regarding store security (since with self-service and fewer employees per customer than in traditional stores, shoplifting and employee theft are more tempting) and the control of waste and shrinkage.

Perhaps the major point to be learned from the experience of Grant is the fallacy of growth at any cost. Stores were opened without regard either for sound location or for an adequately trained organization. Adding millions of square feet of selling space each year may increase sales, but at what cost? In the extreme case of Grant, the cost was the destruction of the company.

The dilemma that confronted Korvette was by no means unique among the

---

INFORMATION SIDELIGHT

MANAGEMENT DEVELOPMENT

Any growing firm needs competent executives and staff professionals to step into new opening slots. Managerial expansion can come in two ways:

1. From internal management development
2. By recruiting from outside the organization

Internal management development presumes a body of trainees who have the potential competence and motivation to fill important executive slots in the future. But time is needed to give such trainees the experience, coaching, and perhaps formal training to fulfill such expectations. For example, the S. S. Kresge Company at one time planned a five-year program to develop new college graduates—to whom they paid very competitive salaries to recruit—to become small variety-store managers.

The alternative is to conduct a vigorous recruiting campaign and obtain experienced executives from outside the organization. Unfortunately, such an approach, if relied upon primarily, can play havoc with the morale of present employees who see little chance for their advancement. (You may want to review "The Issue of Promotion from Within," earlier in this chapter.) Furthermore, the firm's compensation package and reputation must be attractive enough to woo outsiders. This may mean that the pay scale must be higher than that of competing firms, and this can place an organization at a cost disadvantage. Generally, a commitment to hiring from outside is not prudent on a scale large enough to support vigorous expansion.

Of course, there is another alternative to developing from within or bringing from without. People can be promoted quickly to fill slots, with the hope that they can develop on the job and not make too many mistakes in the process. This is akin to filling responsible positions with "bodies" and characterizes much of the expansion efforts of Korvette and W. T. Grant. The consequences of ignoring management development or of outpacing it can be dire indeed.

---

discounters of the day. Riding a wave of consumer enchantment with lower prices (and the self-service and convenience of parking and store hours), many discount store entrepreneurs found themselves with a few successful stores and developed grandiose plans for expansion. It was natural to bring their friends and relatives in to the good thing as Ferkauf did. (See the following discussion of the perils of nepotism and cronyism.) Many thus overextended themselves, both financially and managerially, and were in trouble. The difference with Korvette was that its attained size was much greater than most of its contemporaries before problems began to overwhelm it. Largely this is a credit to the work-load of a peripatetic Ferkauf, who was able to supervise directly a large number of stores before it became too much for him.

And then there was K mart. Despite the almost unbelievable growth in number of stores—opening as many as 271 huge stores in a single year—K mart had the trained employees to staff them effectively, and most of the funds needed were generated internally without the need for heavy outside financing.

Learning Insight. Simplicity is important for smooth growth.

Simplicity may well be one of the keys to controlled growth. K mart's organization was kept simple; it was hardly more complex than when Kresge had only variety stores. No separate organization was created for the discount operation. And the existing organization found the challenge and opportunity of developing the new venture to be highly motivating, beckoning it to greater responsibilities and advancement. Similarly, the store facilities were geared to simplicity in planning and operating, with standardized sizes of stores, layouts, displays, and so on. The control and the merchandise assortment plans—all were simply adaptations and modifications of those developed over decades of variety store operations.

Learning Insight. It is important to maintain a stable and clear-cut image and undeviating objectives.

As growth and success came to K mart, it resisted the temptation to try to be something it was not, such as upgrading to a department store, thereby confusing its customers and blurring its image. Korvette was not able to resist this temptation, and it succeeded in alienating many of its former customers. Grant was not sure what it should be, nor were its customers. Even Woolworth was confused as to what Woolco should be—a full-fledged discount store or a promotional department store—and developed a fuzzy image.

To be successful, a retailer needs to build a distinctive image. Many years ago the problems of an image deficiency were cited:

> What happens to the retail store that lacks a sharp character, that does not stand for something special to any class of shoppers? It ends up as an alternative store in the customer's mind. The shopper does not head for such a store as the primary place to find what she wants. Without certain outstanding departments and lines of merchandise, without clear attraction for some group, it is like a dull person.[14]

---

[14]Pierre Martineau, "The Personality of the Retail Store," *Harvard Business Review*, January–February 1958, p. 50.

INFORMATION SIDELIGHT

PROS AND CONS OF CRONYISM AND NEPOTISM

Cronyism is the selection of friends for high executive positions. In general, cronyism offers these advantages to an organization:

1. The loyalty of these executives is ensured, because they are already close friends and presumed confidants of the chief executive.
2. Communication and a close working relationship is enhanced.
3. Strengths and weaknesses of each individual should be known factors and not come as unpleasant surprises, as they can be when outsiders are brought into the organization.

The major drawbacks of selecting most or all of the top cadre of executives from close personal friends are:

1. Such a small body of executive candidates may bring very limited expertise and abilities to the organization.
2. A narrow organizational perspective is promulgated, because most of these people will have come from similar backgrounds and probably have similar views on most matters.
3. Morale and motivation of the rest of the organization may atrophy because of the perceived lack of advancement opportunities.
4. Because people have been selected more on a basis of friendship than ability, there may be a real reluctance to pressure them for performance and to discipline or discharge those who are performing poorly.
5. As a result of the above factors, such organizations tend toward complacency and conservatism.

On balance, the drawbacks and dangers of cronyism far outweigh the benefits.

Related to cronyism and a phenomenon of many small and medium-sized family-owned businesses is the reserving of important managerial positions for family members and relatives—*nepotism*. The pros and cons are similar to those of cronyism.

Grant had not really established a desired image when its vigorous expansion effort began. Prices and quality were sometimes competitive and sometimes not. The guiding force of a unified image needed for coordination and expansion was not there.

Learning Insight. *It is very difficult to upgrade an image.*

To upgrade customers' perceptions of a firm is never easy, but that is what Korvette tried. Eugene Ferkauf made his initial entry into the market by gaining a reputation as an aggressive discounter of appliances. But as he expanded he tried to upgrade. These attempts to redefine Korvette as a promotional department store aimed at a higher-income clientele were made for over a decade without any conspicuous success. To attempt to upgrade an image is difficult and can cost a firm its old bargain-conscious customers without gaining a significant number of other customers.

Learning Insight. *For an organization desiring rapid expansion, there are strong arguments for a decentralized management.*

Most discounters, such as Zayre's, Spartans, and Korvette, were centralized with home office executives having major authority for most policies and decisions regarding store operation and merchandise. In the most extreme cases, the store manager only ''carries the keys''; that is, he was responsible for opening and closing the store, seeing that adequate workers were on hand, store maintenance, and displays and other dictates of the home office. There was little opportunity to exert initiative, and accordingly such jobs were neither well paid nor of very high caliber.

A few discount firms, notably K mart, decentralized and gave their store managers much more authority over operations and merchandising. These managers were well trained (seven to ten years before becoming K mart managers, versus one to two years for some other discount chains), and well paid.

The combination of high-caliber field executives (store managers) and decentralized authority to encourage their initiative and motivation is in sharp contrast with the centralized organization, which fosters low-level field executives. Home office supervision under a centralized organization becomes, with expansion, somewhat uneven because an inordinate amount of attention is necessarily focused on opening new outlets. Older stores tend to be neglected, and the growth is not completely digested. With high-level field executives under a decentralized organization such a situation tends to be minimized.

Learning Insight. *Basic merchandising principles must not be neglected in the pursuit of growth through additional outlets.*

Grant violated basic merchandising principles in its rush toward expanding square footage of selling space. Markdowns were not taken when needed; as a result merchandise was no longer fresh, clean, and attractive. Staple or basic merchandise should have been carefully maintained to avoid out-of-stocks, but was not. New merchandise lines should have been tested and planned, rather than being abruptly placed on sale. Signs of deteriorating conditions should have been watched for and corrective actions taken quickly. With Grant, the burgeoning debt, lessening merchandise turnover, the low sales per-square-foot ratios—all these should have alerted management to something seriously amiss. For example, the creeping problem of high inventories should have been detected and prompt action taken; inventory as a percent of sales rose from 18.3 percent in 1969 to 24.3 percent in 1972. In the six years before 1969, this stock-to-sales ratio had never been higher than 19.0 percent. When it reached 20.8 percent in 1970, and certainly when it reached 21.7 percent in 1971, action should have been taken.

Finally, a major issue is raised in these cases. Should we concentrate our efforts, or should we spread them over more alternatives? When we consider the laggard performance of Woolco, the desirability of concentrating rather than diffusing efforts seems confirmed. This strategy is not unlike that facing military commanders: do we concentrate our forces to secure a breakthrough, or do we spread our efforts to cover all sectors?

No sweeping generalization is possible for this dilemma. In the case of K mart versus Woolco, the concentration of efforts worked to perfection. But if the K mart venture had failed . . . ? At what point should you commit your full resources to a new and unproven venture? And if there is misjudgment, a full commitment may mean disaster. Perhaps the prudent approach to discounting was that of Woolworth. But a conservative and prudent approach is bound to fail against the aggressively successful approach. Risks cannot be avoided in decision making.

For Thought and Discussion

1. We have noted that one of the serious problems Korvette faced during its rapid growth was lack of adequate systems and procedures, particularly regarding feedback and controls from the stores. What controls or performance measures would you want to have established in this situation?
2. Personal supervision by Ferkauf was possible when he had only a small number of stores in a limited area. With steady expansion, such personal supervision was no longer possible. What might have been done at this point to assure adequate supervision of stores?
3. Was the major mistake of Woolworth that it did not put sufficient stake into the Woolco operation, that it was reluctant to go all-out as Kresge did? Discuss.
4. How do you think it might have been possible for Grant to expand as vigorously as it did and to do so successfully?
5. The success of K mart, the imitator not the innovator, suggests that being first to the market may be less advantageous than coming later. Evaluate this reasoning.

Invitation to Role Play

1. You are the personnel director of the Kresge Company. The decision has just been made that the firm will shift as rapidly as possible into discounting. You face a major challenge to provide a sufficient number of trained executives at all levels. How would you propose to do this? In particular, address the issue of recruiting experienced discount executives from other organizations.
2. You are a staff assistant to James Kendrick of Grant. He has just assumed leadership of the company. You have been asked by him to develop plans for a course of action to keep the company viable. Be as specific as you can, and be prepared to defend your recommendations.
3. Place yourself in the role of Eugene Ferkauf, a tremendous innovator and leader of the discount movement with Korvette. You have just been proclaimed by famed educator Malcolm McNair as one of the six greatest merchants in U.S. history. You are humble, yet ecstatic at this honor. Now to prove it. How? Be as specific as possible.
4. As the CEO of Woolworth at the time of the Woolco abandonment, how would you support your decision to the board of directors? Be as persuasive as possible—your job as CEO may depend on this.

CHAPTER 9

The Battle of Hamburgers

Such a simple product: a hamburger. What can any reasonably efficient operation do to hurt a hamburger, and jeopardize business? But, alas, we face the vivid contrast between the great success of McDonald's, the premier hamburger maker, and an also-ran, Burger Chef.

The differences between the success and failure of the two firms is hardly one of resources: McDonald's did not have vastly superior financial and managerial resources with which to command mass-media advertising and to open hundreds of additional outlets. In fact, Burger Chef was acquired by General Foods Corporation in 1967 when General Foods was a $3 billion corporation lacking neither resources nor know-how about the marketing of food. Our look at the differences in the two corporations will uncover some important learning concepts with far wider applicability than simply the jockeying of fast-food behemoths.

BURGER CHEF: WHY NOT ANOTHER MCDONALD'S?

In 1967 General Foods Corporation acquired Burger Chef Systems, a fast-food franchising operation of some 700 units, for $16 million. In less than four years, General Foods amassed a pretax loss of $83 million from the venture, while, during the same period, McDonald's net income rose 285 percent. There were some marginal fast-food franchisors that collapsed during this period in which there appeared to be a saturation of hamburger, chicken, and other restaurants. But General Foods was no marginal firm. It was the nation's largest manufacturer of

THE BATTLE OF HAMBURGERS

convenience foods, with sales approaching $3 billion. It was an astute and aggressive marketer and the country's third largest national advertiser, spending over $150 million a year. It had an unbroken string of annual sales increases dating back to 1935. With such backing for an already established and growing franchise chain, how could disaster strike, and in just a few years?

The General Foods Company

General Foods traces its beginning back to C. W. Post Cereals in 1895. It was incorporated in 1922 as the Postum Cereal Company, manufacturers of Post cereals and Postum beverage. In 1925, the firm began consolidating with other companies, including the Jell-O Company and the Maxwell House Coffee Company. In 1929 the Postum Cereal Company changed its name to General Foods.

The company continued to grow and diversify through internal development of new products and by acquisition and mergers with other firms. By 1965 its sales were $1.5 billion and net earnings over $177 million. Well-known brands of this major processor and marketer of packaged food products included: Maxwell House, Yuban, and Sanka coffees; Jell-O desserts; Bird's Eye frozen foods; Post cereals; Swans Down cake mixes; Baker's chocolate; Minute rice; Kool-Aid soft drink mixes; Gaines pet foods; Tang breakfast drink; and Log Cabin syrup.

During the 1960s, however, some performance indicators showed deterioration. While sales revenues increased steadily, profit margins on sales began declining from the high of 6.5 percent in 1963. Returns on stockholders' equity were also showing declines. Still, in 1966 when a new man, C. W. "Tex" Cook, came in as chairman and chief executive, and Arthur E. Larkin became president and chief operating officer, General Foods stood at the forefront of the packaged foods industry with net profits at 6 percent of sales. Of six major food categories, General Foods led sales in all but cereals, with no competitor even close in instant coffee, desserts, and dog food.

Tangible problems emerged in 1968 when the Federal Trade Commission forced General Foods to divest of its S.O.S. soap-pad business, which it had acquired in 1957. Chairman Cook bitterly took umbrage at this decision:

> They laid down some pretty severe strictures regarding what we could and could not do for "X" number of years. For instance, they made it very clear that we were precluded from touching anything of consequence that went through the supermarket on a national basis. Similarly, they would frown on something that depended very heavily on consumer advertising. So that we were almost directed away from the kinds of things where our experience and expertise had, over the years, given us most of our benefits.[1]

[1] "The Rebuilding Job at General Foods," *Business Week*, August 25, 1973, p. 50.

To add to the problems connected with antitrust action, three of General Foods' biggest divisions began running into trouble. The Bird's Eye Division lost ground to Green Giant Company, which developed ready-to-cook vegetables in plastic bags that could be dropped directly into boiling water. Supermarkets were bringing out their own branded products, which they sold below the prices of General Foods' national brands. Consumer acceptance of these private brands cut into General Foods' market share and profit margins.

The sales of Maxwell House Division, which generated more than a third of General Foods' sales revenues, leveled off. This sales decline reflected changing consumer tastes, particularly those of young adults, whose consumption of coffee was less than that of their parents.

INFORMATION SIDELIGHT

PRIVATE BRANDS

Wholesalers and retailers often use their own brands—commonly referred to as private brands—in place of or in addition to the branded goods of manufacturers. Private brands, although offered at lower selling prices than nationally advertised brands, typically give dealers more per-unit profit since they are bought on more favorable terms, partly reflecting promotional savings. Some firms, such as Sears, Penney's, and A & P, stock mostly their own brands. As a result they have better control over repeat business, since satisfied customers can repurchase the brand only through the particular store or chain.

Since private brands directly compete with manufacturers' brands, sometimes at a better price, why do manufacturers sell some of their output to retailers under a private brand? Some manufacturers do so to minimize idle plant capacity, arguing that if they refuse business with private label seekers, someone else will get the business. Other manufacturers welcome private brand business because they lack the resources and know-how to enter the marketplace effectively with their own brands.

Changes in consumer tastes also caused the dry cereal market growth to slow markedly. As a result of a massive promotion by competitor General Mills, General Foods' Post Division (Post Toasties, Grape Nuts, 40% Bran Flakes, etc.) was displaced from second place (behind Kellogg).

Faced with governmental constraints, a tangible loss of profit momentum, and an eroding market share, General Foods began seeking diversification in directions compatible with the company's expertise in food-related activities. During the mid-1960s, food sold away from home was growing at twice the rate of food sold in stores for home consumption.

The decision to acquire Burger Chef Systems, an Indianapolis-based chain of 700 (mostly franchised) fast-food hamburger restaurants, seemed reasonable and expeditious. Six Rix roast-beef sandwich restaurants were also acquired at that time. 1968 was a boom year, and companies like McDonald's were growing at rates in excess of 25 percent a year. Burger Chef was operating in 39 states and selling a million hamburgers per day. Expectations for the fast-food business were high.

Burger Chef under General Foods

A vigorous expansion program was undertaken for Burger Chef. By March 1969, not much more than a year after the acquisition, there were 900 outlets operating across the country. That same month, Burger Chef moved into Canada with an outlet in Toronto.

By December 1969, there were 1022 outlets in the United States and 29 in Canada. One year later, there were more than 1200 outlets in the United States and 36 in Canada, representing an increase of over 70 percent in three years. Some 84 percent of the outlets were franchised and 16 percent operated by Burger Chef. Advertising expenditures averaged $2.5 million a year.

General Foods lost several of its key executives in its fast-food acquisitions. The founder of Burger Chef left to pursue other interests shortly after the acquisition. Another key executive had a heart attack. Other departures for various reasons resulted in an almost complete management turnover during the first two years. But this seemed to pose no severe problems, because General Foods supplied the new management for its acquisition from its own ranks.

The bad news, when it came, was sudden and shocking. In January 1972, General Foods announced a write-down amounting to $83 million pretax dollars, nearly $1 a share after taxes. General Foods informed its stockholders that it was cutting back its ambitious expansion into fast food. It closed all 70 of its Rix roast-beef restaurants. It closed 100 of the 1200 Burger Chef units and announced it was writing off many more. The faster General Foods tried to expand its fast-food operation, the bigger the problems became.

Forbes magazine questioned how so big a company could go so wrong in as simple a business as frying hamburgers and slicing roast beef. In an interview with *Forbes'* reporters, President Larkin explained: "We couldn't get enough people to come into our stores. The kids didn't want roast beef and later the adults didn't want it either. Roast beef was just a fad." Regarding the Burger Chef operation, Larkin admitted the problem was simply management: "The key man had a heart attack. We sent one of our own men and he just did not know his way around this kind of operation."[2]

---

[2]"The Bigger They Are . . . ," *Forbes*, February 15, 1972, p. 21.

Struggle for Survival

For 19 consecutive years, General Foods managed to achieve gains in per-share earnings. But the hamburger and roast-beef disaster broke the trend in 1972. The viability of the multibillion dollar company was not in danger, and the company was still profitable despite the fast-food drain. However, Burger Chef's substantial losses hurt the image of the company, especially with its major food chain customers. This image further suffered when General Foods cut back on some customer services in order to absorb the fast-food losses.

Arthur Larkin, the heir apparent for the chairman's position, took an early retirement. As part of the company-wide efficiency drive, salaried personnel were cut by 10 percent, and General Foods took a hard look at its total marketing operation.

While other aspects of the corporation were also causing problems, the biggest rebuilding job continued to be the Burger Chef chain. The total number of units was pruned to about 1000, and more attention was given to clustering these in major markets to obtain a more efficient sharing of advertising expenditures. More thorough screening and training of franchise owners and managers was instituted. A new building design, new logo, more emphasis on product quality, a more varied menu, and even a new plastic wrapper to keep hamburgers warm longer, were belatedly introduced. Yet, it seemed likely the fast-food division was years away from making a major contribution to General Food's earnings.

Postmortem

Burger Chef seemed such a perfect acquisition in 1968. How could such a compatible union go wrong? In retrospect, a fast-food operation is vastly different from the marketing of packaged food in supermarkets. There were major differences in promotional efforts, in competition, in facilities, and, most important, in management controls. Unfortunately, General Foods did not realize this until much of the damage was done.

No single event can be selected as the cause of the Burger Chef debacle; rather, it was a combination of factors. But these factors were by no means hidden; they were obvious and should have been identified and corrected by management. At the time of the acquisition, Burger Chef suffered from a lack of distinction and identity. McDonald's had its golden arches, Kentucky Fried Chicken had its easily recognized red and white colors, and most of the other successful fast-food establishments were readily identified. Burger Chef, on the other hand, had an undistinguished red and yellow sign that was not universally used, and when used it was inconspicuous among the multitude of other signs proliferating along commercial strips. The outlets themselves were modestly constructed, some with walk-up windows, but few with sit-down accommodations. There was little uniformity in design among the mostly franchised operations.

At the time of acquisition, Burger Chef had a considerable disadvantage in that its 700 outlets were thinly dispersed and spread over 39 states. A major metropolitan area might have only a handful of restaurants, in contrast to McDonald's and some of the other major franchisors. Supervision of such a widespread network was difficult and costly, and the benefits of concentrated promotional efforts, which could have been shared among a number of outlets at relatively low cost, were lost, leaving the competitive advantage to those firms with greater concentration of outlets. The better policy would have been a slower geographical expansion, on a market-by-market basis.

The quality of food and the limited assortment available also contributed to the poor market performance. At a time when competitors were adding fish sandwiches, double- and triple-decker hamburgers, onion rings, and fruit pies to their menu, Burger Chef stood pat. In addition, food quality varied with franchisee and area.

Company spokesmen admitted their selection of franchisees, and their training of them, was questionable. Interest in a Burger Chef franchise, satisfactory character references, adequate financial standing, and some experience in running a filling station or whatever, were all that was necessary for approval. Although new franchise holders were sent to a training school for a brief period, there was no on-the-job training to familiarize them with hiring people, to teach them how to be hospitable, how to handle the problems of a teenage gathering place, and so on.

Major emphasis in the Burger Chef operation was on expanding the number of outlets just as rapidly as possible. In the process, existing outlets and their problems were ignored. As a result, location mistakes, problems of controlling quality of product and service, and other problems were not corrected for the new units being established. The expansion was coming on top of an unstable and even wobbly base.

An economic recession in 1969–1971 should have discouraged pell-mell expansion, or at least caused some introspection and review of the overall marketing strategy for this division. During this time some of the marginal fast-food franchisors went out of business. But the stronger ones survived with little ill effects. With the formidable resources of General Foods, Burger Chef should have strengthened its market share, focusing on upgrading and improving the outlets it had, instead of enlarging its number of mediocre establishments. As president Larkin said: "We moved too far, too fast, under the pressure of the times."[3]

[3]Marylin Bender, "At General Foods, Did Success Breed Failure?" *New York Times*, June 11, 1972, pp. 111–118.

Update

Late in 1981, General Foods sold The Burger Chef subsidiary to Hardee's, a Canadian-owned hamburger fast-food firm with 1396 U.S. outlets. At the time Burger Chef had been pruned to 676 units and, after five years of losses, was finally showing a small profit. The sale to Hardee's resulted in a charge against earnings for General Foods of $12.5 million. The loss was regarded as acceptable to be rid of a burr that had plagued it and that, while showing a profit, was still yielding a lower return on investment than most of its other divisions. The acquisition was viewed by Hardee's as providing additional sales and earnings growth potential to its already substantial fast-food operation.

By the mid-1980s, there was rapid growth in the fast-food restaurant industry in the number of outlets and the variety of offerings. Some 10,000 new franchise chain outlets were opened in nearly two years, 1984 and 1985. New chains were coming on the scene, while the older ones continued to expand. While certain market areas were becoming saturated, considerable expansion was occurring in the international market and in nontraditional domestic sites, such as military bases, college campuses, and various other institutions.

The general public was showing a new concern for nutrition and weight consciousness, and such chains as Burger King and Wendy's emphasized low-calorie menus. Demand for chicken and seafood was increasing, "gourmet" hamburgers, gourmet pizza (nontraditional toppings on a thin crust), and gourmet croissants were doing well. Ethnic food restaurants, particularly Mexican, were finding strong demand.

While General Foods failed with its Burger Chef acquisition, in recent years large food-related corporations eagerly diversified successfully into fast-food restaurants. Pepsico had Pizza Hut and Taco Bell; General Mills owned Red Lobster; Pillsbury was successful with its Burger King and Godfathers chains; and RJR Nabisco had Kentucky Fried Chicken.

And still, McDonald's remained at the top of the heap, with 1985 sales of $3.7 billion and net profits of $433 million.

MCDONALD'S: SUCCESS WITH SUCH A SIMPLE PRODUCT

Ray Kroc faced a serious dilemma. He was 57 years old and all his life had dreamed of becoming rich. And how he had tried. Ever since he came back from World War I (at 15, he had falsified his age when he joined), he had worked hard at getting rich. He played piano with dance bands; he sold paper cups for Lily-Tulip; and moonlighted at a Chicago radio station (WGES) playing the piano, arranging the music programs, and accompanying singers. The Florida land boom in the mid-1920s brought him from Chicago where he tried selling land. A year later he returned to Chicago almost broke. Lily-Tulip gave him back his old job, and he stayed there more than 10 years. In 1937 he stumbled onto a new gadget, a simple electric appliance that would make six milkshakes at the same time. He quit Lily-Tulip again, made a deal with the inventor, and soon became the world's exclusive agent for the Price Castle Multi-Mixer. Over the next 20 years he traveled all over the country peddling it. He earned a fair living, but did not become rich.

Now Kroc had stumbled onto the opportunity of a lifetime. But he needed $1.5 million to make it work. Unfortunately, he had neither money nor credit. His main source of income had dried up when he was forced to sell his mixer business for $100,000 to pay for a divorce. Now his total assets, including his house, were $90,000.

Prelude

In 1954 Kroc received an order for eight Multi-Mixers from a hamburger stand in San Bernardino, California. The order was unusual enough that he decided to get a first-hand look at an operation that needed to make 48 milkshakes at a time.

Maurice and Richard McDonald had come to California from New England in 1928, thinking California was the land of opportunity. They opened their first restaurant in Pasadena in 1940, and in 1948 opened a self-service hamburger stand in San Bernardino. They had trouble staffing their restaurant after World War II: unskilled job seekers were primarily drunks and drifters. Dick McDonald recalled thinking:

> Let's get rid of it all. Out went dishes, glasses, and silverware. Out went service, the dishwashers, and the long menu. We decided to serve just hamburgers, drinks, and french fries on paper plates. Everything prepared in advance, everything uniform.[4]

These operations proved so successful that they had offers to buy them out or work out franchising deals. But they were conservative and cautiously sold only six franchises in California while passing up other deals. The brothers lived in a small town, netted $75,000 a year, and were afraid of getting too big.

When Ray Kroc arrived, he was amazed. He saw crowds of people waiting in line under the Golden Arches. He estimated the hamburger stand's gross at $250,000 a year. He was even more impressed with the speed of service and the cleanliness. The McDonalds served a standard hamburger for 15¢, and the french fries, kept warm under infrared heat lamps, were always fresh and crispy. Since customers moved in and out quickly, only a small facility was needed to generate the substantial sales volume.

Ray Kroc badly wanted in on this business. He hounded the McDonald brothers for two days until they relented and allowed him to sell franchises. The agree-

[4]"What McDonald's Had, the Others Didn't," *Forbes*, January 2, 1973, p. 26.

ment was to charge 1.9 percent of revenues for each franchise, of which Kroc got 1.4 percent and the McDonald brothers 0.5 percent.

At first Kroc was most interested in expanding the chain in order to sell more Multi-Mixer machines. But by 1960 he had sold 200 franchises, providing him gross franchise income of about $700,000 per year. He had taken a partner, Harry Sonneborn, a former vice president of Tastee Freez, who was drawing $100 a week. Kroc's secretary was taking her wages in stock. (When she retired, she had an estimated 1 million shares of McDonald's stock.)

Sonneborn convinced Kroc to take a wholly new approach. All new franchises would be tenants: the company would select the site, build the store, provide the equipment, and rent the total package to an operator. McDonald's would receive the rental from the lease as well as the franchising fee. A great plan, but it required money—about $1.5 million. And with Kroc's meager assets, bank credit was unattainable.

Franchising

Franchising is a contractural arrangement in which the franchisor extends to independent franchisees the right to conduct a certain kind of business according to a particular format. Although the franchising arrangement may involve a product, a common type of franchise involves a service, with the franchisors providing a carefully developed, promoted, and controlled operation.

Franchising dates back at least to the turn of the century. General Motors very early established its first independent dealer to sell and service automobiles. Coca-Cola and the other soft-drink makers granted franchises to their independent bottlers. By 1910, franchising was the principal method of marketing automobiles and petroleum products. By 1920 it was used by food, drug, variety, hardware, and automotive parts firms. The major growth of franchising began after World War II. Soft ice cream outlets typified this growth: in 1945 there were 100 soft ice cream stands in the United States; by 1960 there were almost 18,000. Franchise sales of goods and services comprise almost 30 percent of all retail sales, with half a million franchise establishments in the United States employing over 4 million workers.[5]

Fast-Food Restaurant Franchising. Franchised fast-food restaurants have made a major impact on the food service industry since World War II. Employment in fast-food franchising by the 1970s accounted for almost 30 percent of total franchising employment and for over 30 percent of all persons employed in eating and drinking places in the United States.

Advantages of Franchising. A firm has two major advantages in expanding through franchised outlets rather than company-owned units. First, expansion can

---

[5]U.S. Department of Commerce, *Franchising in the Economy, 1972–1979* (Washington, D.C.: Superintendent of Documents, U.S. Government Printing Office, 1979), pp. vi, 1.

be rapid because the franchisees are putting up some or most of the money; almost the only limitations to growth are the need to screen applicants, to find suitable sites for new outlets, and to develop the managerial controls necessary to ensure consistency of performance. Second, more conscientious people normally can be obtained to operate the outlets, since franchisees are entrepreneurs with a personal stake in performance rather than hired managers.

The major advantage to a franchisee or licensee is the lower risk of business failure or, to put it positively, the greater chance of success. The entrepreneur has a business with proven consumer acceptance and wider recognition. The franchisee can also benefit from well-developed managerial and promotional techniques and from group buying power.

Onward to Success

Ray Kroc got the money he needed and propelled McDonald's to a huge success. In only 22 years his firm reached the billion-dollar milestone. It took corporations such as IBM and Xerox 46 and 63 years, respectively, to reach this milestone. And Kroc boasted in his autobiography that the company is responsible for the making of over 1000 millionaires—the franchise holders.[6]

Kroc obtained the $1.5 million from several insurance companies. As a premium on the loan, they took 20 percent of the company; this they later sold for a $7 million profit. A year later, Kroc bought out the McDonald brothers, paying them $2.7 million for everything—trademarks, copyrights, formulas, the Golden Arches, and the name. The brothers took their money and quietly retired to their hometown in New Hampshire. A few years later, when Sonneborn's health began to fail, Kroc offered him $10 million in cash, and $100,000 a year for life, and Sonneborn retired to Florida.

Figures 9.1 and 9.2 show the extraordinary growth of McDonald's in number of outlets and in sales from 1955 to 1975. An investment of $5000 in McDonald's in 1967 was worth $100,000 by 1973.

The Marketing Strategy

Ray Kroc saw a market opportunity in catering to "budget-conscious families on wheels who want quick service, clean surroundings, and high-quality food."[7] This was seen as an alternative to drive-ins with car hops, jukeboxes, tipping, waiting,

---

[6]Ray Kroc and Robert Anderson, *Grinding It Out: The Making of McDonald's* (New York: Berkley Publishing, 1977), p. 200.

[7]Carol White and Merle Klingman, " 'Hamburger.' McDonald's Takes It Seriously," *Advertising Age*, May 22, 1972, p. 117.

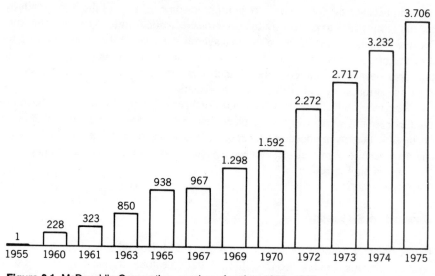

Figure 9.1. McDonald's Corporation, number of outlets 1955–1975.

and food of inconsistent and questionable quality. Kroc defended his approach because

> . . . all of those things create unproductive traffic in a store and encourage loitering that can disrupt customers. This would downgrade the family image we wanted to create for McDonald's. Furthermore, in some areas the vending machines were controlled by the crime syndicate, and I wanted no part of that.[8]

As the executive vice president, Fred L. Turner, said, "We want young families in the tricycle and bicycle neighborhoods—the station wagon set, or one car going on two."[9]

During the company's early years, Ray Kroc used the company airplane to spot good locations; he would fly over a community looking for schools and church steeples and follow with site surveys. The company favored above-average-income and residential areas, preferably near shopping centers. New store sites should contain 50,000 residents within a three-mile radius. This changed by the 1970s when marketing research revealed that three-fourths of McDonald's customers stopped by in conjunction with some other activity. As a consequence, stores were located according to pattern of customer activity and traffic flows.

[8]Ray Kroc and Robert Anderson, *Grinding It Out: The Making of McDonald's* (New York: Berkley Publishing, 1977), p. 200.

[9]"McDonald's Makes a Franchise Sizzle," *Business Week*, June 15, 1968, p. 107.

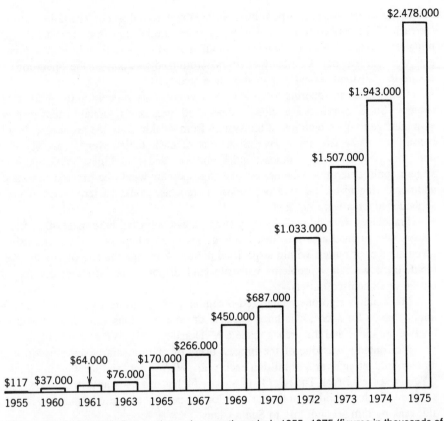

Figure 9.2. McDonald's Corporation, sales growth analysis 1955–1975 (figures in thousands of dollars).

Kroc offered the public a clean family atmosphere in which service was quick and cheerful. Cleanliness of outlets, including the toilets, and friendliness of salespeople became major competitive advantages. These characteristics were not obtained without great pains. At Hamburger University, a special McDonald's training school for managers and owners, heavy emphasis was given customer service. A 350-page operating manual required adherence to strict standards, not only in preparation of food but also in care and maintenance of the facilities. For example, the manual called for door windows to be washed twice daily. There was even an employee dress code, with men required to keep their hair cropped to military length and their shoes highly polished. Women were to wear dark, low shoes, hair nets, and only very light makeup. All employees wore prescribed uniforms.

Food preparation was completely standardized: a pound of meat was to have less than 19 percent fat; buns were to measure 3½ inches wide, no more than one-quarter ounce of onions was permitted per hamburger, and so on. The holding time for each of the cooked products was set by corporate headquarters: french fries, 7 minutes; burger, 10 minutes; coffee, 30 minutes—after these time limits the products were thrown out. Company auditors scrutinized this part of the operation to ensure that all food served was of the same quality.

Consistency in adhering to these high standards was inherent in the marketing strategy. Store operation was closely supervised by strong regional offices to prevent damage to the reputation of the system from weakness in one restaurant. Field consultants made two three-day inspections of each outlet every year, grading operators on quality, cleanliness, quick service, and friendliness. This grading system could determine whether an existing operator would be granted desirable additional franchises. On rare occasions, a franchise could be terminated if prescribed standards were not met.

Franchises were granted store by store. This contrasted with most other franchisors who granted area franchises to large investors who promised to establish a given number of outlets within a specified period. Although the rate of growth was rapid, there were few problems with substandard conditions at either company-owned or franchised outlets.

McDonald's rigorously analyzed potential sites to ensure each unit the maximum chance for success; failures because of poor locations were few. The distinctive buildings and the arches made a McDonald's unit visible from a distance.

McDonald's was one of the biggest users of mass-media advertising of any retailer, budgeting over $50 million each year. Who is not familiar with the jingle "You Deserve a Break Today"? How successful has this mass advertising been? In a survey of schoolchildren in the early 1970s, 96 percent identified Ronald McDonald, ranking him second only to Santa Claus.

The Maturing Years

In 1968 Ray Kroc stepped aside and appointed 35-year-old Fred Turner president of the company. Turner had been Kroc's understudy for several years, starting as a cook and working his way up.

Despite Turner's allegiance and admiration for Kroc, he began instituting a number of changes in established policies. The red-and-white tile exteriors were replaced by dull-brown brick, more plate glass windows, and a shingled roof. The garish neon Golden Arches gave way to a more sedate logo. The interiors were modified so that people could more comfortably eat on the premises, and the hamburger stands were now called restaurants. Certain outlets were permitted more flexible decor, such as a nautical theme in Boston and a campus theme at UCLA.

As McDonald's gained financial strength, efforts were made to increase the number of company-owned units. An aggressive buy-back policy encouraged old franchise-holders to sell out to McDonald's. Company stores proved to be more desirable because of their higher profitability and more centralized control. In 1968, McDonald's owned only 15 percent of the outlets, but by 1974 40 percent were company owned.

As choice highway locations became scarce, McDonald's moved into downtown locations and shopping malls, zoos, office buildings, hospitals, and even a high school. Central city locations involved some adjustments. Salaries and occupancy costs were higher, and selling hours shorter with little business on weekends. But much higher volume—averaging twice the volume of the suburban stores—offset these drawbacks. Along with the central city expansion came the overseas market. By 1980, 1050 stores were located abroad, of which 250 were in Japan and 50 in England; 19 percent of total company sales volume came from this international operation.

McDonald's continued with its traditional Saturday morning television ads promoting Ronald. According to a McDonald's official, "It takes only one child to influence a meal out."[10] McDonald's also developed ads aimed at specific segments of the public, such as blue-collar workers, a group that had been hard for McDonald's to draw. Special promotions and giveaways aimed at children also influenced sales—for example, Kid's Day, featuring free sundaes, premiums in "play value" packages, and even a "Fun Bus" that takes schoolchildren on field trips with, of course, a stop at a McDonald's restaurant for lunch.

The traditional product offering of McDonald's is simplicity itself. In the early days, the product line was only hamburgers, french fries, milkshakes, and soft drinks. The first successful menu expansion came with the Filet-o-Fish in 1962, invented by an operator in Cincinnati, Ohio, located in a large Catholic neighborhood and faced with weak Friday sales. Before introducing the sandwich chainwide (not until 1965), McDonald's developed standards on how long to cook it, what type of breading to use, how thick to make it, and the kind of tartar sauce to use. It was then test-marketed, being offered on Fridays in a limited number of outlets. Similarly, chicken was intensively tested, beginning in 1971, and not made generally available until 1981. Even the Big Mac was tested for several years before being made widely available.

The most notable success with product expansion was the breakfast menu. The Egg McMuffin was first tested in 1972, with other breakfast items added shortly after. Initially, breakfast menus were tested in Chicago, Pittsburgh, and Washington, D.C. They proved so successful there that the breakfast menu became available nationwide in 1976 and by 1977 accounted for 10 percent of the company's sales. A major advantage of these breakfast sales is that they bring additional business during a time when these outlets would otherwise be idle. In addition, the breakfast menu lured older customers not previously attracted to the restaurant. In

---

[10]Christy Marshall, "McDonald's '79' Plan: Beat Back the Competition," *Advertising Age*, February 2, 1979, p. 88.

1971, only one year after introduction of the breakfast menu, patronage from customers over 35 years of age jumped from 18 percent to 22.5 percent. Thoroughly testing a few selected menu additions has been a hallmark of the product strategy. The company uses its company-owned stores to test-market new-product candidates before making them more widely available.

Keys to Success

Many franchise firms faded in the late 1960s and 1970s because of oversaturation. Competitors established more outlets than the market could support, and marginal operations faltered. Some franchisors failed because of difficulty in obtaining qualified franchisees or licensees. McDonald's believed that a key factor for success was for a licensee initially to work full time in the business. The unsuccessful franchisors failed to attract or insist on licensees who met prescribed qualifications. They tended to be interested primarily in getting the initial franchise fee. Business was viewed as a quick-buck scheme, to be milked dry with the franchisor then exiting.

Poor site selection plagued some operations. Too fast an expansion led to indiscriminate site selection, sometimes influenced by opportunistic realtors. Another factor leading to poor locations was lack of capital to purchase the more desirable sites.

When business and the economy are going well, ineffective management controls are not always readily apparent. However, when the economy experiences a downturn and competition intensifies, lack of effective controls can be fatal.

In order to gain quick public attention and recognition, many fast-food franchisors used the name of either an entertainer or a professional sports figure to lure potential licensees: Minnie Pearl's Chicken, Here's Johnny Restaurant (Johnny Carson), Al Hirt Sandwich Saloon, Broadway Joe's (Joe Namath), Jerry Lucas Beef'n Shake, and Mickey Mantle's Country Cookin' Restaurant. Although the public would pay to see the entertainer or sports figure perform, they do not necessarily frequent a fast-food outlet simply because of the famous name—unless the food and service warrant their patronage.

The ingredients of success for McDonald's were simple, but few competitors were able to emulate them:

- A brief menu of consistent quality with hundreds and thousands of outlets.
- Strictly enforced and rigorous operational standards for service, cleanliness, and all aspects of the operation.
- Friendly employees, despite a high turnover of personnel because of the monotony of automated food handling.
- Heavy mass-media advertising, directed mostly to families and children.
- Identifying a fertile target market—the family—and directing the market-

ing strategy to satisfying it: product, price, promotional efforts, and site locations.

MCDONALD'S AND BURGER CHEF: WHAT CAN BE LEARNED?

In most areas of operation, Burger Chef compared poorly with McDonald's. It lacked image, consistency in its product, and a diversified product line. Its promotional expenditures—$2.5 million annually during the growth years versus $50 million for McDonald's—were insufficient to bring it recognition. It had neither a well-planned and organized selection procedure for franchisees nor a training program to assure efficient operational procedures. Its controls and auditing compared in no way with the thoroughness and strictness practiced by McDonald's.

There is nothing exotic about success. It consists simply of doing customer-pleasing things better and more consistently than the competition. A unique product is not an essential ingredient for success, although it can certainly help. But a hamburger is a hamburger is a hamburger.

Franchising is significantly different from other types of business operations, and the differences present powerful opportunities as well as lurking dangers. Rapid growth is possible through franchising—far more rapid than a firm can achieve on its own, even with substantial resources. Because somebody else is putting up most or all of the capital for an outlet, the major requirements for expansion are finding and wooing sufficient investor-licensees and locating attractive sites for additional units. Both requirements can be met *carelessly* in the quest for wild expansion or *carefully* for controlled expansion.

In franchising, a few poor operations hurt the other outlets since all operate under the same format and logo. This is similar to the situation of any chain operation (a few bad stores can hurt the image of the rest of the chain), but a franchise system is composed of independent entrepreneurs who tend to be less controlled than the hired managers of a chain operation.

Learning Insight. The benefits of rapid growth may be illusory.

The rapid growth made possible through a franchise system can be its downfall. Because growth in the number of units can occur easily and quickly, it is tempting to rush headlong into opening more units to meet the demand of prospective licensees. Emphasis on growth often means that existing operations are ignored. As a consequence, they are undercontrolled, and emerging problems do not receive adequate attention. Screening of people and locations tends to become superficial. Eventually the bubble bursts, and the firm is forced to recognize that many outlets are marginal and must be drastically pruned. Growth must be prudent and controlled in order to achieve adequate assimilation.

Learning Insight. Controlled growth requires tight controls.

All firms need to maintain tight controls over far-flung outlets in order to be sufficiently informed about emerging problems and opportunities, to optimize their use of resources, and to maintain a desired image and standard of performance. In a franchise operation, tight controls are all the more essential since franchisees often are independent entrepreneurs rather than hired managers.

The establishment of a control process requires three basic steps:

1. Standards of performance must be set and communicated to those persons involved.
2. Performance should be checked against these standards.
3. Corrective action should be taken when needed.

Burger Chef's performance would have been greatly improved had it set up standards for the quality and preparation of food, cleanliness and service, menus, general operations, and personnel. Also helpful would have been accounting standards for budgeting cost or expenses, size of servings, number of employees, payrolls, and the like. Better-run franchised operations have extensive standards and specifications for all aspects of their operations in minute detail—remember the 350-page operating manual of McDonald's?

When standards are specifically designated and communicated to those responsible for adhering to them, the next step of the control process can be imposed—measuring performance against the standards. Performance is best measured by outside auditors, inspectors, or district and home-office executives visiting the premises unannounced, perhaps with a checklist in hand, and grading actual against expected performance. All aspects of the operation should be checked—from the grease content of the french fries to the soap supply in the restrooms.

After deviations from the standards are identified and their importance assessed, measures should be taken to correct the situation, perhaps through better training, more motivation, or even threat of dismissal or demotion. Although franchise operations involve independent owners of outlets, the franchisor still has authority to impose sanctions on deviant behavior. Such sanctions typically consist of warnings, placing on probation, and finally, if performance still does not meet standards, removing the franchise.

Learning Insight. All firms need to develop a distinctive image, and they must guard against a negative one.

A unique and distinctive image is highly important in a competitive environment. Distinction is not always easy to achieve, especially where many competitors have already adopted the more obvious possibilities. Burger Chef was unable to achieve any distinction. Distinction can come from a design or logo, a roof, or a building style; it can come from a menu, services, or the promotional approach; it can even be achieved by appealing to a different segment of the market.

The hardest task in achieving a distinctive image is with a commodity-type product, such as grain, beef, or chicken. Since such products can hardly be differentiated from competing brands, it is difficult to advertise a particular brand effectively. But it is possible. Consider the case of Perdue Chickens.

Frank Perdue produced and marketed chickens. He differentiated his product in two ways:

1. He fed his chickens special feed. Along with high-nutritional ingredients, he added some marigold flowers, giving the broiler a golden-yellow appearance instead of the usual pale flesh color.
2. He sold fresh rather than frozen birds. Consumers considered his chickens to be more flavorful and desirable than competitors' frozen birds. Eventually more than 600 vehicles left Perdue facilities each day to ensure fresh produce in all the markets served.

By 1980 Frank Perdue was spending $5,000,000 a year on advertising and appearing in his own commercials. Perdue chickens dominated the New York City market area, and, indeed, the Northeastern United States, accounting for 20 percent of total retail sales of almost $2 billion.

Worse, of course, than an unexciting image is a negative image, such as the one Nestle developed and which we examined in the first case in this book.

Learning Insight. Imitation should not be disdained.

A willingness to imitate may appear inconsistent with the need to develop a distinctive image, but it need not be so. McDonald's management and operational procedures were not unknown; indeed, they were highly publicized. It required no genius to recognize the merits of McDonald's operational procedures or to put these procedures into effect. But most of the other fast-food operations—such as Burger Chef, and even Burger King in its early years—either failed to imitate the successful strategy or did so only belatedly.

When a firm has developed a proven and successful format, why not imitate it? Creativity can be reserved for other aspects of the operation. A firm can still maintain its own distinctive image while basing its operations on successful management and control practices.

Learning Insights. In diversifying, a firm should seek a strategic fit.

Strategic fit refers to the mutually reinforcing effects that different business activities can have on the organization's overall effectiveness. Sometimes this idea is graphically referred to as "2 + 2 = 5"; that is, the sum of the benefits of the combined operations is more than if they had remained separate.

Several forms of fit can be recognized. *Product-market fit* is obtained when the different products can use the same distribution channels, sales promotion techniques, and can be sold to the same customers with the same sales force. *Operating fit* results from economies of purchasing, warehousing, overlapping of technology and engineering, production compatibility, and the like. *Management fit* occurs when existing management know-how and experience can be effectively transferred to the newly acquired activities. The common thread of strategic fit can provide a unifying focus and the company can build on joint managerial, financial, and technological strengths.

The popularity of conglomerate mergers, in the late 1960s, the early 1970s, and later in the 1980s, involving little or no fit or similarity, cast doubt on the necessity for fit. Some of these conglomerates have been successful: for example, International Telephone and Telegraph (ITT) products and subsidiary companies range from Sheraton Hotels, Wonder Bread, and Avis Rent-a-Car to finance companies, chemicals, lawn care, and even business schools.

But other conglomerates found that trying to manage many unrelated product markets and technologies brought severe problems, as with the General Foods and the Burger Chef operation. In some cases, such acquisitions resulted in "2 + 2 = 3" [for example, Mobil Oil and its Marcor (Montgomery Ward) acquisition]. Many conglomerates, after the initial acquisition spree, have been forced to sell off some of their subsidiaries in order to get on the profit track again.

With the benefit of hindsight we can question the judgment of General Foods' decision to diversify into a fast-food franchised restaurant operation. While fast-food marketing at first appeared within General Foods' experience in food marketing, in retrospect it proved dissimilar and difficult for General Foods' executives to manage effectively.

We conclude that, although a common thread or strategic fit is not absolutely essential for all of a firm's business activities, it increases the probability of successful assimilation and synergy.

For Thought and Discussion

1. Playing the devil's advocate (one who takes the opposing viewpoint for argument's sake), criticize the acquisition of Burger Chef by General Foods as thoroughly as you can.
2. Would you advocate changing the name of Burger Chef? Why or why not?
3. How do you account for the reluctance of competitors to imitate successful examples of other firms in their industry?
4. To date, McDonald's has shunned diversification into other related and unrelated food retailing operations. Discuss the desirability of such diversification efforts.

Invitation to Role Play

1. Assume the role of the General Foods' executive responsible for Burger Chef after the acquisition. Be as specific as you can in formulating a marketing strategy for the growth of this venture.
2. As a McDonald's executive, you are strongly in favor of significantly expanding the menu offerings. In particular, you have been very critical of the slow (four to five years) testing of the breakfast menu before its widespread adoption. Array as many arguments as you can for expanding the menu in specific ways. Be prepared to defend your position against other skeptical executives.

10

THE CREST RIDERS OF THE RUNNING BOOM

Adidas had been the innovator in its industry, running shoes, and later, in ancillary apparel and athletic equipment. It had set the standards that subsequently were followed by almost all its competitors.

Somehow, the innovator and standard-bearer allowed itself to be overtaken and passed by upstart foreign firms—this time, U.S. firms, of whom the most notable was Nike—in its biggest and most rapidly growing market. And the wonder is that these interlopers did nothing distinctive or innovative. They simply followed the tried and tested strategy of the old master.

How could this be?

ADIDAS: OPENING THE DOOR FOR COMPETITORS

In the early 1970s, Adidas dominated the running-shoe industry. It had done so for decades. Now it stood on the threshold of one of the biggest surges of popularity ever known in any recreational pursuit. Tens of millions of people were to take up running or jogging in the next few years; other millions of nonrunners would be buying running shoes because they were comfortable and conveyed an aura of fitness and youth.

Did Adidas cash in on the recreational boom of the century? Unfortunately for Adidas, the answer is *no*. In a classic error of miscalculation and conservative planning, it underestimated the U.S. market. Even worse, it underestimated the aggressiveness of U.S. competitors, most of whom had not even been around at the beginning of the decade. A few years later Adidas was pushed aside by one of the fastest-growing firms outside the computer industry: Nike.

Historical Background

Rudolf and Adolf Dassler began making shoes in Herzogenaurach, West Germany, shortly after World War I. Adolf, known as Adi to his family, was the innovator, and Rudolf was the seller of his brother's creations. The brothers achieved only moderate success at first, but in 1936 made a big breakthrough. Jesse Owens agreed to wear their shoes in the Olympics and won his medals in front of Hitler, the German nation, and the world. The lucrative association of shoes with a famous athlete triggered a marketing strategy that Adidas—and other athletic shoe manufacturers—practiced from that point on.

In 1949 the brothers quarreled, never to speak to each other again outside of court. Rudolf took half the equipment and left his brother to go to the other side of town and set up the Puma Company. Adolf established the Adidas Company from the existing firm ("Adidas" was derived from his nickname and the first three letters of his surname). Rudolf and his Puma never quite caught up with Adolf's Adidas, but they did become number 2 in the world.

Adolf constantly experimented with new materials and techniques to develop stronger, yet lighter shoes. He tested thorny sharkskin in attempts to develop abrasive leather for indoor flats. He tried kangaroo leather to toughen the sides of shoes. The first samples of Adidas footwear were shown at the Helsinki Olympic Games of 1952. In 1954 the German soccer team, equipped with Adidas footwear, won the World Cup over Hungary. The shoes were definitely a factor in the win, as Dassler had developed a special stud to screw into the shoes that allowed good footing on the muddy playing field that day; Hungary's shoes did not give the same traction.

Dassler's many innovations in the running-shoe industry included four-spiked running shoes, track shoes with a nylon sole, and injected spikes. He developed a shoe that allowed an athlete to choose from 30 different variations of interchangeable spike elements that could be adapted to an indoor or outdoor track as well as to natural or artificial surfaces.

With its great variety of superior products, Adidas wearers dominated the widely publicized international showcase events. For example, at the Montreal games, Adidas-equipped athletes accounted for 82.8 percent of all individual medal winners.[1] Amid the tremendous publicity for the company, sales rose to $1 billion worldwide.

But competitors were emerging. Prior to 1972, Adidas and Puma practically constituted the entire athletic shoe market. Adidas seemingly had built up an insurmountable lead, providing footwear for virtually every type of sporting activity as

---

[1]Norris Willett, "How Adidas Ran Faster," *Management Today*, December 1979, p. 58.

well as diversifying into other sports-related product lines: shorts, jerseys, leisure suits, and track suits; tennis and swimwear; balls for every kind of sport; tennis racquets and cross-country skis; and the popular sports bag that carried the Adidas name as a prominently displayed status symbol.

Strategic Planning

The strategic planning originated by the Dassler brothers became the guiding influence for the entire industry. The Dasslers had long used international athletic competition as a testing ground for their products. Feedback from the athletes led to continual design changes and improvements. Agreements were entered into with professional athletes to use their products. However, Adidas' strength was in international and Olympic events in which the participants were amateurs, and such endorsement contracts were more often made with national sports associations rather than the individuals.

Following the lead of Adidas and Puma, endorsement contracts with athletes have become commonplace. For example, every player in the National Basketball Association is under contract to at least one manufacturer. The going rate for an endorsement contract today ranges from $500 to $150,000. The athlete must wear a certain brand and appear in various promotional activities. It has become an industry practice to spend about 80 percent of the advertising budget for endorsements and 20 percent for media advertising. The distinctive logos that all manufacturers have developed is the key to the effectiveness of these endorsement contracts. Such logos permit immediate identification of the product; fans and potential customers can see the product actually being used by the famous athlete. These logos also permit effective product diversification into apparel, bags, and so on.

To increase volume quickly, production facilities were sought in areas such as Yugoslavia and the Far East, where shoes could be made cheaply and in great quantities. Medium-sized firms in such countries were signed up as licensees, and goods were produced to specifications. Great outlays for plants and equipment were avoided and costs kept low.

Adidas led the running-shoe industry in offering a wide variety of shoe styles—shoes to fit all kinds of running activities, from various kinds of races to training shoes. Shoes were also offered for every type of runner and running style. The great variety of offerings, more than a hundred different styles and models for Adidas, was to be exceeded only by Nike as it charged to capture the U.S. market.

The 1970s Running Market

During the late 1960s and early 1970s the environment affecting the running-shoe industry changed dramatically and positively. Americans increasingly were concerned with physical fitness. Previously unathletic people were searching for ways to exercise. The spark that ignited the booming interest may have been the 1972 Munich Olympics. Millions of television viewers watched Dave Wottle defeat Russian Evgeni Arzanov in the 800-meter run and Frank Shorter win the prestigious marathon. But the groundwork for the running boom was laid before. The idea of fitness perhaps first came to the attention of the general public in a trailblazing book by Dr. Kenneth Cooper, *Aerobics*, which sold millions of copies and gave scientific evidence of the physical benefits of a running (or jogging) regimen. A little less than 10 years later, another book with monumental impact, *The Complete Book of Running* by James Fixx, also sold millions of copies and was on the best-seller list for months.

Through the decade of the 1970s the number of joggers increased. Estimates by the end of the decade indicated that 25 to 30 million Americans were joggers, while another 10 million wore running shoes around home and town. The number of shoe manufacturers also increased. The original three—Adidas, Puma, and Tiger— were joined by new U.S. brands: Nike, Brooks, New Balance, Etonic, and even J.C. Penney, Sears, and Converse. To sell and distribute these new shoes, specialty shoe stores such as Athlete's Foot, Athletic Attic, and Kinney's Foot Lockers sprouted up nationwide. New magazines catering to this market were starting up and showing big increases in circulation: *Runner's World, The Runner*, and *Running Times*. These provided the advertising media to reach runners with no wasted coverage.

Relinquishing Market Dominance

The decline of Adidas during the upsurge in running popularity is best depicted by the phenomenal growth of Nike. Figure 10.1 shows that Nike's sales rose from $14 million in 1976 to $694 million six years later. Figure 10.2 shows the United States'

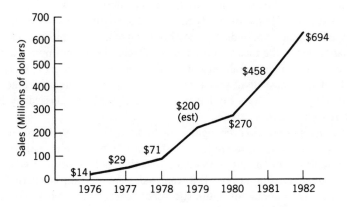

Figure 10.1. Nike sales growth, 1976–1981. (Source: Company annual reports.)

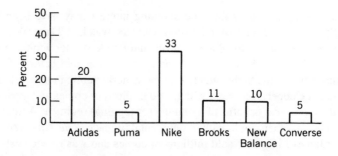

Figure 10.2. Domestic running-shoe market shares, 1978. (Source: Compiled from "The Jogging-Shoe Race Heats Up," *Business Week*, April 9, 1979, p. 125, by special permission, ©1979, McGraw–Hill, Inc.)

competitive positions as of 1979. By then Nike was the leader with 33 percent of the market; within two years it accounted for 50 percent. As Adidas' share continued to fall, well below that of Nike, it had U.S. firms such as Brooks and New Balance also to worry about.

Adidas' Mistakes—What Went Wrong?

Adolf Dassler died in 1978. Perhaps this was a factor in Adidas' waning aggressiveness, although the management transition after his death appeared to go smoothly. Actually, Nike had made its big inroads by this time. No, we must seek further to find a suitable explanation for a front-runner's stumbling to give the lead to someone coming from far back in the pack.

Undoubtedly Adidas underestimated the growth of the market for running shoes. The firm had four decades of experience in the business, and had always seen slow, stable growth. Skepticism about the extent and the duration of the "boom" undoubtedly appeared reasonable. Adidas was not alone in misjudging the potential and the opportunity. Some of the U.S. firms that traditionally were strong in the lower-priced athletic shoe industry, notably Converse and Uniroyal's Keds, were caught flat-footed in the race to bring new and technologically improved models to the market. These major producers of tennis shoes and sneakers (Converse made two-thirds of U.S. basketball shoes) also vastly underestimated the potential, and did not direct strong efforts until they were completely outclassed by Nike and several other U.S. manufacturers.

In gearing an operation for rapid growth, sales forecasting becomes vital. All aspects of a firm's operation are necessarily based on the sales estimates for the coming period(s): for example, production planning and facilities, inventories, and sales staff and advertising efforts. But when sales are reaching uncharted territory, the firm faces the dilemma of optimistic versus conservative sales projections, as discussed in the boxed information.

Adidas not only underestimated the market, it also underestimated the aggressiveness of Nike and other U.S. manufacturers. Perhaps this was a natural consequence of being the market leader with a seemingly unassailable position. After all, foreign brands in many product lines commanded a mystique and attraction unmatched by domestic brands. How could small U.S. manufacturers, starting practically from scratch, pose any serious threat to the more than three decades of seasoned experience of Adidas?

But the U.S. manufacturers were not weak opportunists striving for a stray bone. Nike among others saw an opportunity, seized it. and charged. Perhaps Nike's success is less a reflection of Adidas' deficiencies than a credit to Nike. But should not Adidas have been more alert in such an easy-to-enter industry? Neither technology nor plant investment requirements were such as to preclude other firms from entering the arena. Should not the front-runner have recognized the ease of competitive entry and acted aggressively to discourage it—especially where demand was increasing geometrically? Strong promotional efforts, new product introductions, a step-up in research and development, sharper pricing practices, expansion of the dealer network—these actions might not have prevented competition, but, given the resources of the market leader, they could have lessened the inroads.

OPTIMISTIC VERSUS CONSERVATIVE SALES PLANNING:

CONSEQUENCES OF INACCURATE SALES FORECASTS

The sales forecast—the estimate of sales for the period(s) ahead—serves a crucial role since it is the starting point for all planning and budgeting. When the market is volatile and growing rapidly, forecasting poses some high-risk alternatives: should we be optimistic or conservative?

If the planning is conservative, the danger to the firm is that, when the market begins to boom, it cannot keep up with demand and cannot expand its resources sufficiently to handle the potential. It does not have the manufacturing capability and sales staff. The result invariably is to abdicate a good share of the growing business to competitors who are willing and able to match their capability and strategic planning efforts to the demands of the market.

On the other hand, a firm facing burgeoning demand must decide if the increase in demand is a short-term fad or a long-term trend. A firm can easily permit itself to become overextended in the buoyancy of booming business, only to see the collapse of such business actually jeopardizing its viability.

When a firm is operating under extreme conditions of uncertainty, forecasted and actual results should be carefully monitored and the forecast adjusted upward or downward as indicated by sales data.

NIKE: BEARDING FOREIGN COMPETITION

The success of Nike propelled its founder, Phil Knight, into the ranks of the Four Hundred Richest Americans, as identified by *Forbes* magazine. There he joined another young man, to be discussed in the next section, Steven Jobs, the founder of Apple Computer.

Phil Knight and the Beginning of Nike

Phil Knight was a miler of modest accomplishments. His best time was 4:13, but he had trained under the renowned coach, Bill Bowerman, at the University of Oregon in the late 1950s. Bowerman had put Eugene, Oregon, on the map in the 1950s, when year after year he turned out world-record-setting long-distance runners. He was constantly experimenting with shoes, because of his theory that an ounce off a running shoe might make enough difference to win a race.

In the process of completing his MBA at Stanford University, Phil wrote a research paper based on the theory that the Japanese could do for athletic shoes what they were doing for cameras. After receiving his degree in 1960, Knight went to Japan to seek an American distributorship from the Onitsuka Company for Tiger shoes. Returning home, he took samples of the shoes to Bowerman.

In 1964 Knight and Bowerman went into business. They each put up $500, formed the Blue Ribbon Sports Company, sole distributor in the United States for Tiger running shoes. They put the inventory in Knight's father-in-law's basement; they sold $8000 worth of these imported shoes the first year. Knight worked by day as a Cooper & Lybrand accountant; nights and weekends he peddled shoes to high school athletic teams.

Knight and Bowerman finally developed their own shoe, and in 1971 decided to manufacture it themselves. They contracted the work out to Asian factories where labor was cheap. They named the shoe Nike (rhymes with psyche), after the Greek goddess of victory. They also developed the highly distinctive "Swoosh" logo which was placed on every Nike product. The Nike shoes' first appearance in competition came during the 1972 Olympic trials in Eugene, Oregon. Marathon runners persuaded to wear the new shoes placed fourth through seventh, whereas Adidas wearers finished first, second, and third in these trials.

Nike faced severe competition in the athletic-shoes industry. Knight and Bowerman realized that they had no hope for capturing a large share of the market unless they could develop a product better than what was currently available. And up to then American-made running shoes just did not match most foreign shoes, particularly Adidas.

On a Sunday morning in 1975, Bowerman, tinkering with a waffle iron and some urethane rubber fashioned a new type of sole—a "Waffle" sole whose tiny rubber studs made it springier than those of other shoes currently on the market. This product improvement gave Knight and Bowerman an initial impetus. The marketing strategy they used to propel Nike to the top of the U.S. market was more imitative than innovative. It was patterned after that of the very successful Adidas, but the result was that the imitator outdid the originator.

Nike's Charge

The new Waffle sole developed by Bowerman proved popular with runners. This popularity along with the favorable and rapidly expanding market brought 1976 sales to $14 million, up from $8.3 million the year before and $2 million in 1972.

Nike stayed in the forefront of the industry with its careful research and development of new models. By the end of the decade Nike employed almost 100 people in research and development. Over 140 different models were offered in the product line, some of these the most innovative and technologically advanced on the market. The diversity came from models designed for different foot types, body weights, running speeds, training schedules, sexes, and different levels of skills.

Some 85 percent of Nike's shoes eventually were manufactured in 20 different overseas locations, while factories in New Hampshire and Maine made 15 percent of Nike's shoes. By the late 1970s and early 1980s, the demand for Nikes was so great that 60 percent of its 8000 department store, sporting goods, and shoe store dealers gave advanced orders, often waiting six months for delivery. This gave Nike a big advantage in production scheduling and inventory costs.

Figure 10.1 in the preceding section shows the phenomenal growth of Nike, with sales rising from $14 million in 1976 to $694 million six years later. Figure 10.2 shows the market shares in the U.S. market for the beginning of 1979. By then Nike was the leader with 33 percent of the market; within two more years it commanded 50 percent of the market. In 1981 *Forbes* asked 150 junior high students in a middle-class Dallas neighborhood what their favorite athletic shoe was. All 150 listed Nike first, often citing its status as an expensive "designer" shoe.[2]

Nike remained in the forefront of technological development. In early 1979 it introduced the revolutionary "Tailwind." Called the "next generation in footwear," and advertised as "air travel," the Tailwind was developed by a former aerospace engineer from Rockwell International and used a sole cushioned with polyurethane-encapsulated air chambers. The three-year R&D effort involved exhaustive testing by everyone from "policemen to podiatrists." At $50, it carried the highest price tag in the industry, but demand was so great that Nike was forced to allocate it to dealers.

In 1980 Nike went public, and Knight became an instant multimillionaire with a net worth estimated at just under $300 million. Bowerman, age 70, had sold most

---

[2]"Nike's Fast Track," *Forbes*, November 23, 1981, pp. 59–62.

of his stock earlier, and owned only 2 percent of the company, worth a mere $9.5 million.

As the running boom matured and no longer offered the growth of a few years earlier, Nike began moving into children's shoes and apparel and athletic bags. Nonshoe products especially appeared to offer considerable potential, as Adidas derived an estimated 40 percent of its sales from such products as apparel and athletic bags, which had been of minuscule value for Nike up to 1980. Nike also diversified into other kinds of shoes. By the end of 1980, basketball shoes accounted for 24 percent of Nike's sales, with tennis and other racquet-sport shoes adding another 18 percent. (See Table 10.1 for the approximate breakdown of U.S. sales by major product types for the three years 1978 through 1980.) Plans were readied to expand into hiking and deck shoes and to invade the overseas markets, especially Western Europe, long the domain of Adidas.

In the January 4, 1982, edition of *Forbes,* in the "Annual Report on American Industry," Nike was rated number 1 in profitability over the previous five years, ahead of all other firms in all other industries.[3]

Ingredients of Success

Unquestionably Nike faced an extraordinarily favorable primary demand during the 1970s. Jogging and keeping fit were sweeping the nation as few sports or activities ever had. Nike was positioned to take advantage of this trend, and indeed most of the running-shoe manufacturers had impressive gains during these years. But Nike's success went far beyond simply coasting with a favorable primary demand. Nike outstripped all its competitors, including the dominant Adidas.

Nike, as it began to reach its potential, offered a broader product line than even Adidas. A broad product line can have its problems; it can hurt efficiency and add to costs. Most firms are better advised to prune their weak products so that adequate attention and resources can be directed to the winners. But in its disavowal of such a policy, Nike achieved one of the great successes of the decade in choosing an incredibly wide product mix.

By offering a great variety of styles, prices, and uses, Nike appealed to all kinds of runners and conveyed the image of the most complete running-shoe manufacturer of all. This image was very attractive in a rapidly evolving industry that was attracting millions of runners of all kinds and abilities. Nike provided shoes to fit every runner's needs, running styles, and special problems. And no other shoe manufacturer, not even Adidas, offered as much. In a rapidly expanding market, Nike found that it could tap the widest possible distribution with its breadth of product line. It sold its shoes to conventional retailers, such as department stores and shoe stores, and it sold its shoes to specialized running-shoe stores. There were

---

[3]"Annual Report on American Industry," *Forbes,* January 4, 1982, p. 246.

Table 10.1 Nike's Dollar and Percentage Sales by Product Categories, 1978–1980

	Year Ended May 31					
	1978		1979		1980	
	Dollars (in Thousands)	Percentage	Dollars (in Thousands)	Percentage	Dollars (in Thousands)	Percentage
Running	39,000	55	80,500	55	107,600	43
Basketball	14,300	20	27,800	19	61,800	24
Tennis and other racquet	12,200	17	25,500	17	46,700	18
Children's	1,600	2	5,500	4	21,400	8
Apparel	1,300	2	2,200	2	8,100	3
Field sports	900	1	1,900	1	4,300	2
Leisure	1,000	2	1,200	1	1,600	1
Other	300	1	1,000	1	1,700	1
Total	70,600	100	145,600	100	253,200	100

Source: Company prospectus.

183

enough styles and models to go around—different models for different types of retail outlets.

Short production runs and many styles generally add to production costs, but apparently not in Nike's case. Most shoe production was contracted out, 85 percent to foreign, mostly Far Eastern, factories. Short production runs were less of an economic deterrent where many foreign plants were contracting for part of the production.

Nike emphasized research and technological improvement. It sought more flexible and lighter-weight running shoes that would be protective and give the athlete—whether world-class or slowest amateur—the utmost advantage that running-shoe technology could provide. Nike's commitment to research and development is tangibly evident in its 100 research and development employees, many holding degrees in biomechanics, exercise physiology, engineering, industrial design, chemistry, and other related fields. The firm also engaged research committees and advisory boards, including coaches, athletes, athletic trainers and equipment managers, podiatrists, and orthopedists, who met periodically with the firm to review designs, materials, and concepts for improved athletic shoes. Activities included high-speed photographic analyses of the human body in motion, the use of athletes on force plates and treadmills, wear-testing using over 300 athletes in an organized program, and continual testing and study of new and modified shoes and materials. Some $2.5 million was spent in 1980 on product research, development, and evaluation, and the 1981 budget was approximately $4 million.

As a final point-of-sale testing, Nike maintained seven retail outlets, called "The Athletic Department." The outlets were established to bring product information to the consumer as well as provide feedback to Nike's research and development teams. The outlets served as sensors and helped Nike monitor the market and provided an additional distribution channel.

Nike made good use of the industry-wide strategy of persuading athletes to promote its brand. Knight made a rather well-publicized statement that one can pay $50,000 for a full-age advertisement in *Sports Illustrated,* but it is impossible to buy the front cover. But by getting top athletes who make the cover of *Sports Illustrated* to wear Nike shoes, Knight essentially "makes" the front cover. When such athletes are seen on television, in person, or on the cover of *Sports Illustrated* wearing the familiar Nike logo, the publicity gained for Nike is almost inestimable. Viewers will readily emulate the famous athlete by choosing Nike for their own use. An impressive list of athletes have been under contract to wear Nike products: John McEnroe, Nolan Ryan, Alberto Salazar, Sebastian Coe, Henry Rono, half a dozen Los Angeles Dodgers, and the defensive line of the Dallas Cowboys, among others. In 1979, Coe was the first individual to hold the world records for the 800-meter, 1500-meter, and 10-mile runs. Rono was the first individual to hold world records in the 3000-meter steeple-chase, and the 3000-, 5000-, and 10,000-meter runs.

This use of athletes was certainly followed by all such manufacturers; however, Nike was able to gain the best in many cases, partly through its R&D efforts, which placed it in the forefront of technological improvements, and because of the momentum it had built up as the fastest growing and soon the biggest firm in the industry. "The secret to the business," explained Knight, "is to build the kind of shoes professional athletes will wear, then put them on the pros. The rest of the market will follow."[4]

Some U.S. firms, as well as Adidas, underestimated the strength and longevity of the running boom. And not all U.S. firms had sufficient production savvy to take advantage of the heated market. Brooks, which had attracted initial market success, dissipated its opportunity with poor quality control. Defective shoes and shoe returns destroyed its momentum both with consumers and with dealers.

Finally, Nike made a strong commitment to diversification as the running market began to mature. Children's shoes, apparel, leisure shoes, and field sport shoes expanded the product diversity. Also, Nike began strenuous efforts to expand geographically, to Europe in 1981, and Japan by January 1982.

Nike Postscript—The Pendulum Swings

It is difficult for firms to maintain a pattern of success. A few firms have done so year after year, even decade after decade—McDonald's, K mart, and Honda. More firms have their time of success, find success slipping way, and become ordinary enterprises. Occasionally, as with Korvette, the pattern of success turns into disaster. With Nike, the pendulum began swinging back in 1983, and in 1984 one notable business periodical headlined an article: "Nike Loses Its Footing on the Fast Track: Earnings Are Dismal, Management Is Shuffling, and Many Wonder if Founder Philip Knight Has Run Out of Breath."[5]

The running-shoe industry peaked in 1983, with sales of about 19 million pairs of shoes, a significant jump over the nine million sold in 1977. In 1984, the number of units sold rose only 2 percent, and the next year the bottom fell out. Nike was no longer a successful company.

Nike supposedly had recognized years before that the running boom could not possibly continue forever, and it had diversified into apparel in 1979 and began pushing overseas in 1981. By 1984, apparel accounted for 21 percent of U.S. revenues, up from 3 percent in 1980, while foreign sales were 18 percent of total sales. But profits proved to be disappointing in both these areas of diversification.

In view of the tapering of demand, Nike was surprised and overextended. The

---

[4]"Nike's Fast Track," *Forbes*, November 23, 1981, pp. 59–60.

[5]"Nike Loses Its Footing on the Fast Track: Earnings Are Dismal . . . ," *Fortune*, November 12, 1984, p. 74.

decline in running-shoe demand was not so much a result of fewer people running but was more a consequence of less use of running shoes for casual dress. In addition, the market began to fragment, with shoes for aerobics, basketball, and tennis competing with running shoes for shelf space. As it turned out, Nike made the same mistake as Adidas had a decade earlier: understimating an opportunity. Nike was late into the fast-growing market for shoes worn for the aerobic dancing that was sweeping the country, fueled by best-selling books by Jane Fonda and others.

Eventually, Nike's inventories reached 22 million in mid-1983, forcing heavy price-cutting with many shoes dumped below cost. Earnings plummeted 29 percent to $40.7 million in fiscal 1984, the first drop in a decade. By 1984, Nike's stock was worth less than half its value of the year before, as the investment community quickly lowered its esteem for this former star. The slide worsened in fiscal 1985, with net income falling to a bare $10.3 million.

Nike's management style came under attack. Phil Knight had recruited many athletes for his executive positions, so much so that the company resembled a fraternity according to some critics. In the summer of 1983, Knight turned over the presidency to Robert Woodell, a former long-jump champion. Fifteen months later, Knight took back his job. The loose, paternalistic management structure developed by the company in its early entrepreneurial days appeared inadequate for Nike now that it was almost a billion-dollar firm.

Upon resuming the presidency and direct involvement with day-to-day operations, Knight began tightening the management structure and aggressively cutting costs. About 400 people were laid off, some 10 percent of the work force, and the excessive inventory was pruned. By the fourth quarter of fiscal 1985, profits were increasing, and it appeared the corner had been turned. Nike began trying to change its image from that of a running-shoe company to a total-fitness orientation, while maintaining its 50 percent share of the running-shoe market. The company achieved a major advertising and marketing coup in late 1985. Knight shifted the promotional emphasis from many to only a few well-known athletes. He signed Chicago Bulls basketball player Michael Jordan for a reputed $2.5 million to promote "Air Jordan" shoes. This shoe, introduced in July 1985, was a runaway success as orders exceeded $90 million during the balance of the year.

ADIDAS AND NIKE: WHAT CAN BE LEARNED?

Usually we attribute the success of a firm to one or more of the following: doing things differently from competitors and in such a way as to meet customers' needs better; recognizing opportunities or market sectors previously unrecognized; or plowing more resources into the effort than hapless competitors are able to muster. The Mustang was a somewhat different car, meeting the needs of a large group of consumers better than anything had previously; Honda recognized opportunities for an expanded motorcycle market that no one else had even dreamed of; and K mart and McDonald's were more aggressive than their competitors in placing resources into their efforts. But the source of Nike's success was different.

Learning Insight. Effective imitation without innovation or greater resources can lead to success.

Of course, imitation must be judicious. A strategy worth imitating should be historically successful. In the case of the running-shoe industry, the successful strategy of Adidas in offering many models, in associating its brand with major athletic events and athletes themselves, in constantly seeking new products, was proven over a long period. All running-shoe manufacturers followed the same strategy, but Nike did it better.

While being imitative, a firm must develop its own identity. Successful imitation is not a slavish effort to be identical. Only the successful policies, standards, and actions are imitated. A tottering Burger Chef could have improved its lot by imitating some of the successful policies of McDonald's, particularly with respect to operational standards; but it would have been a mistake to have copied the golden arches, modifying them to become pink or green. With effective imitation there is still room to develop a distinctive image, trademark, or logo, and to establish an organization and management alert to new opportunities.

Learning Insight. The front-runner is vulnerable, particularly in easy-entry industries with rapidly expanding markets.

We saw earlier that a dominant firm in a supposedly nongrowth industry can still be vulnerable. The ability of Honda to convert motorcycles to a growth industry and outdistance Harley Davidson is a business marvel. The front-runner is much more vulnerable in a rapidly growing industry. If the investment in technological know-how and financial resources to enter the industry are not great, the vulnerability of the front-runner increases. This situation characterized the running-shoe industry in the 1970s.

The industry leader tends toward complacency. Sharply rising demand is reassuring and lulling. Sales will be increasing sharply for the industry leader during such a time, but increasing sales may mask a declining market position in which competitors are gaining at the expense of the dominant firm.

Learning Insight. In an expanding market, beware of judging performance on increases in sales rather than market share.

Market share refers to the percentage of total industry sales accounted for by an individual firm. A market share analysis evaluates company performance by measuring it relative to that of competitors. Changes in market share from preceding periods, especially when these changes show a worsening competitive position, should induce strenuous efforts to ascertain the cause and take corrective action. When a market is expanding, such as the running-shoe market, market share changes need to be carefully monitored to prevent loss of competitive advantage.

The critical lapse of Adidas, faced with the growing strength of Nike and its American contemporaries, and the greatly increasing industry potential, suggests a need for a better monitoring of demand and competitive factors. Alert executives should be able to detect nascent changes by encouraging systematic feedback from those closest to the market—sales representatives, dealers, and suppliers alike—by keeping abreast of latest trade journal statistics and commentaries, and other sources described below. There must also be a willingness to act on significant changes in industry conditions, but such willingness is often difficult for veteran firms since it requires disassociating themselves from perspectives and practices of a different past.

Sources of market share data. Market share analysis requires information on sales of competing brands and firms in the market. Fortunately it is usually not difficult to obtain such information in most industries, although some costs are involved. Trade associations or trade publications provide reasonably accurate sales figures for many industries. While such information may not include brand breakdowns, a firm can determine its share of the total market and define important trends. Government agencies provide data for other industries, such as automotive, liquor, and insurance, from mandatory reports including new car registrations, and excise and other tax data.

There are syndicated services that provide consumer-goods manufacturers various measures of competitive brand position. Two major services are:

1. A. C. Nielsen Company conducts store audits in grocery, drug, and certain other fields, and also buys computer tapes from supermarkets equipped with electronic scanning cash registers.
2. Market Research Corporation of America (MRCA) gathers information on expenditures through a panel of consumers who maintain a record of their purchases in diaries.

Cautions in the use of market share data. Although market share information is a valuable management tool, it should not be used as the primary or only measure of marketing performance. It ignores profitability, and this is a major flaw. Too much emphasis on increasing market share often leads to rash sales growth at the expense of profits. Executives can be motivated in this direction because their prestige is bound up with company size and growth relative to other firms in the industry.

Heavy advertising, or concentration on short-term sales at the expense of more satisfied customers and dealers, will increase market share, but profitability may be adversely affected.

The great value of market share measurements is that they identify possibly problem areas that need further research and investigation. Perhaps there is a satisfactory explanation for an initial decline in market share. For example, it might be caused by a large sale occurring in an adjacent period, or perhaps be due to a temporary production slowdown for a model change. On the other hand, a declining market share may indicate a serious problem that needs prompt corrective action in order to prevent a loss in competitive position that can never be regained.

> **Learning Insight.** *In coping with product life-cycle uncertainties, be flexible in order not to take unacceptable risks.*

Every firm needs to react with its environment and the subtle and not-so-subtle changes taking place. This is especially important when the product life cycle is uncertain in scope and duration. The boxed information discusses product life-cycle uncertainties.

The uncertainties about the extent and durability of the life cycle led Converse and Keds, the two biggest makers of low-priced athletic shoes, to move far too slowly into the running-shoe market, and they never gained much ground. Had the bubble burst, had the running boom been a short-lived phenomenon, would Nike have been able to maintain its viability in a greatly diminished market? We think so. Several years before the leveling-off and maturing of the market, Nike diversified into related but different products. It had kept production flexible by contracting the greater portion of its manufacturing to foreign factories. Consequently, it did not establish a large infrastructure with high fixed costs and vulnerability to falling demand.

Our conclusion reminds us of the opposite situation with the Edsel. The Edsel planners had lofty expectations for their new car, and they planned accordingly. They introduced a wide product line, they established separate dealerships, and they created so much advertising that everyone was familiar with the new car. But no provision was made for what should have been reasonable uncertainties. When sales did not come close to expectations, the whole operation was doomed. There is no escape from product life-cycle uncertainties with new and untried endeavors, but it is possible to build in flexibilities and realistic break-evens in case the expected does not happen.

> **Learning Insight.** *No one is immune from mistakes; success does not guarantee continued success.*

INFORMATION SIDELIGHT

PRODUCT LIFE-CYCLE UNCERTAINTIES

Just as do people or animals, products have stages of growth and maturity—that is, life cycles. There are four stages in a product's life cycle: introduction, growth, maturity, and decline.

Below are representative life cycles for a typical consumer-goods product and for one that is more of a fashion or fad item. Notice how abruptly sales peak and decline for a fad item in comparison with a more standard item. Once the decline begins for a fad or fashion product, it is usually impossible to reverse or even slow it.

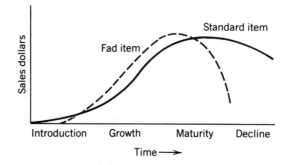

The life cycle for running shoes was influenced by the popularity of running and the transference of running-shoe use from dedicated joggers and runners to others who bought them as a symbol of fitness or because they found them comfortable to wear for casual use.

A major question confronting the industry was whether the purchase of running shoes was a fad or a longer-lasting phenomenon representing a change in the life-style of many Americans. No one could doubt that the growth stage would level out and reach maturity. Less certain, however, was how many millions of runners and others would eventually comprise the market—and how rapid the decline would be. Such uncertainties plagued running-shoe manufacturers. If they geared up for continued growth and a maintenance of high-level demand, the results would be devastating when demand fell drastically. Unless flexibility could be built into the production, and unless alternative markets were identified and targeted, a firm could find itself with so much excess capacity that its viability might be jeopardized. On the other hand, if it did not gear its production to a sufficiently high level, the door was open for competitors to carve out great chunks of market share. The product life cycle, its estimate and realization, was a crucial consideration.

Many executives and administrators fool themselves into thinking success begets continued success. It is not so! No firm, market leader or otherwise, can afford to rest on its laurels, to disregard a changing environment and aggressive but smaller competitors. Adidas had as commanding a lead in this industry as IBM had in computers. But it was overtaken and surpassed by Nike, a rank newcomer, and a domestic firm with few resources in an era when foreign brands (of beer, watches, cars, etc.) had a mystique and attraction for affluent Americans that few domestic brands could achieve. But Adidas let down its guard at a crucial point. In the same way, Nike lagged in its underestimation or unawareness of the marketing opportunity in aerobic dancing.

Would Nike have achieved its success if Adidas had been more aggressive? Was a major part of the Nike success due not to its own efforts but to the deficiencies of Adidas? Perhaps this is a realistic assessment. We would have to answer this hypothetical question by conceding that Nike probably would not have been nearly as successful if Adidas had not dropped its guard. On the other hand, with a rapidly expanding market and easy entry, Nike could have entered successfully and become a viable and profitable operation.

Learning Insight. The reward of entrepreneurship can be great indeed.

The Nike case illustrates the great payoff possible for the entrepreneur of a successful and popularly exciting firm who takes his or her enterprise public and sells shares to public investors. In the next section we will examine another such instance of the fantastic rewards possible in taking a private enterprise public. Entrepreneurship can have the greatest monetary payoff possible of any endeavor in our society.

For Thought and Discussion

1. Do you think Adidas could have successfully blunted the charge of Nike? Why or why not?
2. In what ways does the age and experience of a firm tend to induce myopia and resistance to change?
3. "The success of Nike was strictly fortuitous and had little to do with a powerful marketing strategy." Evaluate this statement.
4. Discuss the pros and cons of optimistic versus conservative sales forecasts for a hot new product.

Invitation to Role Play

1. As an Adidas executive, how would you propose to counter the initial thrusts at your market share by Nike and other U.S. running-shoe manufacturers?

2. As an executive for a medium-sized U.S. running-shoe manufacturer, you recognize that the long-overdue lessening of the popularity of running is beginning to take place. What strategy recommendations would you make now that the primary demand curve is moving down?

11

Wild Success and Plummeting Hopes in the Personal Computer Industry

In this chapter we examine two of the most rapidly growing firms ever seen in the U.S. economy. The sales of one firm rose from $774,000 to $583 million in only six years; the sales of the other rocketed to $100 million in only 18 months. Fantastic success stories. But one firm could not maintain its level of success, and sales plummeted as fast as they had risen. The other firm maintained its growth and market position for almost a decade in an environment of rapid change before encountering problems that it stoutly set out to overcome.

What underlying factors accounted for such contrasts? And what transference do they have to other firms, perhaps in more sedate industries?

OSBORNE COMPUTER: THE ILLUSION OF SUCCESS UNLIMITED

Rarely does a new firm hit the jackpot—A meteoric rise surpassing the most optimistic expectations of founders and investors. In the heady excitement anything seems possible. It appears that the enterprise is invincible. Alas, sometimes such stars come tumbling back to earth, and reality. Perhaps there is no better example in modern business annals than the almost vertical rise and collapse of Osborne Computer Corporation. Founded in 1981, the business was booming at a $100 million clip—in barely 18 months. But on September 14, 1983, the company sought protection from creditors under Chapter 11 of the Bankruptcy Code.

Adam Osborne

Adam Osborne was born in Thailand, the son of a British professor, and spent his earliest years in India. His parents were disciples of a maharishi, although he was educated in Catholic schools. Later he was sent to Britain for schooling, and in 1961 at the age of 22 he moved to the United States. He obtained a Ph.D. in chemical engineering at the University of Delaware and then worked for Shell Development Company in California.

Osborne and Shell soon parted company, the bureaucratic structure frustrating him. He became interested in computers, and in 1970 he set up his own computer consulting company. The market for personal computers began to mushroom in the mid-1970s, and he emerged a guru. He had a computer column, "From the Fountainhead," for *Interface Age,* and he began making speeches and building a reputation. He wrote a book, *Introduction to Microcomputers,* geared to the mass market. When it was turned down by a publisher, Osborne published it himself and sold 300,000 copies. By 1975 his publishing company had put out some 40 books on microcomputers, nearly a dozen of which he had written himself. In 1979 he sold his publishing company to McGraw-Hill, but agreed to stay as a consultant through May 1982.

Osborne was thus in a position to take full advantage of the growth of the microcomputer industry. But he also angered many in the industry by his stinging criticisms and bold assertions. In particular he spoke out sharply against the pricing strategies of the personal computer manufacturers, contending that they were ignoring the mass market by raising prices with every new feature added.

Osborne himself was the subject of some of the most colorful copy of the industry. Tall and energetic, he possessed a strong British accent to go along with his volubility, charm, and supreme confidence. He epitomized the new breed of entrepreneurs drawn to the epicenter of high-tech industry, the Silicon Valley in California.

Early in 1981 Osborne put his criticisms and assertions to the test. To a chorus of skeptics he announced plans to manufacture and market a new personal computer priced well below the competition. His first machines were ready for shipping by that July, and before long the skeptics were running for the hills. Osborne was showing that he was a doer, and not merely a talker.

The Osborne Strategy

Osborne discerned a significant niche in the personal computer market. "I saw a truck-size hole in the industry, and I plugged it," he said.[1] He hired Lee Felsenstein, a former Berkeley radical, to design a powerful unit that weighed 24 pounds,

---

[1]"Osborne: From Brags to Riches," *Business Week,* February 22, 1982, p. 86.

could be placed in a briefcase, and was small enough to fit under an airline seat. It was the first portable *business* computer; the other portable computers were much less sophisticated. Portable computers are a subset of personal computers. As the name implies, they are lightweight and relatively easy to carry. Actually, there are three categories of portable computers recognized by the industry: (1) hand-held computers; (2) portable computers, which have a small screen, limited memory, and weight 10 to 20 pounds; and (3) transportable computers, which have bigger screens and memories, and weigh more than 20 pounds. Osborne Computer was in the third group.

Osborne priced his computer at $1795, hundreds of dollars less than most other business-oriented computers. He was able to sell for this price by running a low-overhead operation. For example, he hired Georgette Psaris, then 25, and made her vice president of sales and marketing, putting her office in a chilly former warehouse. He achieved economies of scale and capitalized on the declining prices of semiconductor parts. Assembled from standard industry components, the display screen was small, only five inches across, and there was no color graphics capability. Osborne himself admitted, "The Osborne had no technology of consequence. We made the purchasing decision convenient by bundling hardware and needed software in one price."[2]

To cut costs on software, Osborne, in a drastic departure from other personal computer makers, relied entirely on independent software companies to provide programs written in the popular programming language. To reduce software costs still further, Osborne gave some software suppliers equity in the company. As a result, Osborne provided almost $1500 worth of software packages as part of the $1795 system price.

Osborne had a flair for showmanship. One of his first triumphs was in the 1981 West Coast Computer Faire in San Francisco. In place of the rather ordinary booths and displays of the other computer makers, he took a substantial part of his venture capital to build a Plexiglass booth that towered toward the ceiling. The Osborne Company logo, the "Flying O," dominated the show.

He believed that mass distribution was a key to success. By 1982 he had signed an agreement with Computerland Corporation, the largest computer retailer. This extended Osborne's distribution by doubling in one swoop the number of retail stores carrying his computer. The Osborne 1 proved to be a hot item, with sales hitting $10 million by the end of 1981, the first year of operation. By the end of 1982, after only 18 months of operation, annual sales soared to $100 million. There were predictions that "most of the Osborne management team would be millionaires by the time they're 40 or even 30."[3] At this point the bare-bones operating style was abandoned.

---

[2]"Osborne Bytes the Distribution Bullet," *Sales & Marketing Management*, July 4, 1983, p. 34.
[3]Steve Fishman, "Facing Up to Failure," *Success*, November 26, 1984, p. 48.

By 1983 some 750 retail outlets stocked the company's portables: the Computerland chain, Xerox's retail stores, Sears' business centers, and various department stores. Early in 1983, the company added 150 office-equipment dealers with experience in selling the most advanced copiers, enabling Osborne to reach small and medium-sized businesses. While Osborne was not the originator of the portable computer, he was the first to sell such computers in mass quantities. He expanded the targeted market greatly, from key people in data processing departments to every office desk.

Marching into 1983

By early 1983 Osborne began to loosen his grip on the company, under pressure from his investors. The investors felt that the growing operation—it already had 800 employees—required professional management instead of Osborne and his early hirees. Osborne was an entrepreneur and not an administrator, and the two abilities are quite different. To protect its front-running position—estimated at an 80–90 percent market share—the company hired Robert Jaunich II, president of Consolidated Foods, to become president and chief executive officer. Adam Osborne moved up to chairman. Jaunich turned down offers at Apple and Atari because he felt these firms would not give him enough control. He also sacrificed a $1 million incentive to remain at Consolidated Foods. Obviously he felt strongly that the opportunities and potential of Osborne far surpassed his other options.

Jaunich moved quickly to decentralize the management structure. Georgette Psaris, vice president of marketing, became vice president of strategic planning. Joseph Roebuck, lured from Apple Computer where he was marketing director, replaced her. Fred Brown, the director of sales for Osborne, became vice president of sales, and David Lorenzen, a consultant for Osborne, became director of marketing services, with responsibility for dealer-support programs.

The distribution strategy, on which Adam Osborne prided himself as being one of the strengths of the venture, was refined. The company continued using computer-store outlets, but added alternative channels as well. A major addition was Harris Corporation's computer systems division to act as a national distributor for major firms. Harris was a $1.7 billion minicomputer firm with 70 salespeople and 1200 support personnel, including systems analysts, in its computer systems division. To protect Osborne's smaller clients, Harris agreed to handle only large orders of 50 units or over.

Other sales targets were United Press International (UPI), the news service, to sell Osborne portables to its 1000 subscriber newspapers as personal workstations. Brown, the vice president of sales, began exploring other distribution possibilities, including independent sales organizations, airlines, and hotel chains.

As competitors started to enter the portable market, offering cheaper and fancier machines than the Osborne 1, the firm readied itself to broaden its product line. It prepared an even cheaper version of the Osborne 1, the Vixen. It unveiled an Executive 1 in the spring of 1983, with an Executive 2 planned for late summer. These models offered more storage capacity and larger screens than Osborne 1. The Executive 1 was able to serve as a terminal to communicate with a mainframe, thereby enabling users to work with larger data bases and handle more complicated jobs. The Executive 1 had a $2495 price tag that included $2000 worth of software, covering word and data processing. The Executive 2, at $3195, was promoted as compatible with IBM's hot-selling personal computer, the IBM PC.

In 1982 Osborne spent $3.5 million on advertising, including $1.5 million in consumer magazines, $500,000 on spot TV, and $1.5 million in business publications. Plans were made to continue heavy advertising in order to reinforce the product differentiation. The sales force was expanded to keep pace with the growing firm. An 8-person sales force was to be supplemented by an additional 30 to 40 people, thereby permitting more specialized selling. Instead of being generalists selling to all types of customers, sales were organized by specialists concentrating either on retail or nonretail accounts. Brown explained this rationale:

> Retailers . . . need help on such things as point-of-sale displays to stimulate the guy who comes in off the street. Dealers call on purchasing and data-processing departments and need advice on direct mail campaigns.[4]

The sky seemed the limit. Osborne predicted revenues of $300 million for 1983. And when he made one of his frequent trips abroad, he was received by ambassadors and prime ministers, most of whom wanted stock in his company. He was the head of one of the fastest-growing companies Silicon Valley had ever seen— growing even faster than Apple.

Premonition

The first premonition of trouble came to Adam Osborne on April 26, 1983. He was giving a seminar in Colorado when he received a call. "Over the weekend considerable losses were discovered," he was told. "That's not possible," he is reported to have said.[5] But in the few days Adam was away from the office, the bad news built.

The news that earlier profit figures were in error came at a particularly bad time. On April 29 a public stock offering, designed to raise about $50 million, was planned that would have made the top executives of Osborne rich. Adam Osborne had to wonder how news of losses instead of profits would affect the stock offering.

In the first two months of the fourth fiscal quarter (the fiscal year ended February 1983), pretax profits were reported that were $300,000 ahead of company

4"Osborne Bytes . . . ," p. 36.
5Fishman, op. cit., p. 51.

projections. In February the company racked up an all-time high in shipments, and with supposed high profit margins. Projections for February profits were in the neighborhood of $750,000, and the future seemed euphoric. But it was all an illusion.

By late March the results for February showed, instead of the projected profit, a loss of more than $600,000, reflecting charges against new facilities and heavy promotional spending. For the entire fiscal year there was a loss of $1.5 million, despite revenues slightly more than $100 million.

The worst was yet to come. On April 21, Jaunich learned that the company would have a $1.5 million loss for the February quarter, and a $4 million loss for the full year, brought about chiefly by excessive inventories of old stock, liabilities in software contracts, and the need for greater bad debt and warranty reserves. Although Jaunich planned to move ahead with the stock offering, the attractiveness of stock in the company was rapidly diminishing. But worse news was to come. On April 24, new projections showed that losses would be $5 million for the quarter and $8 million for the year, thanks to further unrecorded liabilities and more inventory problems.

That same day Jaunich decided to scrap the offering, despite heavy pressure to find another underwriter to bring the stock to market. Every report made the situation appear blacker. The final report for the year showed a loss of more than $12 million. Heavy losses continued over the next months, as further adjustments in inventories and reserves became necessary. Adam Osborne's house of cards was collapsing.

Osborne had had no trouble attracting seed money from venture capitalists before; indeed, venture capital firms were clamoring to participate. But when the company's earnings came to light, the funding dried up. A few investors still had hopes, and Osborne found another $11 million in June. But the firm could not find an additional $20 million which the company considered necessary to speed a needed competitive product from drawing board to market.

Black Friday Osborne resorted to sporadic employee layoffs beginning in the late spring as the company desperately tried to improve its cash flow. But the climax came on Friday, September 16. On the previous Tuesday the company had filed for protection from creditor lawsuits under Chapter 11 of the federal Bankruptcy Code. The company did so after three creditors filed two lawsuits saying Osborne owed them $4.7 million. Osborne's petition stated that it owed secured and unsecured creditors about $45 million whereas its assets were $40 million.

Osborne's employees expected the worst when a meeting was abruptly called in the company cafeteria. They soberly listened as top management announced that more than 300, about 80 percent of the remaining company staff, were to be immediately "furloughed." Final paychecks were issued, and workers were given two hours to empty their desks and vacate the company offices.

News of the company's Chapter 11 filing and near shutdown shocked the industry, although Osborne's recently sagging sales and consequent need for cash were well known. The company made strenuous efforts to raise money, especially after the July shipments turned soft. But venture capitalists fled from the industry shakeout; the market was not able to support 150-plus microcomputer companies.

Postmortem

Internal Factors Adam Osborne was an entrepreneur, not a professional manager. Perhaps this accounted for most of the problems that befell his company. Often, it seems, the entrepeneurial personality is incompatible with the manager-type person who must deal with the nitty-gritty details and day-to-day controls over operations. Osborne had never managed more than 50 people, but the organization had grown to almost 20 times that size. He operated with a "fire-fighting" perspective, with no advance planning. "I had no professional training whatsoever in finance or business management," Osborne admitted.[6]

The board of directors of Osborne and the venture capitalists who contributed to the fledgling enterprise brought about sufficient pressure that Adam Osborne stepped aside and turned over the operating responsibilities to a professional manager, Robert Jaunich, early in 1983. But apparently the switch was too late to rectify the damage already done. Perhaps six months earlier . . . ?

Some of the mistakes can be explained by the heady excitement that accompanied the geometrically rising sales. Other mistakes can be credited to simple miscalculations—of which any firm can be guilty—about the impact of competitors of all kinds, and particularly the rapidity with which the awesome IBM could enter the market and dominate it.

Lack of controls was the most obvious failing of the company. Managers did not know how much inventory they had. They did not know how much they were spending, or needed to spend. Ironically, information management was sorely lacking in a company whose product was primarily geared to aiding information management. Other examples of incompetence were unrecorded liabilities, such as bills never handed over to the accounting department; inadequate reserves established for the shutdown of a New Jersey plant that was producing computers with a 40 percent failure rate; and insufficient funds set aside to pay for a new European headquarters on Lake Geneva in Switzerland.

Lack of controls permitted expenses to run rampant. "Everybody was trying to buy anything they wanted," said one former Osborne employee.[7] When Jaunich

---

[6]Jaye Scholl, *Barron's*, July 26, 1984, p. 26.

[7]"Shaken Osborne Computer Seeking Suitor in the Face of Possible Failure," *Wall Street Journal*, September 12, 1983, p. 35.

finally took over the managerial reins, he clamped down hard on expenses, but it was too late.

By spring of 1983 miscalculations had reduced cash flow to a trickle. Osborne made the mistake of announcing the new computer, the Executive, too soon. Upon learning of the new machine in April, many canceled their orders for the Osborne 1, resulting in heavy inventory write-offs. Compounding the problems, the Executive was delayed and not ready for initial shipments until May. April was a month with practically no sales.

Other companies, notably Kaypro and Compaq, entered the market with low-priced computers and at least as much bundled software. But the biggest impact was from IBM. Its personal computer, introduced in late 1981, quickly became the industry standard against which other competitors were judged. Osborne was slow in reacting and adopting IBM's state of the art technology and equally slow in developing a model compatible with the IBM personal computer at home or in the office. While Osborne waited, scores of other computer companies jumped to produce IBM-compatible computers. Hardly a year after coming to market the formerly popular Osborne computer with its tiny screen was obsolete.

Another new product was obsolete before it was introduced—the Vixen, originally scheduled for introduction in December 1982. It was 10 pounds lighter and cheaper than the Osborne 1. A poorly designed circuit board caused production delays, and the project was finally scrapped as company resources were redirected to an IBM-compatible unit with a larger screen. It was difficult to cope with production delays and the speed with which IBM took over the personal computer market.

External Factors. The environment for personal computer makers was becoming unhealthy by 1983. A major shakeout for the more than 150 small manufacturers in this industry was inevitable. A factor behind the proliferation of firms was a tidal wave of venture capital. Early winners such as Apple Computer dazzled investors and led to the perception of a "can't lose" industry. It was almost too easy to start a new computer company. "As a result, a whole series of 'me too' companies started. They are developing products that do not have a unique feature or competitive advantage. They don't stand a chance," one venture capitalist said.[8]

While demand by businesses and consumers for small computers was increasing, so was cutthroat competition. Price-cutting and shrinking profit margins were inevitable. Dealers' shelves could hardly accommodate more than a few brands.

The first presentiment of worsening problems for the industry came early in 1983 when three big manufacturers of low-priced home computers—Atari, Texas Instruments, and Mattel—reported first-half losses totaling more than half a billion

---

[8]"Trouble in Computer Land," *Newsweek,* September 26, 1983, p. 73.

dollars. Makers of higher-priced computers tried to dissociate themselves from this low-end calamitous environment. But other well-known companies such as Victor Technologies, Fortune Systems, and Vector Graphics all reported shocking losses for the second quarter. Even Apple Computer saw its stock price sink nearly 34 points between June and September 1983.

Texas Instruments' 99/4A home computer, which sold for $525 when introduced in 1981, retailed for $100 by early 1983. Yet, each 99/4A cost about $80 in parts and labor not including TI's overhead expenses, dealer profits, and marketing costs.

Other computer makers were desperately struggling to revamp their production and marketing efforts. For example, Vector Graphic, after losing $1.7 million in the second quarter of 1983, obtained a new $7 million line of credit to help tailor its computers to such specialty markets as agriculture.

Update

Under Chapter 11 of the federal Bankruptcy Act, a company continues to operate, but has court protection against creditors' lawsuits while working out a plan for paying its debts. By the end of 1984 Osborne was emerging from bankruptcy with most of its debts paid and two new machines to sell. Its retail network had shrunk from 800 dealers to about 50. Suppliers now demanded cash on delivery. And the firm was anathema to venture capitalists who lost $31 million when the company collapsed. Gone are the factories, the 1000-worker payroll, and the swank executive offices. But the lean, trimmed-down company had $10 to $30 million worth of tax credits to offset future income taxes. Its name and still-extant dealer network in Europe was a plus. Perhaps the biggest challenge it now faced was redeveloping its retail network. "Competition for shelf space is hot even for companies with no strikes against them. Retailers were left with a bad taste when the company went Chapter 11," noted an executive of a 40-store chain. The new president was Ronald J. Brown, the former vice president of international operations who engineered the company's restructuring.

Adam Osborne left the company to try his entrepreneurial talents in the marketing of software, as well as organizing a defense against investor lawsuits. He wrote a book (publishing it himself) called *Hypergrowth: The Rise and Fall of the Osborne Computer Corporation* (with John Dvorak), soundly criticizing Robert Jaunich. Georgette Psaris, Osborne's former vice president, noted: "I've gone from being a multimillionaire to being in the hole,"[9] but she joined Adam Osborne in his new entrepreneurial endeavor.

[9]Ibid., p. 74.

APPLE COMPUTER: BLENDING TECHNOLOGY AND MARKETING

Apple Computer . . . Steven P. Jobs . . . 28, Single . . . College dropout . . . saw potential in fellow computer freak's home-built personal computer. With partner started production in 1976 in family garage on $1300 from sale of calculator and VW minibus. Went public in 1980. . . . Has 7.5 million Apple shares worth $225 million.[10]

In perhaps the greatest success story of the last half-century, this young man, who was 21 when he turned entrepreneur, became a multimillionaire and one of the richest individuals in America in just a few years. Jobs is the youngest of all those who accumulated their great wealth without inheritance.

Industry Background

In the early 1970s it became obvious that survival in the computer industry requires a large market share and broad customer base. Computers ranged from small units to the very large mainframes affordable only by well-heeled firms. The industry was dominated by one company, IBM, with 70 percent of the market. All the other firms in the industry were scrambling for small shares. IBM seemed to have an unassailable advantage because it had the resources for the greatest marketing and research and development expenditures in the industry. A firm with a masterful lead in a rapidly growing industry has an increasing command over resources in comparison with its competitors who must be content to chip away at the periphery of the market.

The computer industry had experienced rapid technological change since the early 1960s. By the early 1970s, however, the new technology involved peripheral accessories rather than major changes in main units.

Before the advent of microelectronics technology, which made smaller parts possible, computers were costly and complicated. It was not economically feasible for one person to interact with one computer. The processing power existed in a central data processing installation, and for those who could not afford to have their own computer, time-sharing services were available.

The "small" or minicomputer industry began in 1974 when a few small firms used memory chips to produce small computer systems as do-it-yourself kits for as low as $400. These proved popular and other companies built microcomputers designed for the affluent hobbyist and small-business person. In 1975 microcomputer and small-business computer shipments went over the $1 billion mark. The mainframe market was maturing and the microcomputer industry was beginning its rocketing ascendancy.

In 1975 the first personal computer reached the market. Personal computers are

---

[10]"The Richest People in America—The *Forbes* Four Hundred," *Forbes*, Fall, 1982, p. 110.

easy-to-use desktop machines based on microprocessors, have their own power supply, and are priced below $10,000. By using various software packages, these computers can serve the needs of businesses and a variety of professionals such as accountants, financial analysts, scientists, and educators, as well as the sophisticated individual at home. The big three minicomputer makers in 1977 were Data General, Digital Equipment, and Hewlett–Packard. It should be noted that the minicomputer grew up without IBM, the company that dominated mainframe computers and accounted for two-thirds of all computer revenues in 1976.

The Market for Small Computers

By 1977 there were three identifiable segments within the microcomputer market: (1) hobbyists, (2) home users, and (3) professional and small-business users. Table 11.1 shows an industry analysis of this market in 1977. The greatest number of customers was in the hobby segment. A complete hobby system could involve a $2000 investment or more. The systems were sold by mail order and through approximately 300 retail stores.

The home segment was comprised mainly of those interested in video games. During 1977 Commodore introduced the Commodore PET, priced at $495, especially for this market. National Semiconductor and Tandy's Radio Shack also targeted products to this consumer, with distribution through computer stores, consumer electronic shops, and department stores.

Available for the professional and small-business segment were the IBM 5100, Wang 2200, Hewlett-Packard 9830 series, and the Datapoint 2200, with prices ranging from $5000 to $20,000. At the time, there was nothing lower priced that could provide the needed level of reliability. Lack of software and an inadequate network of field service offices were problems for this market segment. Because of these deficiencies, most of this segment relied on time-sharing.

In summary, in 1977 as Jobs and his Apple were making the initial market entry, the hobby market was mature, with little growth. The consumer market seemed ripe for growth but lacked computer equipment simple enough for home use

Table 11.1 Estimates of the Market for Personal Computers, 1977

| Segment | Potential Market | | |
	Units	Percent Share	Price Range
Hobby	40,000	57.1	$1,000 to $ 5,000
Home	20,000	28.6	$ 500 to $ 1,000
Professional/business	10,000	14.3	$5,000 to $20,000
Total	70,000	100.0	

Source: "Home Computer Sales Ready to Take off," *Industry Week,* Nov. 7, 1977, p. 98. Reprinted by permission of *Industry Week,* copyright © Penton/IPC. Inc., Cleveland, Ohio.

to achieve mass penetration. For the professional and business sector, the potential was real, but two obstacles existed: (1) product capabilities and prices were not attractive enough for this market, and (2) service, support, and efficient distribution were also lacking. Computers were needed that were more user-oriented and lower priced.

Steven Jobs

Few multimillionaires were more unpromising in their youth than Steven Jobs. He was a loner in school, and his family had to move once because the boy refused to go back to his junior high school. At Homestead High School in Los Altos, California, Jobs became enchanted with technology. He often went to Hewlett–Packard lectures after school. One day he boldly called the president, William Hewlett, to ask for some equipment for a machine he was building. Hewlett was impressed, gave him the equipment, and helped arrange summer employment. While at Homestead High School, Jobs became acquainted with Stephen Wozniak, also profoundly interested in technology.

After graduating from high school, Jobs went to Reed College in Oregon, but dropped out before the first semester was over. He decided college was not for him, and he experimented for a year with fruitarianism and Hare Krishna. Next he took a job at Atari, a small electronics firm only two years old. Steve soon left Atari. With the money he had saved, he took a trip to India and spent the rest of 1974 trying to decide what to do with his life.

Meanwhile, Wosniak went to the University of Colordao and DeAnza College in Cupertino. After a year of designing software, he enrolled at the University of California at Berkeley. He dropped out in 1975 to become an engineering designer at Hewlett–Packard. In his free time he worked at building a small computer, something that had fascinated him from his childhood when his father taught him to design logic circuits.

Jobs often visited Wozniak where he was building small computers and circuits to show other computer buffs. At one such visit Jobs envisioned the potential that Wozniak devices might have in the marketplace, and the germ of the idea was born that was to make the two college dropouts multimillionaries.

The Beginning

In March 1976 Jobs and Wozniak formed a partnership and by June were selling pint-sized circuit boards. They pestered electronics suppliers for credit; they even tried to get backing from Atari and Hewlett–Packard but were unsuccessful. The two young men finally raised $1300 by selling Jobs' Volkswagen bus and Wozniak's Hewlett–Packard hand-held calculator. They purchased $10,000 in parts on credit and soon found that orders for their circuit boards outnumbered their ability to manufacture them. By that summer they were well into the design of an advanced version, which they called the Apple II, a personal computer. By the end of 1976, sales were $200,000 with a 20 percent net income—all this from a $1300 investment.

In late 1976 and early 1977 Jobs and Wozniak made some major moves. They placed a technical article in a leading trade journal that gave them considerable visibility. They established a distribution agreement with several computer retailers. They persuaded an attorney to provide legal services in a pay-later plan. But they still needed vastly more capital if they were to tap what seemed to them an almost unlimited potential, and they badly needed marketing expertise.

Jobs called a major semiconductor company in the area to find out who did their advertising. The agency, Regis, McKenna, at first refused to consider Apple as a client because of their insistence on a pay-later plan. But Jobs continued to pester Regis, and the ad agency finally agreed to the proposition and remained the Apple agency until 1986.

Jobs and Wozniak found the answer to their financial and marketing needs in A. C. Markkula, marketing manager of Intel Corporation, a leading semiconductor manufacturer. He was made an equal partner in return for his services and a $250,000 personal investment. (Markkula is now also one of the *Forbes'* Four Hundred Richest People in America.)

Markkula helped arrange a credit line with Bank of America. The firm, beginning to look impressive at this stage, attracted the attention of strong financial venture capitalists. Two such financial backers were Venrock Associates (the Rockefeller family), and Arthur Rock. Apple now had over $3 million, enough to begin major production.

The Charge of Apple

In March 1977 Apple incorporated and moved out of a garage into a plant. The Apple II was introduced at a trade show in April and was an instant success. It was the first fully programmable personal computer. It was designed to function as a home system and was simple enough for a beginner but easily adaptable to the expert programmer. The name ''Apple'' was chosen because it was believed that computers intimidated the lay user, but ''Apple'' conveyed a friendly and ordinary image that could be targeted to the home user.

The total marketing budget for 1977 was $162,419, close to the total sales of the previous year. Sales for 1977 surged to $774,000, but the amazing growth caused corporate structural problems. The company leadership needed to be formalized, with a president and chairman. Jobs and Wozniak balked at the day-to-day operating responsibilities. They nominated Markkula as chairman and brought in Michael Scott, president of National Semiconductor, to be president. Scott saw the growth potential of Apple and took a 50 percent pay cut to come on board. Jobs became vice chairman, and Wozniak vice president of research and development. The firm remained privately held and primarily employee-owned until December 12, 1980, when it made a $96.8 million public offering. The stock was snapped up and rose quickly in market value. Three years after the founding, Jobs and his colleagues were multimillionaires.

Growth burgeoned again in 1978 as the Apple II found wide acceptance among small businesses and professionals. The international market opened up as IT&T agreed to handle overseas sales of Apple computers. Sales for 1978 were almost 8 million.

By 1979 Apple and its major competitor, Tandy, dominated the market for personal computers. Apple had 500 retailers selling its computers in the United States, whereas Tandy with its Radio Shacks had 8000 outlets. Because of its retail network, Tandy led the personal computer industry, but Apple was second and closing fast. Many other computer makers were gearing up to invade the personal computer market, with rumors that mighty IBM might soon put in an appearance, too. Atari, a company gaining success in the video arcade market, was ready to invade, and Texas Instruments entered the market early in the year. By the end of 1979, approximately 30 companies were making personal computers.

In 1979 Apple added 100,000 square feet of manufacturing capacity to its 22,000 square feet in order to keep pace with the growing market potential and not lose market share to eager competitors. Apple sales in 1979 rose to almost 48 million, a sixford increase over the previous year. Apple was now marketing through five independent distributors who in turn sold to dealers and other customers.

In 1980 the Apple II was still selling well at $1435 for the basic model. This same year the company introduced the more expensive and heralded Apple III. The new computer was targeted to the small business and professional market and not meant for the home, but this Apple was plagued with one technical flaw after another. Overheating problems in the main circuit board resulted in a lab overhaul, leaving 850 U.S. dealers empty-handed because of the unavailability of the Apple III. Fortunately, many customers turned to the II. The company was forced to recall the 1400 units it had sold to be reengineered. It was not brought to market again until November 1981. If the Apple II had not been held in such high esteem, the Apple III debacle could have jeopardized the entire company.

In March, Apple set up its own network of four regional replenishment centers. It now controlled its entire channel of distribution except the 800 retail outlets. The marketing budget for 1980 reached $12.1 million. Some 135,000 Apple IIs were sold, with total yearly sales reaching $117 million and a $12 million net profit.

The Apple III fiasco resulted in some changes in 1981. The product manager of the Apple III and president Scott resigned, and 40 employees were dismissed. The Apple III, redesigned and vigorously tested, was reintroduced with some sales success.

In the fall, IBM came into the market. Apple, now ahead of Tandy in the race

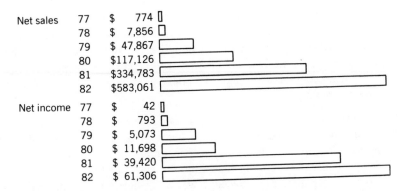

Figure 11.1. Sales and income, Apple Computer, 1977–1982 (in thousands of dollars). (Source: Company annual reports.)

for market share, became IBM's target. To increase customer and dealer service, Apple opened three more distribution centers. The Apple II was upgraded and named the Apple II plus. About 15,000 units per month were sold through 1981. Total sales in 1981 were $334.7 million, again a phenomenal increase.

Sales in 1982 again increased spectacularly. Net sales rose 74 percent to $583.1 million, and earnings increased by 56 percent. Although more than 100 manufacturers had entered the personal computer market, Apple pulled ahead with a 24 percent market share. The company strengthened its retail distribution network, increased its research and development expenditures, and spent more for marketing. It added two service centers to bring the worldwide total to 12.

The entry of IBM, however, cast shadows over the optimism of Apple. *Forbes* analyzed the situation in the following terms:

> Apple's essential problem is that it could find itself squeezed from below by Atari, Commodore, and Tandy, and from above by the big battalions of IBM, Xerox, H-P, and others.[11]

In 1983 Apple unveiled its new computer, "Lisa," a $10,000 unit that Apple hoped would attract the corporate market. Late in 1983 the MacIntosh was introduced, aimed at the home and professional markets. While the aggressive efforts of IBM blunted the impact of these new products, nevertheless, in the 1977 through 1982 period, Apple achieved an extraordinary success story (see Figure 11.1).

Ingredients of Success

Environmental. The success of Apple might be attributed to having the right idea at the right time. But this is far too simplistic. It took no genius to recognize that there

[11]Kathleen K. Wiegner, "Tomorrow Has Arrived," *Forbes*, February 15, 1982, p. 119.

was a latent demand for a simple personal computer. But it took a young computer buff, Wozniak, to design the computer and an entrepreneurial whiz to maneuver the idea and the early prototypes into a half-a-billion-dollar company, wedging in through entrenched, well-heeled, experienced, and aggressive competitors.

The following conditions created a favorable environment for introduction of the personal computer:

- Interest in computers was growing among business people and the general public, while the need to improve business productivity through better information flow and analyses was becoming more apparent.
- Simple equipment offering reliability was not available.
- Lack of programming knowledge was a big deterrent for many potential users. People wanted a product that would let them program without being computer experts.
- Microcomputers were available in the market in the form of kits, so the technology and interest was emerging.
- Software was lagging behind the hardware, and manufacturers such as Commodore and Heath were entering the market unaware of this gap. The situation was aggravated by an incompatibility of language support.

Marketing Mix Coups. Apple responded to almost all the environmental needs of the market with its Apple II. For the first time the end user had access to a low-priced small computer that was easy to use but with the technical capabilities of a more expensive minicomputer. Software was no longer an obstacle because the company made available to consumers its own programs; and a number of enterprising firms began supplying software packages designed specifically to work with Apple systems. The product was given a friendly, nonthreatening name and logo. It was compact, light and trim, and easily portable. The case for the keyboard and video display was light plastic instead of metal. The video display was smaller than a television but large enough to provide good resolution and clear print. The whole product was light-colored and attractive, rather than the austere and formidable black and silver colors of such brands as Tandy. The instruction manual made it easy to understand the system and the software. The instructions were an early key to success because they added to the ease of operation, the "user-friendliness." All these features reinforced the perception that the computer was easy to use: a friendly computer with a high-quality image at an affordable price.

The company decided to manufacture the Apple with the highest quality control standards possible. A reputation for high quality quickly followed, and Apple was able to command a price premium and maintain its market lead over a host of scrambling competitors.

Apple detected the need to shift the target market for its personal computers away from the general public and home use to which most personal computer firms were catering. Consumers were disillusioned with a lack of suitable software, a fear of machines, and a growing recognition that they did not need such sophisticated machines. Instead, Apple saw professionals and small businesses as the main market. Accordingly, it shifted gears and emphasized software, encouraging independent software developers as well as its own developers to design software products for a vast array of potential users.

Apple's pricing policies also aided its entry into the personal computing-for-profit market. For example, while Tandy offered a 4000-character memory system for $499, Apple offered the II with 16,000-character memory for $1195 or 48,000-character memory for $1495. These products, much more suited to the computing needs of the small business firm, especially in view of the wide array of software now becoming available, were still attractively priced.

Apple's distribution channels and strategies also proved appropriate for the professional and business market. Apple created strong ties to 750 to 800 independent retail outlets, such as Computerland, Inc. It provided toll-free software hotlines for users, a monthly newsletter, and a magazine that focused on different applications in each issue. A cooperative advertising program reimbursed dealers for 3 percent of their dollar purchases. By using these marketing efforts directed primarily to dealers, Apple overturned a key computer industry marketing law established by IBM: that selling computers requires armies of direct sales people schooled in handholding of the end user.

Apple kept its margins high and direct sales costs low by using this method of distribution. By 1981 it eliminated the intermediaries by selling directly to retailers through its own regional support centers. The objectives were better inventory control and better access to end users. The company gave direct training to dealers through sales seminars entitled "Apple Means Business." Apple provided dealers with structured presentations that they could use to educate end users. It also equipped dealers to handle same-day walk-in repairs and free replacement of equipment if needed.

Apple's promotional efforts reinforced the other strong ingredients of the marketing mix. User friendliness was continually stressed. The name Apple fostered wide recognition of the company and product. Heavy emphasis was placed on television. A recognizable and authoritative spokesman, Dick Cavett, helped make millions of people aware of Apple, long before any competitor attempted to achieve such public awareness. In unaided tests in 1981, 79 percent of consumers, asked to name "a company that makes personal computers", named Apple. Since professionals are among the general public, this high awareness proved effective in tapping this market.

Handling Great Growth. The ability of Jobs and the organization he created to handle the phenomenal growth—from $200,000 in 1976 to $583 million in sales in 1982—is one of the most remarkable growth episodes of U.S. business. This growth is the more remarkable since it was accomplished without loss of control of the company or serious dilution of ownership. Table 11.2 compares the six key growth years of Apple with those of K mart and McDonald's during their most rapid growth. Apple's growth rate far surpassed the others, despite their being outstanding successes and the dominant influences in their industries. Of course, a small firm can much more easily double and triple its sales from year to year than larger firms with a much greater base. But McDonald's, even in its embryonic years, did not come close to matching the growth of Apple.

Apple did, of course, have some problems in handling its growth. Management of creative employees is an important and often difficult task because such people tend to be nonconformists. Jobs attempted to encourage a creative, risk-taking spirit, one in which high motivation and embracing of challenges prevailed. He used techniques that deviated from orthodox management thinking with its insistence on formal lines of authority and well-designated policies. But infighting

Table 11.2   Comparisons of Growth in Sales for Kresge (K mart), McDonald's, and Apple during the Six Greatest Growth Years

Year	Sales (in Millions of Dollars)	Percent Change from Previous Year
	Kresge	
1965	851.4	25
1966	1090.2	28
1967	1385.7	27
1968	1731.5	25
1979	2185.3	26
1970	2558.7	17
	Apple	
1977	0.8	286
1978	7.9	915
1979	47.1	510
1980	117.1	145
1981	334.8	186
1982	583.1	74
	McDonald's	
1965	35.4	37
1966	42.7	21
1967	53.7	26
1968	97.8	82
1969	143.3	47
1970	200.3	40

Source: Company records.

and power struggles caused the departures of several key people, most notably Stephen Wozniak, co-founder of Apple, and Michael Scott, the former president. Apple was described as disorganized and incompetent in its management.

The problems with Apple III, which could have scuttled the company, were perhaps caused by the loose management controls and bickering, or may simply have reflected the strains of great growth amid fantastic market potential and the eagerness to tap the potential before competitors.

Not the least of the success factors for Apple was its handling of adversity. The significant failure of the Apple III was dealt with as well as was possible. The danger with any highly heralded product that fails because of quality problems is the potential damage to the rest of the product line. Such danger is especially acute for the new firm with little tradition of quality to sustain it.

But Apple handled this quality dilemma very well. As soon as the magnitude of the problems with Apple III surfaced, it withdrew the product, despite extensive preintroductory promotional efforts. The product was not reintroduced until many months later when the problems were corrected. A potential catastrophe was averted.

Update—Another Swinging Pendulum

Apple, as had Nike, encountered trouble maintaining its pattern of success. By 1985 and 1986 problems at the core of the Apple were evident. One involved a major personality conflict; others showed up in operating statistics.

In mid-1983, John Sculley came to Apple as president, leaving the presidency of the Pepsi Cola subsidiary of PepsiCo, Inc., and passing up a chance to become chairman of the $7.5 billion conglomerate. He was intrigued by the challenge and opportunity of personal computers, and he was impressed with the charismatic Steven Jobs.

Sculley soon felt the reluctance of chairman Jobs to let him run the company. In the spring of 1985, Apple faltered, incurring its first quarterly loss ever. In addition, the MacIntosh Division with which Jobs was most directly involved experienced chronic developmental delays. At this point, Sculley persuaded Apple's directors to remove Jobs from operating responsibilities and turn these completely over to him.

Relegated largely to a titular role as chairman, Jobs informed Apple's board on September 12, 1985 that he was starting a new company that would work closely with universities in developing a computer system to fill their research needs, and that five key Apple people would join him. The board was outraged and demanded Jobs' resignation. Amid a highly publicized legal confrontation, there were allegations that Jobs had abrogated his fiduciary responsibilities as chairman and had taken trade secrets with him.

In terms of sales and profit performance, sales were $1.9 billion in 1985, up 51 percent from the year before, while profits were $69.7 million, an 86 percent improvement over a rather poor year. But there were some ominous portents. Market share, expressed as a percentage of worldwide sales of computers costing $1,000 to $10,000, slipped from almost 19 percent to less than 11 percent in only two years. The nine-year-old Apple II contributed 65 percent of Apple's revenues and most of its profits, and this in an industry priding itself on rapid technological advances. The Lisa, designed to tap the business segment of the market, failed along with the Apple III. The MacIntosh, the company's hope for the future, sold at only one-fourth the level of company expectations. And Apple's stock price, which had been as high as 63 in 1983, managed only to climb into the 30s from a low of 14 during the great stock market rally. President Sculley predicted 1986 sales would only match those of 1985, although he did expect that severe cost-cutting would boost profits. He pledged to make Apple products compatible with IBM personal computers, which had come to dominate the business market.

While the company remained a major factor in the personal computer industry, it still needed to regain a solid position in the business market, the fastest-growing area for personal computers. Without this, Apple would have to content itself with the slower-growing education and home markets, and perhaps never become a major computer company. In an attempt to recapture some of its lost momentum, Apple budgeted $50 million for advertising in 1986 and changed the advertising agency to BBDO. The company announced that it expected to introduce more new products over the coming year than it had in the previous 10 years.

APPLE AND OSBORNE, THE GREAT CONTRASTS: WHAT CAN BE LEARNED?

We have examined two rapidly growing entrepreneurial endeavors—one which made venture capitalists and other investors ecstatic, and the other which graphically illustrated the risks inherent in new enterprises.

Learning Insight. Venture capital is usually available for the "right kind" of concepts.

Perhaps the first thing we can learn from these two cases is that venture capital is available for the idea that can be persuasively presented to well-heeled investors. Apple could have achieved only limited success without the investment of outsiders convinced that it stood on the threshold of opportunity. And the success of Apple made additional venture capital available for other new high-tech enterprises, such as Osborne.

For any small business an aggressive and attractive concept helps in winning seed money. Many venture capitalists look more at the person than the idea: "Nearly every mistake I've made has been because I picked the wrong people, not the wrong idea," says Arthur Rock, a renowned venture capitalist.[12] Venture capital exists; some $1 billion a year is flooding into venture capital for innovative entrepreneurs from pension funds, corporations, and wealthy individuals.

Let us also consider several insights that affirm ones discussed earlier in this book. That they are again relevant confirms their significance.

Learning Insight. The financial rewards of entrepreneurship can be great indeed.

In Chapter 10 we noted the rewards coming to the founders of Nike, and how in less than a decade both Phil Knight and his old mentor, Coach Bill Bowerman, became multimillionaires. Apple provides an even more notable example of the quick attainment of great wealth, this time in less than five years. The trigger to such wealth lies in taking a private enterprise public. To do this successfully, the business must have an attractive concept, an idea that seems innovative in a perceived growth area, as Apple did; or the enterprise must be seen as having an attractive similarity to another successful newcomer, as Osborne appeared to have. After a brief period of burgeoning sales, such an enterprise when taken public can command strong investor interest and a high offering price.

Learning Insight. Embrace growth opportunity, but beware of uncontrolled growth.

Apple proved that great growth is possible, that it can be managed without losing control, even if the organization and human relations may be a bit flaky during some of the wildly escalating years. It shows that we "need to run with the ball" when we get that rare opportunity. But there are times when caution is required. We saw another firm, Korvette, that was unable to cope with the demands of increasing size, even though its growth rate was far less than Apple's. And we know that Osborne could not cope with its heady growth.

Risks lie on all sides as we reach for these opportunities. When a market begins to boom and a firm is unable to keep up with demand without greatly increasing capacity and resources, it faces a dilemma: stay conservative in the expectation that the burgeoning potential will be short-lived, and thereby abdicate some of the growing market to competitors, or expand vigorously and take full advantage of the opportunity. If the euphoria is short-lived, and demand stops exponential increases, or even tapers off, the firm is left with expanded capacity, more resource commitment than is needed, high interest and carrying costs, and perhaps even a jeopardized viability because of overextension. This is the dilemma that firms such as Apple and Osborne, Nike and Adidas, and K mart and Woolworth faced, and there

---

[12]"Have You Got What It Takes?" *Forbes,* August 3, 1981, pp. 60–61.

is no firm answer or solution to it. Decision making in the chaotic times of technological breakthroughs and environmental changes is risky, challenging, and tremendously exciting.

Regardless of the commitment to a vision of great growth, a firm must build in organizational, accounting, and financial standards and controls, or find itself on treacherous footing. Inexperienced entrepreneurs tend to fall into the quicksand of expanding operations faster than they can build up the organization and controls necessary for larger enterprises. As a result, costs get out of hand, inventory buildup becomes an albatross, customer accounts may imprudently be allowed to become excessive and overdue, and, in the excitement of increasing sales, assumed profits in reality are losses. Tight controls, especially over inventories and expenses, are essential.

Learning Insight. Build an image of quality, and guard it zealously.

The great importance of guarding a quality image is vividly illustrated with Apple. In only a few years it established a quality product among its many competitors. But it stood to lose all with its inferior Apple III. Drastic action was required if the company's reputation was not to be tarnished, perhaps irrevocably, especially with IBM standing in the wings. Apple quickly withdrew the product and made restitution to all purchasers without delay. All firms should heed this example. To find excuses, to try to dismiss the reality of a defective product, is flirting with disaster. If the problems cannot be quickly remedied, for the sake of customer relations and protection of the vital quality image, any such product should be withdrawn immediately.

Learning Insight. In an industry with rapidly changing technology, heavy commitments to research and development are necessary.

Youthful industries are often characterized by rapidly changing technology. Technological breakthroughs can come at any time, from any firm. The competitor who lags in research and development (R&D) faces serious problems that may well jeopardize its continuing in the industry. Technological breakthroughs may bring improvements or modifications that make existing products obsolete, or they may increase production efficiency and lower costs. Figure 11.2 shows the increasingly heavy expenditures for R&D by Apple from 1977 to 1982, as it sought to avoid vulnerability and to achieve further breakthroughs.

Learning Insight. In many situations the selection of the right customer segment is crucial to success.

In the Miller Beer case we noted an effective use of *segmentation strategy* for Lite beer. A segmentation strategy divides the total market into smaller, homoge-

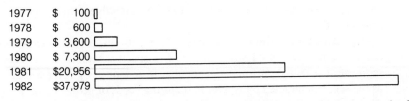

1977	$ 100
1978	$ 600
1979	$ 3,600
1980	$ 7,300
1981	$20,956
1982	$37,979

Figure 11.2. Apple research and development expenditures, 1977–1982 (in thousands of dollars). (Source: Company annual reports.)

neous submarkets (or segments) with marketing efforts directed to specific groups, whereas a mass marketing strategy approaches the total market rather than a piece of it. A segmentation approach is geared to reaching and satisfying a specific group of potential customers. However, the right customer segment must be selected; otherwise the strategy fails. Apple did not direct its efforts to the home market, which had been the target of previous personal computer efforts. Rather, Apple identified the small business and professional market as the one with the greatest potential for its product, and wholeheartedly went for this market.

There are several relevant criteria to consider when deciding what specific segments to seek:

1. **Identifiability.** Is the particular segment identifiable so that its members can be isolated and recognized? Some of the bases for segmentation fail on this count. It may be ascertained, for example, that persons unsure of themselves in social situations make up one large segment for heavy deodorant use. But how are those with such behavioral propensities recognized?

2. **Size.** The segment must be of sufficient size that it is worth the marketing efforts to tap it. A large firm needs a large segment to justify its commitment of resources; a small firm might better direct its efforts to a small segment because of a limited productive capacity and to minimize the likelihood of bigger competitors finding it attractive.

3. **Accessibility.** For a segmentation strategy to be practical, it must be possible to reach the segment(s) with promotional media without much wasted coverage. Generally, with geographic segmentation, appropriate media are available. For many kinds of demographic segmentation, selective media are available. For example, a firm can reach Black consumers in a given city by using the radio stations, newspapers, and magazines that cater directly to this market.

4. **Growth potential.** A segment is more attractive if it is growing. For example, at one time the segment of jogging devotees was not very big. By the early 1970s, however, it was growing phenomenally and eventually numbered in the tens of millions. Consequently, it was an

attractive target market in the early period of its growth before competition proliferated.

5. **Competitive vulnerability or absence.** Competition, present and potential, must be considered when choosing a specific segment. The ideal segment of potential customers is one that is unnoticed by competitors—as the segment targeted by Apple. Perhaps the needs of people comprising this segment are not being met by products geared to their specific requirements. Or perhaps promotional efforts are being misdirected.

Learning Insight. New and rapidly growing industries are often characterized by particularly keen competition.

New and rapidly growing industries present dangers far greater than those facing the entrant to more mature industries. Unless entry to the industry is exceedingly difficult because of high startup costs or secure technological expertise, the new, rapidly growing industry is attractive to all kinds of firms and a host of investors. Such new industries are usually characterized by rapid product improvements and by severe price-cutting. A firm in such an industry must beware of the potential shakeout. It may be better to resist expanding so fast that it becomes vulnerable to overcapacity and excessive inventory when the trauma of price-cutting begins. Competition invariably results in price-cutting as production efficiencies and technological improvements are advanced by competing firms. Where many firms enter the industry, the marginal ones will fall by the wayside, leaving the field to the more able firms with better management and greater resources. During the shakeout period, however, virtually all firms may find themselves losing money because of the severe price competition and the dumping of excess inventories. A stayer must be prepared to weather some rough times before the industry stabilizes.

Learning Insight. The advantage of uniqueness may be transitory and quickly countered by competitors.

Uniqueness is usually transitory. Osborne had a unique product offering in its early months. But it vastly underestimated how quickly that uniqueness would be matched by competitors.

Learning Insight. The possibility of cannibalization must be prudently considered.

The Osborne example shows the dangers of cannibalization carried to the extreme. *Cannibalization* refers to the process by which one product of the firm takes sales away from other products of the firm. Generally, the success of a new product to some extent is at the expense of other products in the line, but hopefully there will be enough new business to increase total sales. In Osborne's case, the foolish announcement of the new Executive computer—before it was even ready to go to market—practically killed sales for the older Osborne 1. Encountering a month and more of virtually no sales is more than most firms can endure.

On the other hand, to be so concerned about cannibalization that needed product improvements and additions are delayed or withheld from the market can also be costly. The classic example of the dangers of such delays is that of Gillette. It procrastinated in introducing its higher-quality stainless steel blade for fear that this blade, which afforded more shaves than its highly profitable super blue blade, would seriously cannibalize the other product. Only when aggressive competitors introduced their own stainless steel blades did Gillette do so. Because of this hesitance in bringing forth an innovation and improvement in shaving, Gillette's market share of the double-edge blade market fell from 90 percent to 70 percent. The loss in competitive position was never fully regained.

INFORMATION SIDELIGHT

STRATEGY COUNTERING BY COMPETITORS

Some strategies are easily duplicated or countered by competitors. Price-cutting is the most easily countered. It is easy to match a price cut, and it sometimes can be done within minutes. Similarly, a different package, such as bundling, or an extended warranty, are easily matched by competitors. The low price of Osborne and its bundling of software, and even the portability of its product were quickly and easily met by competitors, with profits severely affected.

Other strategies are not so easily duplicated. Most such strategies pertain to either service considerations or a strong and positive company image. A reputation for quality and dependability is not easily countered, at least in the short run. A good company or brand image is hard to match since it usually results from years of good service and satisfied customers—and here, of course, Osborne was hampered by its newness.

The best strategies are those that offer something not easily countered, that have lasting effect, and that are reasonably compatible with the present image and resources of the company. In a volatile industry comprised of mostly new and unproven firms, however, such insulation from competitors is rarely achieved. Strategy countering has to be expected and euphoric expectations tempered.

For Thought and Discussion

1. What kind of controls would you advise Osborne to have set up to prevent the debacle that befell it?
2. Did Osborne Computer have any unique strengths that could have enabled it to survive in this hotly competitive industry?
3. What factors account for the surge of competitors in the portable computer field? Should this have been anticipated by a prudent executive?
4. Discuss and evaluate the pros and cons of a heavy growth commitment for a small innovator in
   a. A personal computer adaptation
   b. Running shoes
   c. Discount-concept retailing
   d. A fast-food restaurant

Invitation to Role Play

1. Place yourself in the role of Adam Osborne in late 1982. Sales are exceeding the wildest expectations. Yet you sense that IBM will soon be a factor in this market, as well as many smaller firms. Plan your strategy for 1983 to protect the viability of your enterprise and pave the way for further growth.
2. As a management consultant you have been called in by Robert Jaunich in late spring of 1983. Company losses are mounting. You have been charged with developing recommendations to save the company.
3. As an entrepreneur seeking venture capital for a new and innovative personal computer, what persuasive arguments would you propose for a $500,000 initial request for funds? How would you counter the skeptic's query of how you could possibly compete with the might of IBM?

PART Three

A POTPOURRI OF NOTABLE MISCALCULATIONS

CHAPTER 12

Coca-Cola's Classic Blunder

On April 23, 1985, Roberto C. Goizueta, chairman of Coca-Cola, made a momentous announcement. It was to lead to more discussion, debate, and intense feelings than perhaps ever before encountered from one business decision.

"The best has been made even better," he proclaimed. After 99 years, the Coca-Cola Company had decided to abandon its original formula in favor of a sweeter variation, presumably an improved taste, which was named "New Coke."

Not even three months later, public pressure brought the company to admit that it had made a mistake, and that it was bringing back the old Coke under the name "Coca-Cola Classic." It was July 11, 1985. Despite $4 million and two years of research, the company had made a major miscalculation. How could this have happened with such an astute marketer? The story is intriguing and one that provides a number of sobering insights, as well as having a happy ending for Coca-Cola.

THE HISTORY OF COCA-COLA

Early Days

Coca-Cola was invented by a pharmacist who rose to cavalry general for the Confederates during the Civil War. John Styth Pemberton settled in Atlanta after the war and began putting out patent medicines such as Triplex Liver Pills and Globe of Flower Cough Syrup. In 1885 he registered a trademark for French Wine Coca, "an

Ideal Nerve and Tonic Stimulant.'' In 1886 Pemberton unveiled a modification of French Wine Coca which he called Coca-Cola, and began distributing this to soda fountains in used beer bottles. He looked on the concoction less as a refreshment than as a headache cure, especially for people who had overindulged in food or drink. By chance, one druggist discovered that the syrup tasted better when mixed with carbonated water.

As his health failed and Coca-Cola failed to bring in sufficient money to meet his financial obligations, Pemberton sold the rights to Coca-Cola to a 39-year-old pharmacist, Asa Griggs Candler, for a paltry $2300. The destitute Pemberton died in 1888 and was buried in a grave that went unmarked for the next 70 years.

Candler, a small-town Georgia boy born in 1851 (and hence too young to be a hero in the Civil War), had planned to become a physician, but he changed his mind after observing that druggists made more money than doctors. He struggled for almost 40 years until he bought Coca-Cola, but then his fortunes changed profoundly. In 1892 he organized the Coca-Cola Company, and a few years later downgraded the therapeutic qualities of the beverage and began emphasizing the pleasure-giving qualities. At the same time, he developed the bottling system that still exists, and for 25 years he almost singlehandedly guided the drink's destiny.

Robert Woodruff and the Maturing of the Coca-Cola Company

In 1916, Candler left Coca-Cola to run for mayor of Atlanta. The company was left in the hands of his relatives who, after only three years, sold it to a group of Atlanta businessmen for $25 million. Asa was not consulted, and he was deeply distraught. The company was then netting $5 million. By the time of his death in 1929, annual profits were approaching the $25 million sale price. The group who bought Coca-Cola was headed by Ernest Woodruff, an Atlanta banker. Coke today still remains in the hands of the Woodruff family. Under the direction of the son, Robert Winship Woodruff, Coca-Cola became not only a household word within the United States, but one of the most recognized symbols the world over.

Robert Woodruff grew up in affluence, but believed in the virtues of personal achievement and effort. As a young man, he ignored his father's orders to return to Emory College to complete the remaining years of his education. He wanted to earn his keep in the real world, and not "waste" three years in school. Eventually, in 1911 he joined one of his father's firms, the newly organized Atlantic Ice & Coal Company, as a salesman and a buyer. But he and his father violently disagreed again, this time over the purchase by Robert of trucks from White Motors, to replace the horse-drawn carts and drays of the day. Ernest fired his son and told him never to return home again. So Robert promptly joined White Motors. At the age of 33, he had become the nation's top truck salesman and was earning $85,000 a year. But then he heeded the call to come home.

By 1920 the Coca-Cola Company was threatened by bankruptcy. An untimely purchase of sugar just before prices plummeted had resulted in a staggering amount of borrowing to keep the company afloat. Bottler relations were at an all-time low because the company had wanted to raise the price of syrup, thus violating the original franchise contracts in which the price had been permanently fixed. In April of 1923, Robert was named president, and he cemented dealer relationships, stressing his conviction that he wanted everyone connected with Coca-Cola to make money. A quality control program was instituted and distribution was greatly expanded: by 1930, there were 64 bottlers in 28 countries.

During World War II, Coke went with the GIs. Woodruff saw to it that every man in uniform could get a bottle of Coca-Cola for five cents whenever he wanted, no matter what the cost to the company. Throughout the 1950s, 1960s, and early 1970s, Coca-Cola ruled the soft drink market, despite strong challenges by Pepsi. It outsold Pepsi by two to one. But this was to change.

BACKGROUND OF THE DECISION

Inroads of Pepsi, 1970s and 1980s

By the mid-1970s, the Coca-Cola Company was a lumbering giant. Performance reflected this. Between 1976 and 1979, the growth rate of Coca-Cola soft drinks dropped from 13 percent annually to a meager 2 percent. As the giant stumbled, Pepsi Cola was finding heady triumphs. First came the "Pepsi Generation." This advertising campaign captured the imagination of the baby boomers with its idealism and youth. This assocation with youth and vitality greatly enhanced the image of Pepsi and firmly associated it with the largest consumer market for soft drinks.

Then came another marketing coup, the "Pepsi Challenge," in which comparative taste tests with consumers showed a clear preference for Pepsi. This campaign led to a rapid increase in Pepsi's market share, from 6 to 14 percent of total U.S. soft-drink sales.

Coca-Cola, in reaction, conducted its own taste tests. Alas, these tests had the same result—people liked the taste of Pepsi better, and market share changes reflected this. As Table 12.1 shows, by 1979 Pepsi had closed the gap on Coca-Cola, having 17.9 percent of the soft-drink market, to Coke's 23.9 percent. By the end of 1984, Coke had only a 2.9 percent lead, while in the grocery store market it was now trailing 1.7 percent. Further indication of the diminishing position of Coke relative to Pepsi was a study done by Coca-Cola's own marketing research department. This showed that in 1972 18 percent of soft-drink users drank Coke exclusively, while only 4 percent drank only Pepsi. In 10 years, the picture had changed greatly: only 12 percent now claimed loyalty to Coke, while the number of exclusive Pepsi drinkers almost matched, with 11 percent. Figure 12.1 shows this graphically.

What made the deteriorating competitive performance of Coke all the more

Table 12.1   Coke and Pepsi Shares of Total Soft-Drink Market 1950s–1984

	Mid-1950s Lead	1975 % of Market	Lead	1979 % of Market	Lead	1984 % of Market	Lead
Coke	Better than 2 to 1	24.2	6.8	23.9	6.0	21.7	2.9
Pepsi		17.4		17.9		18.8	

Sources: Thomas Oliver, *The Real Coke, the Real Story* (New York: Random House, 1986), pp. 21, 50; "Two Cokes Really Are Better Than One—For Now," *Business Week,* September 9, 1985, p. 38.

worrisome and frustrating to Coca-Cola was that it was outspending Pepsi in advertising by $100 million. It had twice as many vending machines, dominated fountains, had more shelf space, and was competitively priced. Why was it still losing market share?

The Changing of the Guard

J. Paul Austin, the chairman of Coca-Cola, was nearing retirement in 1980. Donald Keough, the president for Coca-Cola's American group, was expected to succeed him. But a new name, Roberto Goizueta, suddenly emerged.

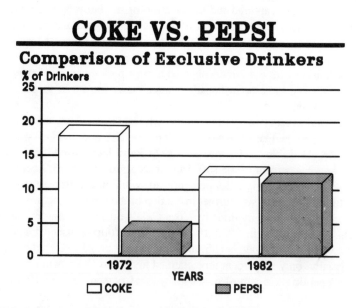

Figure 12.1. Coke versus Pepsi: Comparison of exclusive drinkers.

Goizueta's background was far different from that of the typical Coca-Cola executive. He was not from Georgia, was not even Southern. Rather, he was the son of a wealthy Havana sugar plantation owner. He came to the United States at 16 to enter an exclusive Connecticut preparatory school, Cheshire Academy. He spoke virtually no English when he arrived, but by using the dictionary and watching movies, he quickly learned the language—and became the class valedictorian.

He graduated from Yale in 1955 with a degree in chemical engineering, and returned to Cuba. Spurning his father's business, he went to work in Coke's Cuban research labs.

Goizueta's complacent life was to change in 1959 when Fidel Castro seized power and expropriated foreign facilities. With his wife and their three children, he fled to the United States, arriving with $20. With Coca-Cola, he soon became known as a brilliant administrator, and in 1968 was brought to company headquarters. In 1980, Goizueta and six other executives were made vice chairmen, and began battling for top spot in the company.

CEO J. Paul Austin, soon to retire because of Alzheimer's disease, favored an operations man to become the next CEO. But he was overruled by Robert Woodruff, the 90-year-old patriarch. In April 1980, the board of directors approved Austin's and Woodruff's recommendation of Goizueta for the president. When Goizueta became chairman of the board in March 1981, Donald Keough succeeded him as president.

Shortly after, Goizueta called a worldwide manager's conference in which he announced that nothing was sacred to the company anymore, that change was imminent, and that they had to accept that. He also announced ambitious plans to diversify beyond the soft-drink industry.

In a new era of change announced by a new administration, the sacredness of the commitment to the original Coke formula became tenuous, and the ground was laid for the first flavor change in 99 years.

Marketing Research

With the market share erosion of the late 1970s and early 1980s, despite strong advertising and superior distribution, the company began to look at the product itself. Evidence was increasingly suggesting that taste was the single most important cause of Coke's decline. Perhaps the original secret formula needed to be scrapped. And so Project Kansas began.

Under Project Kansas in 1982 some 2000 interviews in 10 major markets were conducted to investigate customers' willingness to accept a different Coke. People were shown storyboards, comic strip-style mock commercials, and asked series of questions. One storyboard, for example, said that Coke had added a new ingredient and it tasted smoother, while another said the same about Pepsi. Then consumers were asked about their reactions to the "change concept": e.g., "Would you be upset?'', and "Would you try the new drink?" Researchers estimated from the responses that 10 to 12 percent of Coke drinkers would be upset, and that half of these would get over it, but half would not.

While interviews showed a willingness to try a new Coke, other tests disclosed the opposite. Small consumer panels or focus groups revealed strong favorable and unfavorable sentiments. But the technical division persisted in trying to develop a new, more pleasing flavor. By September 1984, they thought they had done so. It was a sweeter, less fizzy cola with a soft, sticky taste due to a higher sugar content from the exclusive use of corn syrup sweetener that is sweeter than sucrose. This was introduced in blind taste tests, where consumers were not told what brand they were drinking. These tests were highly encouraging, with the new flavor substantially beating Pepsi, whereas in previous blind taste tests Pepsi had always beaten Coke.

As a result, researchers estimated that the new formula would boost Coke's share of the soft-drink market by one percentage point. This would be worth $200 million in sales.

Before adopting the new flavor, Coca-Cola invested $4 million in the biggest taste test ever. Some 191,000 people in more than 13 cities were asked to participate in a comparison of unmarked various Coke formulations. The use of unmarked colas was intended to eliminate any bias toward brand names. Fifty-five percent of the participants favored New Coke over the original formula, and it also beat out Pepsi. The research results seemed to be conclusive in favor of the new formula.

The Go Decision

While the decision was made to introduce the new flavor, a number of ancillary decisions had to be reconciled. For example, should the new flavor be added to the product line, or should it replace the old Coke? It was felt that bottlers generally would be opposed to adding another cola. After considerable soul-searching, top executives unanimously decided to change the taste of Coke and take the old Coke off the market.

In January 1985 the task of introducing the new Coke was given to the McCann-Erickson advertising agency. Bill Cosby was to be the spokesman for the nationwide introduction of the new Coke scheduled for April. All departments of the company were gearing their efforts for a coordinated introduction.

On April 23, 1985, Goizueta and Keough held a press conference at Lincoln Center in New York City in order to introduce the new Coke. Invitations had been sent to the media from all over the United States, and some 200 newspaper, magazine, and TV reporters attended the press conference. However, many of them came away unconvinced of the merits of the new Coke, and their stories were generally negative. In the days ahead, the news media's skepticism was to exacerbate the public nonacceptance of the new Coke.

The word spread quickly. Within 24 hours, 81 percent of the U.S. population knew of the change, and this was more people than were aware in July 1969 that Neil Armstrong had walked on the moon.[1] Early results looked good; 150 million people tried the new Coke, and this was more people than had ever before tried a new product. Most comments were favorable. Shipments to bottlers rose to the highest percent in five years. The decision looked unassailable. But not for long.

AFTERMATH OF THE DECISION

The situation changed rapidly. While some protests were expected, these quickly mushroomed. In the first four hours, the company received about 650 calls. By mid-May, calls were coming in at a rate of 5000 a day, in addition to a barrage of angry letters. The company added 83 WATS lines, and hired new staff to handle the responses. People were speaking of Coke as an American symbol and as a long-time friend that had suddenly betrayed them. Some threatened to switch to tea or water. Here is a sampling of the responses:[2]

> The sorrow I feel knowing not only won't I ever enjoy real Coke, but my children and grandchildren won't either. . . . I guess my children will have to take my word for it.

> It is absolutely TERRIBLE! You should be ashamed to put the Coke label on it. . . . This new stuff tastes worse than Pepsi.

> It was nice knowing you. You were a friend for most of my 35 years. Yesterday I had my first taste of new Coke, and to tell the truth, if I would have wanted Pepsi, I would have ordered a Pepsi not a Coke.

In all, more than 40,000 such letters were received that spring and summer. In Seattle, strident loyalists calling themselves Old Coke Drinkers of America laid plans to file a class action suit against Coca-Cola. People began stockpiling the old Coke. Some sold it at scalper's prices. When sales in June did not pick up as the company had expected, bottlers demanded the return of old Coke.

The company's research also confirmed an increasing negative sentiment. Before May 30, 53 percent of consumers said they liked the new Coke. In June, the vote began to change, with more than half of all people surveyed saying they did not like the new Coke. By July, only 30 percent of the people surveyed each week said that they liked the new Coke.

Anger spread across the country, fueled by media publicity. Fiddling with the formula for the 99-year-old beverage became an affront to patriotic pride. Robert Antonio, a University of Kansas sociologist, stated, "Some felt that a sacred

---

[1]John S. Demott, "Fiddling with the Real Thing," *Time*, May 6, 1985, p. 55.
[2]Thomas Oliver, *The Real Coke, the Real Story* (New York: Random House, 1986), pp. 155–156.

symbol had been tampered with."[3] Even Goizueta's father spoke out against the switch when it was announced. He told his son the move was a bad one and jokingly threatened to disown him. By now company executives began to worry about a consumer boycott against the product.

Coca-Cola Cries "Uncle"

Company executives now began seriously thinking about how to recoup the fading prospects of Coke. In an executive meeting, the decision was made to take no action until after the Fourth of July weekend, when the sales results for this holiday weekend would be in. Results were unimpressive. The decision was then made to reintroduce Coca-Cola under the trademark of Coca-Cola Classic. The company would keep the new flavor and call it New Coke. The decision was announced to the public on July 11th, as top executives walked onto the stage in front of the Coca-Cola logo to make an apology to the public, without admitting that New Coke had been a total mistake.

Two messages were delivered to the American consumer. First, to those who were drinking the new Coke and enjoying it, the company conveyed its thanks. The message to those who wanted the original Coke was that "we heard you," and the original taste of Coke is back.

The news spread fast. ABC interrupted its soap opera, *General Hospital,* on Wednesday afternoon to break the news. In the kind of saturation coverage normally reserved for disasters or diplomatic crises, the decision to bring back old Coke was prominently reported on every evening network news broadcast. The general feeling of soft-drink fans was joy. Democratic Senator David Pryor of Arkansas expressed his jubiliation on the Senate floor: "A very meaningful moment in the history of America, this shows that some national institutions cannot be changed."[4] Even Wall Street was happy. Old Coke's comeback drove Coca-Cola stock to its highest level in 12 years.

On the other hand, Roger Enrico, president of Pepsi-Cola USA, said: "Clearly this is the Edsel of the '80s. This was a terrible mistake. Coke's got a lemon on its hands and now they're trying to make lemonade."[5] Other critics labeled this the "marketing blunder of the decade."[6]

WHAT WENT WRONG?

The most convenient scapegoat, according to consensus opinion, was the marketing research that preceded the decision. Yet, Coca-Cola spent about $4 million and

---

[3]John Greenwald, "Coca-Cola's Big Fizzle," *Time,* July 22, 1985, p. 48.
[4]Ibid., p. 48.
[5]Ibid., p. 49.
[6]"Coke's Man on the Spot," *Business Week,* July 29, 1985, p. 56.

devoted two years to the marketing research. About 200,000 consumers were contacted during this time. The error in judgment was surely not from want of trying. But when we dig deeper into the research efforts, some flaws become apparent.

Flawed Marketing Research

The major design of the marketing research involved taste tests by representative consumers. After all, the decision point involved a different-flavored Coke, so what could be more logical than to conduct blind taste tests to determine the acceptability of the new flavor, not only versus the old Coke but also versus Pepsi? And these results were significantly positive for the new formula, even among Pepsi drinkers. A clear "go" signal seemed indicated.

But with the benefit of hindsight some deficiencies in the research design were more apparent—and should have caused concern at the time. The research participants were not told that by picking one cola, they would lose the other. This turned out to be a significant distortion: any addition to the product line would naturally be far more acceptable to a loyal Coke user than would be a complete substitution, which meant the elimination of the traditional product.

While three to four new tastes were tested with almost 200,000 people, only 30,000 to 40,000 of these tests involved the specific formula for the new Coke. The research was geared more to the idea of a new, sweeter cola than the final formula. In general, a sweeter flavor tends to be preferred in blind taste tests. This is particularly true with youth, the largest drinkers of sugared colas, and the group that had been drinking more Pepsi in recent years. Furthermore, preferences for sweeter-tasting products tend to diminish with use.[7]

Consumers were asked whether they favored change as a concept, and whether they would likely drink more, less, or the same amount of Coke if there were a change. But such questions could hardly probe the depth of feelings and emotional ties to the product.

Symbolic Value

The symbolic value of Coke was the sleeper. Perhaps this should have been foreseen. Perhaps the marketing research should have considered this possibility and designed the research to map it and determine the strength and durability of these values—i.e., would they have a major effect on any substitution of a new flavor?

Admittedly, when we get into symbolic value and emotional involvement, any researcher is dealing with vague and nebulous attitudes. But various attitudinal measures have been developed to measure the strength or degree of emotional involvement, such as the semantic differential.

[7]"New Coke Wins Round 1, But Can It Go the Distance?" *Business Week*, June 24, 1985, p. 48.

INFORMATION SIDELIGHT

MARKETING TOOL—THE SEMANTIC DIFFERENTIAL

An important tool in attitudinal research, image studies, and positioning decisions is the *semantic differential*. It was originally developed to measure the meaning that a concept—perhaps a political issue, a person, a work of art, or in marketing, a brand, product, or company—might have for people in terms of various dimensions. As first presented, the instrument consisted of pairs of polar adjectives with a seven-interval scale separating the opposite members of each pair. For example:

Good — — — — — — — Bad

The various intervals from left to right would then represent degrees of feeling or belief ranging from extremely good to neither good nor bad, to extremely bad.

This instrument has been refined to obtain greater sensitivity through the use of descriptive phrases. Examples of such bipolar phrases for determining the image of a particular brand of beer are:

Something special	— — — — — — —	Just another drink
American flavor	— — — — — — —	Foreign flavor
Really peps you up	— — — — — — —	Somehow doesn't pep you up

The number of word pairs varies considerably, but may be as many as 50 or more. Flexibility and appropriateness to a particular study are achieved by constructing tailormade word and phrase lists.

Semantic differential scales have been used in marketing to compare images of particular products, brands, firms, and stores against competing ones. The answers of all respondents can be averaged and then plotted to provide a "profile," as shown below for three competing beers on four scales (actually, a firm would probably use twenty or more scales in such a study).

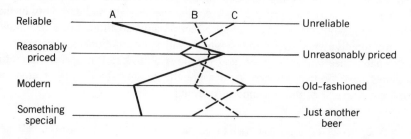

In this profile, brand A shows the dominant image over its competing brands in three of the four categories; however, the negative reaction to its price should alert the company to review pricing practices. Brand C shows a negative image, especially regarding the reliability of its product. The old-fashioned image may or may not be desirable, depending on the type of customer being sought; at least the profile indicates that brand C is perceived as being distinctive from the other two brands. Probably the weakest image of all is that of brand B; respondents viewed this brand as having no distinctive image, neither good nor bad. A serious image-building campaign is desperately needed if brand B is to compete successfully; otherwise, the price may have to be dropped to gain some advantage.

Simple, easy to administer and analyze, the semantic differential is useful not only in identifying segments and positions where there might be opportunities because these are presently not well covered by competitors, but it is also useful to a well-established firm—such as Coca-Cola—to determine the strength and the various dimensions of attitudes toward its product. Semantic differential scales are also useful in evaluating the effectiveness of a changed marketing strategy, such as a change in advertising theme. Here the semantic differential could be administered before the campaign and again after the campaign, and any changes in perceptions pinpointed.

Herd Instinct

A natural human phenomenon asserted itself in this case—the herd instinct, the tendency of people to follow an idea, a slogan, a concept, to "jump on the bandwagon." At first, acceptance of the new Coke appeared to be reasonably satisfactory. But as more and more outcries were raised—fanned by the press—about the betrayal of the old tradition (somehow this became identified with motherhood, apple pie, and the flag), public attitudes shifted vigorously against this perceived unworthy substitute. And the bandwagon syndrome was fully activated. It is doubtful that by July 1985 Coca-Cola could have done anything to reverse the unfavorable tide. To wait for it to die down was fraught with danger—for who would be brave enough to predict the durability and possible heights of such a protest movement?

Could, or should, such a tide have been predicted? Perhaps not, at least as to the full strength of the movement. Coca-Cola expected some resentment. But perhaps it should have been more cautious, and have considered a "worst case" scenario in addition to what seemed the more probable, and been prepared to react to such a contingency.

WHAT CAN BE LEARNED?

The Inconstancy of Taste

Taste tests are commonly used in marketing research, but I have always been skeptical of their validity. Take beer, for example. I know of few people—despite their strenuous claims—who can in blind taste tests unerringly identify which is which among three or four disguised brands of beer. We know that people tend to favor the sweeter in taste tests. But does this mean that such a sweeter flavor will always win out in the marketplace? Hardly. Something else is operating with consumer preference other than the fleeting essence of a taste—unless the flavor difference is extreme.

Brand image usually is a more powerful sales stimulant. Advertisers consistently have been more successful in cultivating a desirable image or personality for their brands or the types of people who use them, than by such vague statements as "better tasting."

Don't Tamper with Tradition

Not many firms have a 100-year-old tradition to be concerned with, or even 25, or even 10. Most products have much shorter life cycles. No other product has been so widely used and so deeply entrenched in societal values and culture as Coke.

The psychological components of the great Coke protest make interesting speculation. Perhaps, in an era of rapid change, many people wish to hang on to the one symbol of security or constancy in their lives—even if this is only the traditional Coke flavor. Perhaps many people found this protest to be an interesting way to escape the humdrum, by "making waves" in a rather harmless fashion, and in the process to see if a big corporation might be forced to cry "uncle."

One is left to wonder how many consumers would even have been aware of any change in flavor had the new formula been quietly introduced without fanfare. But, of course, the advertising siren call of "New!" would have been muted.

So, do we dare tamper with tradition? In Coke's case the answer is probably not, unless done very quietly; but then Coke is unique.

Don't Try to Fix Something That Isn't Broken

Conventional wisdom may advocate that changes are best made in response to problems, that when things are going smoothly the success pattern or strategy should not be tampered with. Perhaps. But perhaps not. Remember Harley Davidson? It dominated the U.S. motorcycle market before Honda entered, and it typified the 3 C's syndrome of failure: conservatism, complacency, and conceit.

Actually, things were not going all that well for Coke by early 1985. Market share had steadily been declining to Pepsi for some years. Vigorous promotional efforts by Pepsi featuring star Michael Jackson had increased market share of regular Pepsi by 1.5 percent in 1984, while regular Coke was dropping 1 percent.[8] Moreover, regular Coke had steadily been losing market position in supermarkets, dropping almost 4 percent between 1981 and 1985. And foreign business, accounting for 62 percent of total soft-drink volume for Coca-Cola, was showing a disappointing growth rate.[9]

So there was certainly motivation for considering a change. And the obvious change was to introduce a somewhat different flavor, one more congruent with the preference of younger people who were the prime market for soft drinks. I do not subscribe to the philosophy of "don't rock the boat" or "don't change anything until virtually forced to." However, Coca-Cola had another option.

Don't Burn Your Bridges

The obvious alternative was to introduce the new Coke, but still keep the old one. This could be called "don't burn your bridges." Of course, in July Roberto Goizueta brought back the old Coke after some months of turmoil and considerable corporate embarrassment and competitive glee—which was soon to turn to dismay. The obvious drawback for having two Cokes was dealer resentment at having to stock an additional product in the same limited space, and bottler concern at having a more complicated production run. Furthermore, there was the real possibility that Pepsi would emerge as the number one soft drink due to two competing Cokes— and this would be an acute embarrassment for Coca-Cola.

The Ineffectiveness of Sheer Advertising Dollars

Coca-Cola was outspending Pepsi for advertising by $100 million, but its market share in the 1970s and early 1980s continued to erode to Pepsi. Pepsi's campaigns featured the theme of the "Pepsi Generation" and the "Pepsi Challenge." The use of a superstar such as Michael Jackson also proved to be more effective with the target market for soft drinks than Bill Cosby for Coca-Cola. Any executive has to be left with the sobering recognition that the sheer number of dollars spent on advertising does not guarantee competitive success. A smaller firm can still outdo a larger rival.

The Power of the Media

The press and broadcast media can be powerful influencers of public opinion. With new Coke, the media undoubtedly exacerbated the herd instinct by publicizing the

---

[8]"Pepsi's High-priced Sell Is Paying Off," *Business Week*, March 4, 1985, pp. 34–35.
[9]"Is Coke Fixing a Cola That Isn't Broken?" *Business Week*, May 6, 1985, p. 47.

Table 12.2   1986 Family of Cokes

Kinds	Millions of Cases
Total of one cola in 1980	1,310.5
1986	
Coca-Cola Classic	1,294.3
Diet Coke	490.8
Coke	185.1
Cherry Coke	115.6
Caffeine-Free Diet Coke	85.6
Caffeine-Free Coke	19.0
Diet Cherry Coke	15.0

Source: "He Put the Kick Back into Coke," *Fortune,*
October 26, 1987, p. 48.

protests to the fullest. After all, this was news. And news seems to be spiciest when an institution or person can be criticized or found wanting. The power of the press should also be sobering to an executive and ought to be one of the factors considered along with certain decisions that may affect the public image of the organization.

Update

Forced by public opinion into a two-cola strategy, the company found the results to be reassuring. By October 1985 estimates were that Coke Classic was outselling New Coke by better than 2 to 1 nationwide, but by 9 to 1 in some markets; restaurant chains, such as McDonald's, Hardee's, Roy Rogers, and Red Lobster had switched back to Coke Classic.

For the full year of 1985, sales from all operations rose 10 percent and profits 9 percent. In the United States Coca-Cola soft-drink volume increased 9 percent, and internationally 10 percent. Profitability from soft drinks decreased slightly, representing heavier advertising expenses for introducing New Coke and then reintroducing old Coke.

Coca-Cola's fortunes continued to improve steadily if not spectacularly. By 1988 it was producing five of the 10 top-selling soft drinks in the country, and now had a total 40 percent of the domestic market to 31 percent for Pepsi.[10]

Because the soft-drink business was generating about $1 billion in cash each year, Roberto Goizueta had made a number of major acquisitions, such as Columbia Pictures and the Taylor Wine Company. However, these had not met his expectations and were disposed of. Still, by 1988 there was a hoard of $5 billion in new cash and debt capacity, and the enticing problem now was how to spend it.

[10]"Some Things Don't Go Better with Coke," *Forbes,* March 21, 1988, pp. 34–35.

The most successful diversifications were in the soft-drink area. As recently as 1981 there had been only one Coke, and not too many years before, only one container—the 6½-oz. glass bottle. Today, only one-tenth of 1 percent of all Coke is sold in that bottle.[11] Now Classic is the best-selling soft drink in the United States, and Diet Coke is the third largest selling. New Coke is being outsold by Classic about seven to one. Table 12.2 shows the total sales volume, expressed as millions of cases, of the Family of Coke.

The future for Coca-Cola looks bright. Per capita soft-drink consumption in the United States has been rising significantly in the 1980s:[12]

	Per Capita Consumption	Percent Increase
1980	34.5 gal.	
1986	42 gal.	22%

The international potential is great. The per capita consumption outside the United States is four gallons. Yet 95 percent of the world's population lives outside the United States.

Conclusion

Some called new Coke a misstep, others a blink. At the time there were those who called it a monumental blunder, even the mistake of the century. But it hardly turned out to be that. As sales surged, some competitors accused Coca-Cola of engineering the whole scenario, in order to get tons of free publicity. Coke executives stoutly denied this, and admitted their error in judgment. For who could foresee, as *Fortune* noted, that the episode would "reawaken deep-seated American loyalty to Coca-Cola."[13]

For Thought and Discussion

1. How could Coca-Cola's marketing research have been improved? Be as specific as you can.
2. When a firm is facing a negative press, as Coca-Cola was with the new Coke, what recourse does the firm have? Support your conclusions.
3. Do you think Coca-Cola would have been as successful if they had introduced the new Coke as an addition to the line, and not as a substitute for the old Coke? Why or why not?

[11]"He Put the Kick Back into Coke," *Fortune,* October 26, 1987, pp. 47–56.
[12]*Pepsico 1986 Annual Report,* p. 13.
[13]"He Put the Kick . . . ," p. 48.

Introduction to Role Play

1. Assume that you are Roberto Goizueta, and are facing increasing pressure in early July 1985 to abandon the new Coke, and bring back the old formula. However, your latest marketing research suggests that only a small group of agitators are making all the fuss about the new cola. Evaluate your options and support your recommendations to the board.

2. You are the public relations director of Coca-Cola. It is early June 1985, and you have been ordered to "do something" to blunt the negative publicity. What ideas can you offer that might counter or replace the negatives with positive publicity?

13

J. C. Penney
Company—
Unchanging Policies

At sunrise on a spring morning in 1902, a young man, Jim Penney, opened a tiny dry goods store in Kemmerer, a frontier town in the southwest corner of Wyoming. He called the store the Golden Rule, remembering his father's admonitions to deal with people according to the Biblical injunction: "Therefore all things whatsoever ye would that men should do to ye, do ye even so to them."[1] The opening day was advertised by handbills distributed throughout the town. Penney remained open that day until midnight, and his sales were $466.59. After that he opened at 7 a.m. on weekdays and 8 a.m. on Sundays, and remained open as long as there was a miner or sheepherder on the street. Sales for the first year were $28,898.11.[2]

Penney faced a tough competitor in Kemmerer. The town was dominated by a mining company, and a company-owned store had practically a local monopoly with most business done on credit or with the scrip issued by the mining company. Penney did not offer any credit, nor could he accept the scrip. What he did was offer values so much better that customers were willing to pay cash and carry home their purchases. He had no fancy fixtures, all the merchandise was piled on tables where customers could see and touch, and there was one price for all. Penney also had a return-goods policy; if customers were not satisfied, they could return the purchase and get their money back.

---

[1]Tom Mahoney and Leonard Sloane, *The Great Merchants* (New York: Harper & Row, 1966), p. 259.

[2]Ibid., p. 259.

Jim Penney had not always been successful in his business dealings. He was born on a farm in Missouri in 1875 into the big family of a poor Baptist minister. Upon graduating from high school he worked as a clerk in a local dry goods store. His salary was $2.27 a month. But poor health forced him to resign and move West. Not wanting to work for someone else, he scraped up enough money to open a butcher shop in Longmont, Colorado. However, he soon lost this along with all his savings. His first venture into entrepreneurship had failed. The second venture would not fail; the little store in the small mining town in Wyoming became the seed of the J. C. Penney Company.

THE SUCCESSFUL GROWTH YEARS

Penney was not content to run just one store. As the store in Kemmerer prospered he thought of opening other stores. By 1905 he had two stores with total sales just under 100,000 dollars. In 1910, Penney changed his company's name from the Golden Rule to the J. C. Penney Company. By this time the chain had grown to 26 stores in six Western states. He kept to the same strategy that had worked well in Kemmerer. He tried to give his customers honest values, which usually meant the lowest possible prices; he stayed with a cash-only policy, and he had no fancy fixtures or high overhead expenses. Thus he could offer low prices and still make money. Not the least of the success factors at this time was the environment Penney had chosen for his business. He confined his stores to small towns where the Penney managers could be well known, friendly, and respectable members of the community. The lack of strong competition that would have been encountered in larger cities helped the burgeoning growth, a growth from one store to almost 1500 in only 30 years.

Something else, another unique Penney policy, was also necessary for such a growth rate to be achieved. Where could Penney possibly find the trained, competent, and honest managers to run the hundreds of stores that were being opened? And almost as important, where could he find the financial resources to open so many stores in such a short period of time and stock them with sufficient merchandise?

Jim Penney both financed and created the managerial resources needed by taking in "partner associates." As each store manager was able to accumulate enough capital out of his store's earnings, he could buy a one-third partnership in a new store, *if* he had trained one of his employees to the point where he could go out and effectively manage such a new store. Here then we have the great incentive to provide the resources needed by such a growing company: motivation by each store manager to find the best-qualified employees and give them the best possible training. And profits would often be plowed back into the company to pay off partnership interests or to back new outlets.

By 1924 there were 570 stores and partners. Now, in order to get the outside financial help needed to sustain further growth, the partnerships were formed into a corporation under which the stores became company-owned. The days of managers getting one-third shares of stores were over, and the complexion of the company now underwent a major change.

Up to this time, store operations had been highly individualized, with each manager making his own decisions within rather general policies. Such looseness of organzation now gave way to more centralized policies and activities, a trend that was to continue in the decades to come. Operations were made more uniform, with strict budgeting systems, improved operational methods, store arrangements, merchandise, and promotions planned by experts and followed by all stores. Central buyers had more authority over managers as to what goods and prices they would carry. And store managers were now evaluated against other store managers as to their performance; promotions to better stores or to the home office went to the better producers. Penney's was beginning to shape itself into a unified and efficient organization. Growth continued, despite the depression of the 1930s, as shown in Table 13.1.

EMERGING PROBLEMS

Despite the substantial growth of the Penney Company and the firm entrenchment it had achieved in Middle America, by the 1950s some questions were beginning to be raised about the heretofore successful policies. Did they need to be changed? Were they archaic for today's society? Was the Penney Company vulnerable to competition as perhaps never before?

General merchandise firms were customarily compared with Sears. Sears was the benchmark, the model for efficient, progressive, large-scale enterprise. Montgomery Ward and Company found itself stacking up poorly against Sears due to a

Table 13.1   Growth of J. C. Penney Company by Stores and Sales

Year	Number of Stores	Sales (Dollars)
1902	1	28,898
1905	2	97,653
1912	34	2,050,641
1919	197	28,783,965
1926	747	115,957,865
1933	1,466	178,773,965
1940	1,586	302,539,325

Source: Normal Beasley, *Main Street Merchant* (New York: McGraw–Hill, 1948), p. 222.

nonexpansion policy after World War II. And now the J. C. Penney Company, in looking at comparative sales statistics with Sears, found itself wanting.

Significant as Penney's achievement was in leading his company through difficult years of adolescence and rapid growth, the conservatism of his associates caused a long delay in the market adaptations needed for the two decades following World War II—credit, merchandise diversification, and catering to the urban market. Table 13.2 shows the growth of credit during this period, a period in which the Penney Company stuck resolutely with its cash-and-carry philosophy. Initially such a policy had been compatible with the needs of a population dissatisfied with the lethargic inefficiencies of many independent stores and their high prices. But four decades later a reevaluation was sorely needed.

Diversification of merchandise lines was also long delayed. Penney's remained only a dry goods and clothing operation until the 1960s. Appliances, furniture and carpeting, sporting goods, auto supplies—merchandise categories long carried by other general-merchandise chains such as Sears and Wards and by department stores—were ignored by Penney's.

Finally, most of the Penney stores were in the more sparsely settled, smaller communities west of the Mississippi. The populous and growing East and burgeoning metropolitan areas were not Penney's domain.

A reassessment of policies was needed, indeed long overdue. While the viability of the firm was yet in jeopardy, its stature as a competitive entity in the mainstream of American retailing was. At this point, in 1957, the assistant to the president of Penney's, William M. Batten, wrote a memo to the board of directors that had far-reaching consequences.

The Batten Memo

Probably one of the most influential and widely publicized memos in modern corporate history was that penned by William Batten. He had started with the

Table 13.2 Trend in Consumer Credit, 1940–1970 (Billions)

	1940	1950	1955	1960	1965	1970
Installment: Consumer goods, other than automobiles	$1.8	$4.8	$7.6	$11.5	$18.5	$31.5
Noninstallment charge accounts	1.5	3.4	4.8	5.3	6.4	8.0
Ratio of total consumer credit to disposable personal income	10.9%	10.4%	14.1%	16.0%	19.0%	18.4%

Source: Compiled from the *Satistical Abstract of the U.S.*

company as an extra salesman 26 years before, and had come a long way. He was ready to stake everything on what he saw was a desperate need for change. He sent a memo to the board of directors criticizing the conservatism of the company for not reacting to a changing America.

In the 1950s, population growth was centering in the metropolitan areas. Incomes per capita were rising, and consumer buying power was being attracted toward "want" rather than "need" type of merchandise. Fashion consequently was becoming more important, and Penney's was extremely weak here. The memo bluntly stated that the world in which the Penney Company had prospered was fast disappearing and that if Penney's hoped to survive, it would have to change.

Batten suggested conducting a merchandising character study to define the kinds of stores that should be operated. He suggested the study should concern three basic areas:

1. To assess Penney's immediate position in merchandising compared with chief competitors such as Sears and Wards.
2. To forecast market opportunities through examining changes in population and trends in shopping, work, and leisure.
3. To spell out desired changes in goods and services and voids in the marketplace that required filling.

Penney's had no formal market research or market intelligence[3] until after Batten's memo. After two years, in 1959, the Merchandising Character Study was completed. The conclusions were that Penney's was selling only soft goods and limited home furnishings, and that most of the advertising appeals were to women. It was decided that Penney's needed to pull in the entire family in areas having the greatest population growth. As one vice president commented in regard to the preponderance of apparel and home furnishings:

> We had no browsing areas for men while their wives shopped, like paint and hardware departments. We had nothing to attract the kids, like a toy department. We realized we needed to tend more toward the one-stop shopping idea.[4]

The year following his audacious memo, Batten was made president of Penney's with the mandate to implement the changes necessary. The question was whether it was now too late to catch up with its competitors, to regain the ground lost during the years of conservative and unchanging policies. The problems were at last defined and known to all. But could they be overcome, and quickly?

---

[3]*Editors note.* Some marketers consider marketing research as only one aspect of a complete marketing intelligence system that provides information flow for decision making. For our purposes here we will use the term *marketing research* for all formal and systematic marketing information-gathering.

[4]Alfred Law, "From Overalls to Fashion Wear," *Wall Street Journal,* October 22, 1964, p. 1.

AT LAST, CHANGE

In September 1958, Penney's began testing the feasibility of offering credit. At first, only 24 stores were the object of this experiment. More than three years were required for Penney's to establish its credit operation chainwide. But at least the necessity of credit to keep up with changing times, and to do well with the big-ticket items such as television and washing machines, was realized.

Coming late into the consumer credit field, however, afforded Penney's certain advantages. An almost completely computerized system was designed, in contrast to other retailers who had started with manual systems and then were forced to computerize at an enormous cost. In order to operate its credit system manually, 37 centers would be needed to serve all the stores. However, with the use of advanced IBM computers, only 14 regional credit offices had to be set up. At the time of Penney's installation, Sears was the only other retailer who could allow customers to shop in any store across the country and receive one bill.

By 1962 all stores offered credit. By 1964 the results were notable: 28 percent of Penney's sales volume was done on credit. Revenues in 1964 amounted to $600 million from more than five million active accounts. By 1966, credit sales were responsible for 35 percent of all sales; by 1973 credit sales were over 38 percent of total sales. By 1967 Penney's had 12 million charge accounts, twice the number of Diners Club and American Express combined.

As intended, the establishment of credit led the way for Penney's to diversify its merchandise mix. It began to follow Sears into carrying hard goods (appliances, furniture, and the like) along with its soft goods. For many years Penney's had been the nation's largest seller of women's hosiery, sheets and blankets, coats and dresses, work clothes, and men's underwear. Prior to 1960, soft goods averaged 95 percent of total sales. Admittedly, soft goods to some extent had shielded Penney's from the ups and downs in the economy, since soft goods normally are the last thing people cut down on during hard times; appliances and furniture, on the other hand, can usually be postponed or deferred until times look better. But such soft goods typically afford a low markup, and profitability rests on high turnover and sales volume. And there is a limit to how much soft goods the market can absorb, and certainly sales and profit potential is ultimately limited without diversification beyond soft goods.

First attempts at merchandise diversification came as Penney's moved into higher-priced women's dresses, leather goods, and furniture. Merchandise assortment was widened by adding designer dresses and youth-minded sportswear for both men and women. By 1962 Penney's began to add hard goods, with the new merchandise appearing in new or enlarged stores, and to a lesser extent in other stores where space could be found. In 1963 Penney's opened its first full-line department store having such new departments for Penney's as appliances, televisions, sporting goods, paint, hardware, tires, batteries, and auto accessories. The

---

INFORMATION SIDELIGHT

IMPORTANCE OF CREDIT

As an extreme example of the importance of credit in enhancing consumer demand and consequent purchasing, consider the Superior, Wisconsin, Penney store in 1959, one of the early stores experimenting with credit. Superior, an iron-ore shipping port at the far western end of Lake Superior, experienced wide fluctuations in business and income due to weather, strikes, and economic slowdowns. Sales at this Penney store had remained static for over three years. The first year that credit was offered, sales increased over 30 percent.

Admittedly, the Superior example is not a typical Penney store. The need for credit by people with irregular incomes is the greater. Now, in place of credit, Penney's had always offered the "layaway plan." Here a store held the selected goods for a customer until they were completely paid for—often by small weekly or biweekly payments—and only then released them to the customer. This plan was heavily pushed by Penney's for expensive items and for merchandise sold in advance of the season. But increasingly, customers did not want deferred gratification of their wants. Not if some other store was giving credit, thereby permitting them to have the immediate pleasure of a desired product.

---

new stores subsequently allocated about 25 to 30 percent of total floor space to these new lines of hard goods.

By 1965, Penney's had 173 stores with radio-TV departments, 103 with major appliances, 67 with sporting goods, 58 carrying paint and hardware, and 42 centers handling tires, batteries, and auto accessories. Diversification had begun in earnest.

Penney's also sought to offer hard goods in stores that were too small to stock such goods. General Merchandise Company, a small but highly automated mail order company, was acquired in 1962. Catalog centers were then set up in many stores as a means of offering customers a much wider variety of goods. In 1971 catalog sales moved into the black, and Penney's at last had the means to compete on equal terms with the long-established businesses of Sears and Wards.

Replacement of older, smaller soft-line stores averaging from 30,000 to 40,000 square feet with new full-line units was also proceeding in earnest. These new stores ranged in size from 43,000 to 220,000 square feet, averaging 165,000. Other diversifications into discount stores (Treasure Island stores), drugstores (Thrift Drug), and supermarkets proceeded. Overseas expansion was also occurring with a controlling interest in a major Belgian retailing firm, Sarma, S.A., obtained in 1968, while in 1971 Penney's entered the Italian market.

Conservative policies had been abandoned, and replaced with a vigorous growth orientation. But could the sales and profits that were lost ever be completely retrieved? Perhaps the more important question was: could the ground lost to Sears in the decade and a half of outmoded policies ever be regained?

A MISTAKE RECTIFIED?

In the last decade and a half Penney's has acted aggressively; indeed it has at times almost met the expansion efforts of Sears, a firm more than twice as large. Table 13.3 shows the capital expenditures for Sears and Penney's during more recent years, as well as the percentage of these expenditures to sales. You can see from this table the much greater percentage of sales commitment of Penney's to expansion. But has Penney's been able to make up the lost ground?

Table 13.4 shows the sales volume since 1940 of Penney's compared with Sears. It also shows the market share of Penney's relative to Sears, that is, the percent that Penney's sales are to total Sears and Penney's sales. Figure 13.1 shows the market share of Penney's more graphically, as well as the trends during the long period of 1940 to 1974.

You can see from these statistics that the sharp upward trend in market share (or sales relative to those of Sears) in the early and mid-1940s was reversed in the late 1940s. Penney's market share then eroded badly, reflecting its outmoded policies. Not until 1970 was Penney's able to improve its market share and begin a new, favorable upward trend. Even though the actions in the 1960s improved the situation, results are still far below the trend established earlier and the market share previously attained.

The recent growth efforts of Penney's can hardly be faulted or even improved upon. The fact remains, however, that unless major competitors also stumble, a

Table 13.3   Capital Expenditures of Sears and Penney's, 1968–1973

Year Ending January	Sears		Penney's	
	Capital Expenditures (000,000)	Percent of Sales	Capital Expenditures (000,000)	Percent of Sales
1968	$186	2.5	$111	4.0
1969	139	1.8	127	3.8
1970	211	2.4	139	3.7
1971	259	2.8	204	4.9
1972	339	3.1	185	3.8
1973	392	3.2	210	3.4

Source: Adapted from *Moody's Industrials,* and respective annual reports.

Table 13.4 Relative Sales Volumes, Penney's and Sears, 1940–1974

Year	Penney's (000)	Sears (000)	Market Share (Sales as a Percent of Total Penney's and Sears' Sales) Penney's	Sears
1942	$ 490,295	$ 915,058	35	65
1944	535,363	851,535	38	62
1946	676,570	1,045,259	39	61
1948	885,195	1,981,536	32	68
1950	949,712	2,168,928	31	69
1952	1,079,257	2,932,338	28	72
1954	1,107,157	2,981,925	27	73
1956	1,290,867	3,306,826	28	72
1958	1,409,973	3,600,882	28	72
1960	1,437,489	4,036,153	26	74
1962	1,553,503	4,267,678	27	73
1964	1,834,318	5,115,767	26	74
1966	2,289,209	6,390,000	26	74
1968	2,745,998	7,330,090	27	73
1970	3,756,092	8,862,971	30	70
1972	4,812,239	10,006,146	32	68
1974	6,243,677	12,306,229	33	67

Source: Adapted from respective annual reports.

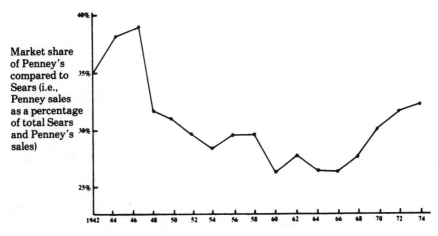

Market share of Penney's compared to Sears (i.e., Penney sales as a percentage of total Sears and Penney's sales)

Figure 13.1. Market share of Penney's compared to Sears, 1940–1974.

substantial lead built up by one firm due to less aggressive or more error-prone efforts of another firm is not likely to be caught.

WHY THE LAPSE OF 1945–1958?

It is one of the anomalies of human endeavor that men of great accomplishment and innovativeness can be both visionary and short-sighted, inspired and blinded. Henry Ford is perhaps the foremost example of such strengths and weaknesses—originating mass production of the automobile, but steadfastly refusing to budge from his original idea of a black Model T.

Jim Penney and his company fell into a similar myopia of resistance to changing times. The policies that worked so well in the early years of the Penney Company became outmoded. But still the temptation is to stick with the historically successful and proven. There is difficulty in breaking from accepted ways of doing things.

Partly accounting for the resistance to change of the Penney Company was the leadership. For the most part, top Penney executives fought their way up through the ranks; the leadership was composed of Penney's associates who had been involved in the company's early growth. For example:

> Earl Sams worked first as James Penney's clerk in Kemmerer, then managed a store for him, and in 1917 became president of the company, serving from 1917 to 1946 whereupon he became board chairman.

> The successor of Sams, Albert Hughes, tutored Penney's sons in Latin, but deciding that retailing would be more exciting, started in the Penney store in Moberly, Missouri, and later managed stores in Utah and Georgia. He was named president in 1946 and served until he stepped aside for Batten (of the famous memo) in 1958.

> Even William Batten, the changemaker, was thoroughly imbued with the traditional Penney philosophy. He first worked for Penney in 1926 while attending high school, and joined the company full time in 1935 as shoe salesman.

> After Batten moved up to chairman in 1964, Ray Jordan became president, culminating a Penney career which began in the small town of Picher, Oklahoma, in 1930.

The Penney Company can boast of its firm policy of promotion from within, and can proudly point out examples of this in the ranks of its top executives. But we might ponder whether such a policy can be carried too far. The absence of new blood can be a negative influence. While trainees may be inspired as to their opportunities and potential attainment, policies tend to become self-perpetuating and innovation stymied without the presence of fresh ideas and even disruptive influences of outsiders.

Marketing research was unknown in the Penney Company until the memo of William Batten in 1957 spurred a thorough study of the needs and opportunities of the environment that Penney's faced. Marketing research can provide a sensor of the market; it can keep a firm's executives apprised on how consumer needs and attitudes are changing, and how competition is adjusting. It is difficult to recognize and be responsive to the dynamics of the environment without it.

Even without a marketing research department, or similar department to provide market intelligence data about changing conditions, Penney executives should have been alerted to looming problems by the sharp drop in market share compared with Sears (as shown in Figure 13.1). For 10 years market share had been shrinking before Batten issued his memo calling for a research study. One wonders what top Penney executives must have thought during these years as they saw their market position relative to Sears relentlessly eroding away. Or did they ever make such a market share analysis? After all, sales were rising during this period—by no means as much as those of Sears—but still there were sales gains. Did this assuage any worries about emerging problems?

Another factor played a role in the myopia of the Penney Company. Penney stores were mostly located in small rural communities, and generally west of the Mississippi. In many such towns the Penney manager was the highest-salaried person in town, and had stature and respect, as did the store he ran. But competition in such rural small towns was certainly less severe than in bigger cities. Perhaps there was a fear of direct competition with big city retailers, such as the major department stores. Was Penney's sophisticated enough to beard such competitors, and on their home ground? Was this perhaps a worry of top Penney executives during this time?

Today, of course, Penney's is in most major metropolitan markets. But this is a relatively new policy, as new as the adoption of credit, of marketing research, and of merchandise diversification. Penney's reluctance to leave small towns may have thwarted the major direction of its growth for a number of crucial years.

Update

As Penney's moved into the 1980s, it had 552 full-line department stores, 1130 smaller units devoted to soft goods (apparel and piece goods), a $1.54 billion catalog business, 361 Thrift drugstores, an insurance business generating $42 million, and a Brussels-based chain of 76 food and general merchandise stores under the Sarma label. It had phased out 37 discount units under the Treasure Island name at the end of 1980. In 1977 it had disposed of several other operations that were not performing satisfactorily profitwise, including its Italian retail stores and the supermarket operations.

By 1981 emphasis was being given to expanding the full-line department stores and upgrading the fashion image of the company.[5] The success of efforts to expand beyond the original soft-line commitment of the company could be seen in the full-line stores, where by 1981 one-third of total sales were accounted for by hard-line departments, such as furniture, appliances, and sporting goods.

Sales and profits for 1987 for the five largest nonfood retailers were:

	1987 Sales ($ millions)	1987 Net Profits ($ millions)
Sears*	48,440*	1,498.9
K mart	25,864	692.2
Wal-Mart	16,065	627.6
Penney	15,332	608.0
Federated Dept. Stores	11,118	313.0

*Sales and profits for Sears include all operations, not just retail operations. Sears' retail volume was $28.1 billion.

As can be seen, Penney's had lost some ground to Sears, with its sales as a percent of total Sears and Penney's sales being 23.8 percent, whereas in 1980 it was 30.6 percent, and in 1974, 33 percent (see Table 13.4). The growth of Sears, however, was more in nonretail operations in recent years. During the decade of the 1970s, K mart had been the big success story, with Wal-Mart close behind.

WHAT CAN BE LEARNED?

Most of the marketing mistakes described in this book are due to a lack of responsive marketing. Changing customer preferences and attitudes are undetected, and adjustments to these are not taken or else long delayed. Now, how does a firm practice responsive marketing? A willingness to act, a disavowal or abandonment of familiar modes of operation, are often necessary. But the changing environment must be recognized and evaluated first. These changes need to be detected, and marketing research can help here. But marketing research alone is no guarantee of responsiveness. It may be used primarily in routine assignments, or its findings may not be accepted and acted upon—or the data may not accurately depict the marketplace. Even with marketing research, decisions may be left to intuition and expediency, or they may not take place at all, despite changing conditions.

The Penney's example suggests the need for fresh blood in an organization. Total reliance on inbreeding and promotion from within tends to foster a narrow and parochial perspective. The traditional way of doing things often prevails in such an environment. (The fact that Batten, in moving up through the ranks, was able to

[5]See "J.C. Penney's Fashion Gamble," *Business Week*, January 16, 1978, pp. 66–74.

point his finger at the flaws and emerging dangers in such an eminent tradition reflects all the more on his strengths, but he was the exception.) We are not suggesting here that the opposite course of action—heavy commitment to filling important executive positions with outsiders—is to be advocated. Such policies play havoc with morale of trainees and lower-level executives. Rather, a middle ground usually is more desirable—filling many executive positions from within the organization, promoting this idea so as to encourage both the achievement of present executives and the recruiting of trainees, and at the same time bringing strong outsiders into the organization where their strengths and particular experiences can be most valuable. Moderation then may be more desirable than major reliance either on promotion from within or from without.

The lack of innovativeness of the Penney Company in the 1940s and 1950s reflects a need in many organizations to foster innovative thinking among employees and executives. Top management support and encouragement of this usually is required. More than this, a receptivity to change and a willingness to change are important, since, if ideas are never acted upon, the creative instincts of an organization are soon atrophied.

Fostering innovation can take many forms. One way is to expose personnel to fresh thinking, either through some mix of sharp new people, or through seminars and institutes where there is exposure to people from other organizations and experiences. Stimulating creativity can also come from quickly recognizing and rewarding creative individuals.

For Thought and Discussion

1. Can you think of other less drastic incentives for store managers to develop trainees than that practiced by the Penney Company in its early years of growth?
2. How might a good marketing research department have alerted Penney top management to the need for credit and merchandise diversification? Could such alerting have been accomplished without formal research?
3. Do you think the growth of the Penney Company in the last decade and a half could have been accomplished any quicker? If so, how?

Invitation to Role Play

1. Place yourself in the position of Batten in 1957. Would you have taken the risk of sending a highly critical memo to the board of directors? What do you think would be the consequences of such a memo in some firms?
2. Assume the role of chief assistant to Batten after he has taken over the presidency in 1958. You have been assigned the responsibility of setting up the diversification into appliances, furniture, sporting goods, hardware, and other hard-line departments new to Penney's. Be as specific as you can as to how you would go about doing this.

14

A & P's WEO—A Price Offensive Backfires

A common failing of large and long-established organizations is a reluctance to take aggressive action. To remain with the tried and true, the established ways of doing things, is much easier. No undue friction is thus created, and the trauma of change and severed little empires can thereby be avoided.

Once in a while a person comes into such an organization and upsets things, gets it moving again, makes major and even risky decisions. In so doing, a giant may be shaken from its lethargy, and a new spirit of innovation and rejuvenation implanted.

This is what happened to the Great Atlantic and Pacific Tea Company, some 113 years old, in the spring of 1972. But sometimes dramatic and forceful decisions do not always turn out for the best; they may reflect poor judgment, or they may be affected by detrimental environmental factors impossible to predict at the time the decision was made.

Is no action better than a major profit-destroying bad decision? Judge for yourself in the following description of the WEO strategy of A & P.

THE DECISION

William J. Kane, 59, took over as chairman and chief executive of A & P in 1971 at a time when sales had leveled and profits were shrinking. In early 1972 he made the decision to convert the chain to superdiscount stores: "We have to start the growth factor in this company right now," Kane was quoted by *Business Week*. "This is a business based strictly on volume, with sales measured in tonnage."[1]

Overnight in various cities across the country, stores were converted to something called "Where Economy Originates" or WEO for short. While stores were not remodeled, two major changes were made:

> Prices were lowered on 90 percent of the merchandise. While some of the reductions were only a few cents, still, percentagewise, they were not insignificant for grocery items where the markup percentage might only be 20 percent.

> The variety of merchandise was pared—from an average 11,000 items in the conventional A & P to around 8,000 in a WEO conversion. This meant fewer sizes and kinds of certain items.

New signs and a profusion of banners were used to acquaint customers with the new policies. Heavy advertising, not only the traditional newspaper advertising of supermarkets, but also radio and television were used to broadcast food prices lower than competitors'.

The decision to convert thousands of A & P stores to the WEO concept did not come easily, especially in a tradition-bound 113-year-old company. Kane, in breaking with the company reluctance to change, ordered a store in Pennsauken, N.J., modified to a low-price discount food operation a month after he took office. It was called a "WEO" store, meaning a "Warehouse Economy Outlet." This first trial WEO store lacked all frills; merchandise stood in open cartons and customers bagged their own groceries, but prices were slashed and the store's volume "increased fantastically."

The second experimental WEO store was opened in Braddock, Pennsylvania, an old, economically depressed steel mill town near Pittsburgh. S. R. Thompson, the store manager, reported: "We were ready to close back in June 1971. We wanted to bring the store back to life again, and WEO did it."[2] For the first six months the store operated as a WEO, average weekly sales rose more than 500 percent over the year before. During 1971, A & P opened ten more WEOs and went back to regular shelf displays and more regular services in them.

The success of the WEO experiments, coupled with the company's first quarterly loss since 1961, helped to make the decision to switch all the stores to the WEO concept.

How much were prices really reduced in the WEO stores? The real impact is best seen in the effect on margins. Margins or markup percentages for most supermarkets, including the regular A & Ps, are around 20 to 22 percent; the WEO

[1]"A & P's Ploy: Cutting Prices to Turn a Profit," *Business Week*, May 20, 1972, p. 76.
[2]Ibid., p. 78.

INFORMATION SIDELIGHT

ADVANTAGES OF CHAINS: OPPORTUNITY FOR EXPERIMENTATION

A & P's testing and modifying of its WEO idea in 1971 shows one of the big advantages multistore organizations have over firms with only a few stores. Prospective strategy changes can be experimented with in a few stores, any desirable adjustments determined, and the success of the strategy ascertained from concrete sales and profits results. All this can be done with relatively little risk since only a few outlets of the total chain are involved, and the strategy can be adopted throughout the company only if the results are good. Experimentation is hardly possible for the firm with one or a few stores, and there is substantial risk in making major strategy changes.

---

margins were estimated to run between 9 and 13 percent. This translated into a can of beef stew being reduced from 67 to 59 cents, for example, while plastic sandwich bags went from 53 to 49 cents. Even if sales volume were to increase dramatically, the question in the fall of 1972 was whether volume would rise fast enough to yield profits at such low margins. But Kane expressed his basic food merchandising philosophy:

> I want to get us back to good, sound, basic fundamentals. This company was built on quality foods sold at low prices.[3]

BACKGROUND

George Huntington Hartford started what was to become A & P in 1859, when he was 26. Tea was selling in New York City at $1 a pound, and Hartford thought this could be reduced to 30 cents by eliminating middlemen. He persuaded his employer, George Gilman, to join him. Wild hoopla was used to promote the first store, such as eight dapple-gray horses pulling a tremendous red wagon through the streets of New York. Gradually spices, coffee, and then other staple grocery items were added, with middlemen bypassed whenever possible. More stores were opened: five by 1865 and 11 by 1869 when the name, The Great Atlantic & Pacific Tea Company (to signify the intention to expand coast-to-coast), was adopted.

Cash and carry, a major innovation by A & P, was introduced in 1912. Doing away with charge-account paperwork and thousands of delivery horses and wagons enabled "economy" stores to sell a large volume at a low markup. (This sounds reminiscent of the 1972 WEO strategy.) For the next two years, economy stores

---

[3]Ibid., p. 76.

were opened at the rate of one every three days. By 1916 there were 1000 A & P stores, each laid out exactly the same. By 1930 there were 19,442 stores, and sales passed the billion-dollar mark.

But in 1930 a "revolution" began in food retailing that would profoundly affect A & P and all the other food chains. The first King Kullen supermarket was opened by Michael Cullen, an former chain-store executive, in August 1930. By the end of 1932 he had eight outlets. More "supermarkets" soon followed as other innovators came on the scene. These first supermarkets often were opened in abandoned warehouses, barns, empty garages and factories; they had crude floors, bare ceilings, unpainted fixtures, and merchandise was piled everywhere. Big compared to regular grocery stores of that time, they were self-service and usually had abundant free parking. Since they had lower operating costs they could offer lower prices than the chain groceries. They also commonly used loss leaders, and customers came from as far as 50 miles to shop in these stores for the bargains they afforded. By 1935, more attractive supermarkets were being opened.

A & P and the other major grocery chains did not respond to this new challenge until 1937. But by then these innovative supermarkets were beginning to dominate the market. Table 14.1 shows the conversion to supermarket operation made by A & P within six years; in the process, thousands of its smaller unprofitable units were abandoned.

After World War II ended, A & P lagged behind in the use of two merchandising ideas that were sweeping the rest of the industry. Nonfood items, ranging all the way from health and beauty aids to toys and certain apparel, were being widely stocked. Goods with high volume and impulse-buying potential that could yield high markups were especially selected. While A & P did not ignore nonfood items, this business was not developed as fully as with most other food chains.

Trading stamps also became extremely popular after World War II. Here

Table 14.1 A & P Changeover to Supermarkets

	Total Number of Stores	Number of Supermarkets
1936	14,446	20
1937	13,058	282
1938	10,671	771
1939	9,021	1,119
1940	7,073	1,396
1941	6,042	1,594

Source: U. S. v. The Great Atlantic and Pacific Tea Co., U. S. Circuit Court of Appeals, 7th district, Docket 9221, Records and Briefs, Vol. 1, p. 323.

again, A & P was slow to act, doing so only after most of its competitors. Finally Plaid Stamps were brought into some stores.

Grocery retailing experienced two additional innovative approaches in the last decade or so: discounting, and the convenience store. While the latter did not directly affect A & P, discounting had considerable influence.

Discounting of general merchandise swept into the retail scene in the 1950s and 1960s. During most of this time it was not a significant factor in food, although some independent stores had tried across-the-board low-margin, high-volume selling with varying degrees of success. The big chains for the most part ignored the discount approach until 1970.

Several things accounted for the slow move into food discounting. Grocery margins were low to begin with—for the most part around 20 to 22 percent, versus 38 to 42 percent for nonfood items. Even when expenses were pared to the limit, it was difficult to reduce grocery markups to much less than 15 percent and still make money; in nonfood items, discount margins were sometimes as low as 20 to 22 percent, or almost half those of regular retailers. This meant that discount prices for appliances, sporting goods, and many other nonfood items could be significantly lower than regular prices and consequently have a strong impact on demand. Since food prices could not be reduced as much, discounting had less impact. Furthermore, the common use by all supermarkets of attractively priced leader items to lure customers into a store often disguised the fact that other items might be proportionately higher.

Besides minimum expenses, another facet of discount operations is lean stocks. Such a decreased assortment ideally consists only of fast-moving items and sizes. But the typical supermarket was geared to offering customers the widest possible variety and so had hundreds of feet of shelf space to fill.

The major chains in the early 1970s finally began moving into discounting, either with separate discount operations or with company-wide low-margin policies. Safeway, the second largest chain (next to A & P), in mid-1970 gradually moved into price leadership or price matching in most markets where it was already dominant. A & P moved more from a position of weakness in a rather desperate attempt to solve a long-standing decline in average store performance. A gradual approach to discounting would not produce results as quickly as needed. Consequently the decision was made for a more drastic and exciting program in order to achieve a shift in its share of the market.

Convenience food stores were also spreading rapidly during the 1960s. These were in marked contrast to discount stores in that they offered higher prices than conventional food stores. They were originally developed in the southwest during the 1930s and were a more sophisticated version of the mom-and-pop neighborhood groceries.

Convenience food stores typically are open seven days a week and often from 7 a.m. to 11 p.m. (the largest convenience food chain is called 7-Eleven, reflecting this). They cater to shoppers between their regular trips to the supermarket and are designed to make shopping quick and convenient. Consequently they are small, afford close-to-the-door parking, and have no long waits at checkouts. There is only a limited selection of merchandise, and this is carefully chosen to yield high turnover. These stores charge at least 15 to 20 percent more than other food stores. But the factor of convenience is a powerful shopping inducement; the number of such food stores grew from 500 in 1957 to 17,000 in 1973. As indirect competitors, convenience food stores were a force to be reckoned with by conventional supermarkets such as A & P.

PRELUDE TO THE WEO DECISION

After being for decades the largest supermarket chain, A & P was finding its position seriously challenged by Safeway; indeed, in 1971 A & P barely nosed out Safeway in total sales. But sales had reached a plateau in the 1960s and were even falling a little in 1970 and 1971, along with a serious erosion of market share. Profits also were faltering during this period and fell drastically in 1971. Tables 14.2 and 14.3 show sales, profit, and market share position of A & P and those of its two largest competitors, Safeway and Kroger, since 1963.

The worsening dilemma of A & P by 1970 reflected a history of bad decisions and a reluctance to make aggressive moves. Many years before, A & P decided not to go into major shopping centers but stuck mostly with free-standing neighborhood stores. A major reason for this policy was a reluctance to pay the higher rents demanded by shopping centers. There was also the belief that A & P was so big and powerful that it could attract people regardless of location. Furthermore, management hesitated to build the bigger stores that were becoming the accepted mode of

Table 14.2 The Long Slide of A & P

	Sales	Income	Market Share[a]
1963	$5,189,000,000	$57,489,000	20.9
1965	5,119,000,000	52,339,000	19.0
1966	5,475,000,000	56,239,000	18.8
1967	5,458,000,000	55,897,000	17.6
1968	5,436,000,000	45,247,000	15.8
1969	5,753,000,000	53,302,000	15.4
1970	5,664,000,000	50,129,000	13.1
1971	5,508,000,000	14,619,000	12.1

[a]Percentage of A & P sales to total grocery chain (11 or more units) sales.

Sources: Based on U.S. Dept. of Commerce reports, and Moody's.

Table 14.3   Comparative Statistics for Safeway and Kroger

	Safeway			Kroger		
	Sales	Income	Market	Sales	Income	Market
	(000,000)		share	(000,000)		share
1963	$2,649.7	$44.82	10.7	$2,102.1	$22.08	8.5
1965	2,939.0	48.18	10.9	2,555.1	31.30	9.5
1966	3,345.2	59.75	11.4	2,660.0	29.38	9.1
1967	3,360.9	50.89	10.8	2,806.1	25.72	9.0
1968	3,685.7	55.06	10.7	3,160.8	34.00	9.2
1969	4,099.6	51.31	11.0	3,477.2	37.39	9.3
1970	4,860.2	68.89	11.2	3,735.8	39.77	8.6
1971	5,358.8	80.18	11.8	3,707.9	36.27	8.1

Sources: U. S. Dept. of Commerce reports, and *Moody's.*

much of the industry. For example, in 1970 A & P stores averaged only 14,000 square feet compared with an average of more than 20,000 for other major chains.

Not the least of A & P's failings had been carelessness with store maintenance and customer service. Many stores were old and poorly lit; displays were unattractive and disordered. Staffing was often so minimal that customers waited for an unduly long time at checkouts. Stores might have cluttered aisles, shelves in need of dusting, and cartloads of sale items might crowd ends of aisles. For example:

> One display with a "Reduced for Quick Sale" sign, included badly dented cans of Ann Page tomato juice and corn, cream cheese with bits of macaroni sticking to the package bottom, packages of breakfast food with already opened pour spouts, and a large box of oatmeal with the lid partly ripped off.[4]

This situation of small, often badly located stores, careless display and housekeeping, and sometimes inadequate service brought an inevitable consequence to A & P—a dowdy, dull, and old-fashioned image. Several other things also conspired to bring this about. Any company over 100 years old would probably have to fight extra hard to escape this image. Furthermore, many of the employees of the company were old—they didn't help counter such a pervasive image.

What kind of customers are attracted to a store with this kind of image? The young suburban families with increasing purchasing power and burgeoning needs? Hardly. A profile of customers would more likely find the preponderance to be old or retired people who grew up on the A & P economy appeal. Is this a healthy type of customer segment to appeal to? It is hardly compatible with growth.

Some of the disaffection toward A & P has been attributed to its emphasis on

[4]Ibid., p. 77.

private labels, including goods produced in its own 24 manufacturing and processing plants and 22 bakeries. Those customers who come to A & P stores looking for nationally advertised brands may find them unavailable and turn to other stores. Undoubtedly, if the quality image of the chain's private label had been successfully sold, this would not be a disadvantage. But there were questions as to how successful A & P had been in selling its private label program.

So the groundwork was laid, the cause established, for drastic action by A & P in the spring of 1972 to generate a new spark in company policies and initiate strong and aggressive action to reverse a stagnant trend of sales and a declining trend of profits. The resulting militant price-cutting was to cause industrywide concern and countermoves, and was to result in deteriorating profits for many firms of the industry, most of all for A & P.

COMPETITIVE REACTION

Competitors could not afford to ignore the aggressive price-cutting and promotion of A & P. Of course, smaller supermarket chains without the financial resources of an A & P found it difficult trying to match prices with the behemoth of the industry. But most attempted to do so and hoped to weather the storm.

For example, Pantry Pride, an Eastern chain, advised customers in advertisements to bring in copies of A & P's ads showing their price leaders, and Pantry Pride would match the prices. Profits dropped drastically. Kroger reported a 63 percent decline in profits for the first three months of 1973, after a 36 percent profit drop for 1972. Food Fair reported profits down 50 percent in two quarters of 1972. The battle raged hardest in Baltimore, Philadelphia, Boston, Chicago, and the state of New Jersey.

But while many chains sought to combat A & P's price assault by matching their prices and by boosting advertising, some also sought new ways to boost earnings. Two in particular found favor: opening longer hours and stocking more nongrocery items.

Some competitors, particularly Jewel, Pathmark, and Arlan's, went to round-the-clock service, open 24 hours a day. The intent, of course, was to attract customers when A & P was closed. But how many customers really are going to shop at midnight? Apparently quite a few. Stuart Rosenthal, assistant to the president of Supermarket General, said, "We get all kinds of people late at night or early in the morning—couples unable to shop together during regular hours, or the wife who trusts her husband to babysit only when the kids are asleep."[5]

But even if only a handful of customers shopped during these extended hours, the cost of maintaining 24-hour operations was not that formidable. Ralph Krueger,

---

[5] "War in the Supermarkets," *Time*, August 14, 1972, p. 60.

vice president of Allied Supermarkets, noted: "It doesn't add much to our labor expense because we must have people in to stock at night anyhow. Certain other expenses, like rent, remain the same whether we stay open or not."[6]

In order to increase profits, more supermarkets turned to additional nonfood items. We know that scrambled merchandising has long been a phenomenon in food retailing, with hosiery, housewares, and even toys being stocked with regularity by many stores. Now guitars, plants, wine shops, sports-clothes boutiques, and even pharmacies began finding space in supermarkets. Such nonfood items were safe from the cut-price actions of A & P; in addition they carried a much higher markup than the typical food item. If an adequate volume could be generated, such nonfood merchandise was well worth carrying.

Competitive Reaction of Jewel

Jewel Companies, a Chicago-based supermarket chain now the fifth largest in the United States, successfully bucked the WEO campaign without really trying to match A & P's prices. In fact it did just the opposite. Shopping hours were extended from 8 a.m. to midnight. Various frills, such as bus transportation for the elderly, were added. A small number of items were sold at discount prices, but the great majority were sold at normal or higher-than-normal prices.

However, Jewel had rather smoothly acquired the image of a discount chain without really being one—and this undoubtedly helped with the price-conscious customers A & P was seeking to win away. In the summer of 1971, when prices were skyrocketing and two days after President Nixon froze prices, Jewel announced its own "Phase I" program. With heavy advertising, the company rolled back its prices to lower than prefreeze levels and did not increase them until months after the 90-day freeze ended. While the price cuts were only token, the publicity value was substantial.

In the late 1960s the company had spread into hard goods and fashion items, drugs, and snack-type restaurants. Many of Jewel's supermarkets are located next to or in the same building as one of its other retailing operations, so that traffic is funneled between. And Jewel's per-store sales volume outstripped A & P's by almost three to one. So, competing with service, integrated retailing, aggressive promotion, and an image of innovativeness but also of low prices (even if hardly justified), the price-cutting assault of A & P was neatly thwarted.

CONSEQUENCES OF THE WEO CAMPAIGN

The WEO strategy was inaugurated early in 1972, although it took some months for all stores to be converted. By August, 3700 of the 4200 stores were ready, with the

[6]Ibid.

rest expected to be by fall. All that remained was to watch for the sales and profits results.

Sales gains were achieved, an increase of $800 million. But A & P also suffered a serious deficit (what would have been catastrophic for many firms) of $51.3 million, the worst in recent history for the company. Table 14.4 updates Tables 14.2 and 14.3, and shows the comparative results of A & P, Safeway, and Kroger for 1972 as well as the preceding two years.

You can see from Table 14.4 that A & P did reverse the falling trend in sales and market share, even though the cost was high. Safeway, despite the aggressive tactics of A & P, not only posted a significant sales gain of $700 million and a major gain in market share, but also substantially increased an already healthy profit base. For a time during 1972, Safeway became the nation's biggest food retailer, as A & P closed more than 400 stores in the name of efficiency while opening up 80 larger units. Kroger was badly affected profitwise by the WEO campaign, although it still had a sales gain. What was of deeper concern to Kroger was the steadily eroding market share.

Because of the loss, A & P was forced to omit a quarterly dividend for the first time since 1925. This broke the proud chain of continuous dividends managed even through the depression of the 1930s. Stockholders were understandably unhappy, and Huntington Hartford, heir to an A & P fortune, criticized management as inefficient.

To add to the woes of A & P, a battle of ownership commenced. Management was challenged by Gulf & Western Industries, an acquisition-minded conglomerate. Gulf & Western sought to win disaffected shareholders to its side with an attractive

Table 14.4 Comparative Statistics for A & P, Safeway, and Kroger, 1970–72

	Sales	*Income*	*Market Share*
A & P:			
1970	$5,664,000,000	$50,129,000	13.1 percent
1971	5,508,000,000	14,619,000	12.1
1972	6,307,000,000	def. 51,280,000	13.1
Safeway:			
1970	4,860,000,000	68,890,000	11.2
1971	5,359,000,000	80,180,000	11.8
1972	6,058,000,000	91,060,000	12.5
Kroger:			
1970	3,736,000,000	39,770,000	8.6
1971	3,708,000,000	36,270,000	8.1
1972	3,791,000,000	23,180,000	7.8

Source: U. S. Dept. of Commerce reports, and *Moody's.*

offer for 3.75 million shares. Others were also interested. But in extended legal maneuvers, Kane and his associates were able to win a court order against the tender offer becoming effective.

Heavy losses were not unexpected by A & P management during the start of the WEO campaign. With margins reduced on thousands of items, increased advertising and refurbishing of stores, and the hiring and training of more employees to handle increased business, some pressures on profits were inevitable. But with virtually no debt, the company was in a position to stick with reduced profits until the WEO strategy had time to prove itself. A dramatic turnaround in profitability was expected by the close of 1972 as greater sales volume and improved market share were achieved.

Unfortunately, an external factor entered the picture and reduced the full impact of A & P's pricing actions. The WEO campaign was begun almost simultaneously with an explosion of food prices. In February 1973, the Consumer Price Index rose 3.9 percent—in one month's time—over 1972, and wholesale food prices increased across the board.

Beset on all sides—by rising food prices, by tremendous stockholder pressure to cut losses, and by the takeover attempt by Gulf & Western—A & P began hiking its prices. The real price war was over by early 1973, even though WEO signs and advertising continued prominently.

Aside from what *Business Week* called a "Pyrrhic victory"[7] (that is, a victory won with staggering losses, based on a victory by Pyrrhus over the Romans in 279 B.C.), what other consequences can be seen in the WEO campaign? Undoubtedly A & P gained the enmity of its competitors and a reputation as a bully in an industry that already had slender profit margins.

As to the efforts to improve market share in some key cities, the results were hardly reassuring. In Chicago, where A & P had an estimated 7 percent of the market, no lasting advantage was gained, although some business was initially taken from smaller independents and from National Tea Company, which had problems of its own before A & P's price war. In Washington, D.C., where A & P also had 7 percent of the market, there was no change, although some thought A & P had been less aggressive there where most of its stores were old and where little money had been spent on new construction. In Pittsburgh, A & P even lost ground, with market share falling from 10 percent to 8.9 percent. But in Philadelphia, a significant gain was initially scored, as market share rose from 13 percent to 16 percent in one year.

While A & P eased its price-cutting tactics early in 1973, the perception of low prices in the minds of some customers appeared to be more lasting. For example, a

---

[7]"A & P Counts the Cost of Its Pyrrhic Victory," *Business Week,* April 28, 1973, pp. 117–119.

limited study by *Business Week* of customers interviewed in WEO stores found 32 were there because of cheaper prices, while 17 of these said they had switched from other chains in the last nine months in order to pare their food costs.[8] This was at a time when several independent studies had found that A & P prices were no longer lower than competitors. For example, a Philadelphia study of 50 key grocery items at WEO and major competitors found only five that cost less at WEO. Another study found that of 10 items advertised in March 1973, seven were the same as competitors', two were slightly higher, and only one was cheaper.[9]

The major question facing A & P in 1973 was whether the hard-won gains would last. Would customers who had been wooed to A & P because of supposed lower prices stay with A & P? Or would they quickly shift when they discovered that WEO prices were comparable with those of other stores?

Time proved the failure of the WEO strategy. The $51 million loss due to severe price-cutting was a wasted effort. While sales rose to $6.7 billion in 1973, and the company went into the black on its higher prices with a $12.2 million profit, this was small compared to past years (see Table 14.2); of even more concern, A & P lost its top spot in sales to Safeway. In 1974 the situation worsened; while sales nudged up 1.9 percent to $6.9 billion, the company plunged to a loss of $157.1 million. To add to its problems, the company was hit with a price-fixing suit and assessed $32.7 million in damages.

In December of 1974, Jonathan L. Scott, chief executive of Albertson's, the fifteenth largest food chain, became the first outsider to head A & P in its entire history. In one of the biggest retrenchments in retailing history, Scott began closing one-third of A & P's 3500 stores at a total write-off of some $200 million. This involved negotiating hundreds of local labor contracts and weakening employee morale. In place of the small, marginal stores, Scott planned to follow the examples of Safeway and other front-running chains and open large stores stocking a wider assortment of foods and nonfoods with higher markups. The prescription for correcting the ills of A & P also included refurbishing other stores, more emphasis on national brands, better displays, and insistence on clean and uncluttered stores.

A & P could never regain its lead over arch-rival Safeway. Results for the two chains for 1974 were as follows:

	Sales	Net Income
Safeway	$8,185,200,000	$79,200,000
A & P	6,874,600,000	−157,100,000

[8]Ibid., p. 117.
[9]Ibid., p. 118.

Update

The new management did not solve A & P's problems. Chairman Jonathan Scott "swung a cruel ax," closing 1700 stores, releasing 10,000 employees, and borrowing heavily to revamp and enlarge the remaining supermarkets. He hired 19 new executives, including Grant Gentry, who left the flourishing Jewel chain to become A & P president. Scott said: "I have a philosophy that you should surround yourself with people better than yourself."[10]

An expensive and self-critical ad campaign, "to put price and pride back together again," was instituted, aimed both at luring shoppers and also at bucking up store employees. But results remained dismal. For the second quarter of fiscal 1977, profits dropped 88 percent below the previous year, and they were hardly breathtaking then. With the release of this news, president Gentry resigned.

By 1978, sales had risen to $7.2 billion; but now Kroger had also surpassed A & P. The company had either lost money or barely made a profit in every year since 1971. Part of the problem was the many central-city stores that were stuck in deteriorating neighborhoods. This situation could not be remedied quickly. Scott made an identifiable mistake in electing to close unprofitable stores one by one in the 36 states serviced, with the result that A & P did not get the distribution savings of quitting an entire region.

Unexpectedly, in early 1979, one of West Germany's largest food retailers, the Tangelmann Group, offered to pay $7.50 a share, a small premium over the market price of $6.75, and far below the book value, for A & P. Thus A & P fell into foreign hands, after 120 years. At first the future looked better for A & P as the German company could supply much-needed capital. It had 2000 stores in Germany and Austria and annual sales of about $3 billion.

But the problems were not to disappear. Jonathan Scott quit in 1980—to start a real estate investment firm in Dallas—and Tangelmann replaced him with James Wood, who was running Grand Union food stores, a subsidiary of English-owned Cavenham Ltd. A & P again reverted to heavy losses, recording $53 million in red ink over five quarters in 1980–1981.

WHAT CAN BE LEARNED?

Where basic weaknesses exist in a company, any strategy not directed to correcting these weaknesses can only be a short-term solution. In A & P's case, a smug, inbred management, too many small, inefficient stores in decaying central city locations, and minimum penetration in affluent suburban markets had to be corrected before price-cutting, heavier emphasis on advertising, or any other strategy could have any lasting impact.

---

[10]"Price and Pride on the Skids," *Time*, December 12, 1977, p. 79.

The strategy of severe price cutting is especially ill-advised in the supermarket industry where markups are small to begin with and where competition is keen.

While A & P increased sales by $800 million during the WEO campaign, this was not nearly enough to compensate for the lower prices, so major losses were incurred. Volume likely cannot be raised sufficiently to compensate for drastically reduced prices and markups, since competition will retaliate and usually attempt to match prices in self-defense.

For Thought and Discussion

1. With the situation facing the new management of A & P in 1971, what alternative actions might have been taken to shake the giant food chain from its waning competitive position? How desirable are these alternatives, rather than the severe price cutting that was decided on?
2. Surveys of customers' motives for shopping particular stores have usually found that lowest prices ranks rather far down the list. For example, one study in 1965 found "low prices" to be 20th on the list, with such things as high quality, reliability, large selection, and friendly employees being much more important.[11] If these surveys have any validity, how wise do you think the reaction was of Kroger, Food Fair, and other supermarket chains matching the price-cutting of A & P, with the result that their profits also dropped drastically in 1972 and early 1973?
3. Did the WEO campaign have any advantageous results?

Invitation to Role Play

1. Place yourself in the role of Jonathan Scott. What specific actions would you initiate to bring the A & P chain back to satisfactory profits as quickly as possible?
2. Place yourself in the role of manager of a fairly run-down A & P store in a deteriorating neighborhood. You have been asked by your district and regional managers to come to the home office to present your views as to how best to bring such stores into profitability. Develop your recommendations carefully and with sound reasoning; your future advancement will undoubtedly depend on the judgment and persuasion you display. (Make any assumptions you need to for this problem, but keep them reasonable and state them clearly.)

[11]F. F. Brown and George Fisk, "Department Stores and Discount Houses: Who Dies Next?" *Journal of Retailing*, Fall 1975.

15

Conclusions—What Can Be Learned?

In considering mistakes, two things are worth noting: (1) even the most successful organizations make mistakes, but survive as long as they can maintain a good batting average, and (2) making mistakes can be an effective teaching tool. The difference in overall success or failure is what is learned from these errors to avoid the repetition of similar mistakes.

We can make a number of generalizations from mistakes, as well as from contrasting successes. Of course, we need to recognize that marketing, as all the social sciences, is a discipline that does not lend itself to laws or axioms. Examples of exceptions to every principle or generalization can be found. However, the marketing executive does well to heed these generalizations. For the most part, these generalizations based on specific corporate experiences are transferable to other situations and other times.

INSIGHTS REGARDING OVERALL ENTERPRISE PERSPECTIVES

Importance of Public Image

As we discussed at some length in Chapter 2 and in the cases in Part One, the image that people (that is, the various publics an organization is involved with) have of the organization and its products or services is of major importance. In particular, we singled out three firms that had serious image problems: Nestle, Coors, and Gilbert.

Nestle tried to ignore a damning reputation having to do with only one part of its diverse and worldwide operation, but unfortunately found the image problem to be both durable and transferable to all other aspects of its operation. The Coors' image of mystique proved to be vulnerable because of a nonaggressive marketing strategy and the onslaught of strong competitors. With Gilbert we saw how very quickly a superior image, a quality image, one built up from decades of well-conceived toys, could be cut down. In Gilbert's case, two or three years of an image-destructive marketing strategy destroyed the positive image, and the company.

But other cases in the book also revealed image problems. For example, the rather negative, old-fashioned image of A & P helped to thwart its price offensive aimed at regaining market share. From the Edsel example we saw that an initial poor reputation for quality, caused by defective cars in the introductory period, plagued Edsel for the rest of its short life and added to its problems of gaining customer acceptance. Burger Chef's lack of a distinctive image placed it at a major disadvantage vis-a-vis McDonald's and other successful fast-food operations, just as the fuzzy images of Grant and Woolco hurt them against the solid and undeviating discounting image of K mart. Adidas' image as the major factor in the athletic shoe industry could not protect it when the guard was lowered during a few crucial years of market expansion. Korvette lost its positive image as a reliable discounter offering greater values than most other firms when the food and furniture operations became questionable. When it tried to upgrade, the low-price, discount image remained and thwarted efforts to move to a higher-quality operation.

A major contributor to a fuzzy or nondistinctive image is that the firm has not clearly determined what it wants to be or in what direction it wants to go.

What Should Our Business Be? An organization's business, its mission and purpose, should be thought through, spelled out clearly, and well communicated to those executives involved in policy making. This is especially true for an organization endeavoring to grow. Otherwise, the organization lacks unified and coordinated goals and objectives. It is like trying to navigate relatively unknown terrain without a map.

However, it is prudent judgment to choose safe, rather than courageous, goals. Mayer, in his presidency of Grant's, wanted the company to grow from $1 billion in sales to $2 billion in barely four years—a courageous goal but hardly safe and prudent.

Determining what a firm's business is or ought to be is a starting point for specifying goals. Several elements help determine this:

The *history* of the organization cannot be disavowed, since it affects employees, suppliers, and customers alike. In view of its history, Grant was unable to translate its future business definition to that of a high-quality and fashion-oriented department-store operation.

The firm's *resources* and *distinctive abilities and strengths* must play a major role in determining its goals. It is not enough to wish for a certain status or position if the firm's resources and competence do not warrant this. To take an extreme example, a railroad company can hardly expect to transform itself into an airline, even though both may be in the transportation business.

Finally, *competitive and environmental opportunities* ought to be considered. The inroads of foreign car makers in the United States reflected environmental opportunities for energy-efficient vehicles and the lack of formidable U.S. competition in this area.

Image can be a lodestone for the organization wishing to expand or upgrade its operation. Improving an image can be a long process requiring great patience and strong resources. For many firms the best course may be to go with the present image rather than radically try to change it. An alternative is to introduce a different brand or a different division, anything to escape the negative or fuzzy image. Occasionally, however, an image can be upgraded. But it takes an inspired type of advertising and strategy, as Honda was able to accomplish in improving the image of motorcyclists.

A favorable image can be an offensive weapon, insulating the organization from most of the rigors of competition, permitting it to charge higher prices, to recruit better employees, to obtain easier financing, and to smooth the way for product expansion or diversification. Such an image needs to be zealously guarded, as Apple was quick to do when one of its products experienced problems. A good image can be quickly destroyed through an episode of poor quality control or servicing.

Power of the Media. Both the Nestle and Coca-Cola examples illustrate the power of the media—a power most often used in a critical sense—to influence a firm's public image. The media can fan a problem or exacerbate an embarrassing or imprudent action. In particular, with well-known firms this can trigger the *herd instinct*, with increasing numbers of people joining in with protests and public criticism.

We can make these key generalizations regarding image:

1. It is important to maintain a stable and clear-cut image and undeviating objectives.
2. It is very difficult and time-consuming to upgrade an image.
3. An episode of poor quality control has a lasting stigma.
4. A good image can be quickly lost if a firm relaxes in an environment of aggressive competition.
5. Well-known firms are particularly vulnerable to critical public scrutiny and must be prudent in decisions and actions that can affect their reputation.

Need for Growth Orientation—But Not Reckless Growth

Only one of the cases treated in this book is one where there was no growth orientation. Harley Davidson was unwilling to change traditional ways of doing things and was content with the status quo. Its comfortable complacency was rudely interrupted by the incursion of Honda.

How tenable is a low- or no-growth philosophy? While at first glance it seems workable, upon closer inspection such a philosophy is seen to sow the seeds of its own destruction. Three decades ago Wroe Alderson pointed out:

> Vitality is required even for survival; but vitality is difficult to maintain without growth, at least in the American business climate. The vitality of a firm depends on the vigor and ambition of its members. The prospect of growth is one of the principal means by which a firm can attract able and vigorous recruits.[1]

A firm uninterested in growth is unable to attract able people and becomes vulnerable to competition. Customers see a growing firm as reliable, eager to please, and getting better all the time. Suppliers and creditors tend to give preferential treatment to a growth-oriented firm, since they hope to retain it as a customer and client when it reaches large size.

Most of the cases in this book—and certainly all of the successes—are growth firms. But an emphasis on growth can be carried too far. Somehow the growth must be kept within the abilities of the firm to handle it. Some of the examples show how firms can grow rapidly without losing control; other cases show how growth can be an instrument of corporate downfall.

McDonald's is an example of the achievement of rapid growth through franchised units rather than company-owned outlets. However, other franchised fast-food operations expanded just as fast and either went out of business or had to cut back drastically and rid themselves of marginal operations. What was the secret of McDonald's handling of rapid growth, while the supposedly shrewd General Foods Corporation's subsidiary Burger Chef could not? The key was very tight controls, careful screening of prospective franchises as well as new locations, and monitoring existing units even during the excitement of opening new ones.

Apple and Nike show that geometric annual growth is possible without losing control of operations. Although Apple had some growing pains, it was able to overcome them and remain a major factor in the rapidly evolving technology of personal computers. Nike experienced almost as rapid growth as Apple, but it had a major problem: the uncertain life cycle of the running boom. It met this challenge

---

[1]Wroe Alderson, *Marketing Behavior and Executive Action* (Homewood, Illinois: Irwin, 1957), p. 59.

by building a very flexible operation, and it also positioned itself to move into related product areas before the running bubble could burst.

Osborne, on the other hand, illustrates the large number of problems associated with growth: no controls established over inventories, expenses, and most other aspects of the operation. As a result, expenses ran amuck, inventory buildup was out of hand, and the incurring of huge losses was not even realized until too late for remedial action.

Perhaps manufacturers such as Nike and Apple can handle rapid growth better than retailers. A geographically expanding retailer has to develop sufficient controls and standards for far-flung operations. Personnel requirements are far greater, also. For example, Nike grew to a half-billion dollar corporation with less than 3000 employees, and Apple with less than 4000. A retail enterprise of the same size employes tens of thousands of employees.

We saw two contrasting examples of rapidly growing retailers. Korvette, the innovator and early leader in discounting, could not cope with its growth, and at the height of its success, faltered. On the other hand, K mart, the imitator rather than the innovator, had the organizational strength to facilitate its growth and became the world's largest discounter and the second largest retailer. And K mart did this while keeping its organization, store facilities, and merchandise plans and controls as simple as possible.

Beware of growth at any cost. W. T. Grant is the premier example of the fallacy of a growth-at-any-cost philosophy. There is prestige in being one of the biggest firms in the industry, prestige especially for top management. Great market share and sales can be achieved if the firm is willing to commit huge expenditures for advertising, or open millions of square feet of selling space as Grant did. Sales increase from such efforts—for as long as the money holds out. Eventually comes the realization that profits are adversely affected, there is towering debt, liquidity has been lost, and the very viability of the enterprise is jeopardized. Profitability and good financial judgment must not be sacrificed to the siren call for growth.

We can make these generalizations about the most desirable growth perspectives:

1.   Growth targets should not exceed the abilities of the organization to assimilate, control, and provide sufficient managerial and financial resources. Growth at any cost—especially at the expense of profits and financial stability—must be shunned. In particular, tight controls over inventories and expenses should be established and performance should be monitored promptly and completely.

2.   The most prudent approach to growth is to keep the organization and operation as simple and uniform as possible, to be flexible in case sales do not meet expectations, and to keep the break-even point as low as possible, especially for new and untried ventures.

3. Concentrating maximum efforts on the expansion opportunity is like an army exploiting a breakthrough. The concentrated strategy usually wins out over more timid competitors who diffuse efforts and resources. But such concentration is not without risk.

4. Rapidly expanding markets face dangers both from too conservative and from overly optimistic sales forecasts. The latter may overextend resources and jeopardize viability should demand contract; the former opens the door to more aggressive competitors. There is no definitive answer to this dilemma, but the firm should be aware of the risks and the rewards.

5. A strategy emphasizing rapid growth should not neglect other aspects of the operation. For example, older stores should not be ignored in the quest to open new outlets. Basic merchandising principles, such as inventory control and new merchandise planning, should not be violated. Otherwise, the sales coming from expansion are built on a shaky foundation, growth is not assimilated, and an illusion is created of strength and success.

6. Decentralized management is more compatible with rapid growth than a centralized organization since it puts less strain on home office executives. However, delegation of decision making to field executives must be accompanied by well-defined standards and controls and executed by high-caliber field personnel.

7. Where growth takes place through additions to the product line, efforts should be made to prevent and reduce cannibalization (taking sales away from other products of the firm). However, cannibalization by one's own products is preferable to losing sales to a competitor.

Innovation

Innovation led to the great success of Apple and Honda. With Apple, product innovation came from humble surroundings and seemingly unpromising individuals—two college dropouts. The innovative product, aggressive marketing efforts, and identification of the most potent customer segment brought great success despite the fact that the mightiest of competitors, IBM, was lurking on the periphery.

With Honda the innovation was partly product: a lightweight, classy model of the old motorcycle. But the important innovation involved changing the image of the motorcycle and catering to an entirely different customer group through effective advertising and revamping the method of distribution.

Desirable as innovative-mindedness is for an organization, major changes are difficult to accomplish in most organizations. This is particularly true for larger and older organizations; major changes usually come from smaller and younger firms. Furthermore, as we saw with the Penney Company, innovation is particularly difficult to foster in an organization firmly espousing promotion from within. Such a policy tends to restrict new ideas and broad perspectives.

Resistance to Change. People as well as organizations are naturally reluctant to embrace change. Change is disruptive, it destroys accepted ways of doing things and familiar authority and responsibility relationships. It makes people uneasy since their routines are disrupted, and their interpersonal relationships with subordinates, co-workers, and superiors modified. Previously important positions are downgraded. And the person who views himself or herself as highly competent in a particular job may be forced to assume unfamiliar duties amid the fear that the new assignments cannot be handled as well.

Resistance to change can be combated by good communication with participants about forthcoming changes. Without such communication, rumors and fears assume monumental proportions. Acceptance of change is facilitated if employees are involved as fully as possible in planning the changes, if their participation is solicited and welcomed, and if assurance is given that positions will not be impaired, only changed. Gradual rather than abrupt changes also make a transition smoother as participants can be exposed to changes without drastic upheavals.

In the final analysis, however, needed changes, embracing different opportunities, should not be delayed or cancelled because of their possible negative repercussions on the organization. If change is desirable, it should be initiated. Individuals and organizations can adapt to change—it just takes a bit of time.

We can make these generalizations regarding innovation:

1. Opportunities often exist when a traditional marketing strategy has prevailed in the industry for a long time.
2. Opportunities often exist when there are gaps in serving customers' needs by existing firms.
3. Innovations are not limited to products but involve such elements as method of distribution.
4. For industries with rapidly changing technologies—these usually are new industries—heavy research and development (R&D) expenditures are usually required if a firm is not to be left behind by competitors.

Power of Judicious Imitation

Some firms are reluctant to copy successful practices of their competitors; they want to be leaders, not followers. But successful practices or innovations may need to be embraced to survive. Sometimes the imitator outdoes the innovator. Success can lie in doing the ordinary better than competitors.

K mart and Nike were imitators. They recognized an effective strategy and rose to dominate their industries. On the other hand, competitors of McDonald's, including Burger Chef, disdained to adopt McDonald's successful format, even though the high standards and rigid controls were obvious to all. Such disavowal probably was due to lackadaisical management. It is no easy task to develop high standards and controls and to insist that they be followed. We can make this generalization:

> It makes sense to identify the characteristics of successful competitors (and even similar but noncompeting firms) that contribute most to their success, and then adopt them if compatible with the resources of the imitator. Let someone else do the experimenting and taking the risks of innovating. The imitator faces some risk in waiting too long, but this usually is far less than the risk of an untested product or operation.

Vulnerability to Competition

Competitive advantage can be short-lived, success does not guarantee continued success, and innovators as well as long-dominant firms can be overtaken and surpassed. This realization should be sobering to any front-runner, and should make the organization alert to possible interlopers. But the "three C's syndrome" of complacency, conservatism, and conceit often blanket the leading firms. We suggest that a constructive attitude of never underestimating a competitor can be fostered by:

- Bringing fresh blood into the organization for new ideas and different perspectives
- Establishing a strong and continuing commitment to customer service and satisfaction
- Conducting periodically a corporate self-analysis designed to detect weaknesses as well as opportunities in their early stages
- Continually monitoring the environment and being alert to any changes

We will discuss environmental monitoring, or sensors in a later section. For now let us emphasize that the environment is dynamic, sometimes with subtle and hardly recognizable changes, and at other times with violent and unmistakable changes. To operate in this environment, an established firm must constantly be on guard to protect its position. Let us examine several internal tools for doing so.

Management by Exception. In controlling diverse and far-flung operations, it becomes difficult to closely monitor all phases of the operation. Successful managers are content to direct their attention to significant performances that deviate from the expected at *strategic control points*. Ordinary operations and less significant deviations can be handled by subordinates. With this approach to control, the manager is not overburdened by a host of details.

Major advantages of management by exception are, first, management efficiency can be improved by freeing time and attention for the more important problems and parts of the job, such as planning; and second, subordinates are permitted more self-management.

In the Korvette example, attention should have been given to deviations from expected performances at important parts of an individual store operation. Deviations that should have received attention included markdowns and shrinkage, merchandise turnover, sales per square foot, and the various categories of expenses. These strategic control points should have been evaluated not only by store but by individual departments. The trends should have been noted. Are conditions getting better or worse? Are we becoming more vulnerable in certain areas of our operations?

The Deadly Parallel. As an enterprise becomes larger and, if a retail enterprise, opens more and more stores, a particularly effective organizational arrangement is one in which operating units of comparable characteristics are established. Sales, expenses, and profits can be readily compared, and strong as well as weak performances can be identified and appropriate action taken. Besides providing control and performance evaluation, the deadly parallel fosters intrafirm competition, and this can stimulate best efforts. For the deadly parallel to be used effectively, the operating units must be as equal as possible in sales potential. This is not difficult to achieve with retail units, as departments and stores can be divided into various sales volume categories—often designated as A, B, and C stores--and operating results of stores within the same volume category can be compared. While the deadly parallel is particularly effective for chain-store organizations, it can also be used with sales territories and certain other operating units where sales and applicable expenses and ratios can be directly measured and compared with similar units.

Following are generalizations regarding vulnerability to competition:

1. Initial market advantage tends to be rather quickly countered by competitors.
2. Countering by competitors is more likely to occur when an innovation is involved than when the advantage involves more commonplace effective management and marketing techniques.
3. An easy-entry industry is particularly vulnerable to new and aggressive competition, especially in an expanding market. In such new industries, severe price competition usually will weed out the marginal firms.
4. Long-dominant firms tend to be vulnerable to upstart competitors because of their complacency, resistance to change, and myopia concerning a changing environment. Careful monitoring of performance at strategic control points and comparison of similar operating units and their trends in various performance categories can detect weakening positions and alert management can take corrective action before competitors intrude.
5. In expanding markets it is a delusion to judge performance by increases in sales rather than by market share; an increase in sales may hide a deteriorating competitive situation.

SPECIFIC MARKETING STRATEGY INSIGHTS

Strengths and Limitations of Advertising

The cases presented in this book provide several insights regarding the power and effectiveness of advertising. But they leave some unanswered questions, and some contradictions. For example, major advertising and promotional expenditures were made for the Edsel, but the car flopped. On the other hand, an equal level of commitment for the Mustang is associated with an outstanding success. And then we have Coca-Cola with its $100 million greater expenditure than Pepsi, all the while with market share steadily declining. Does advertising have much relationship with success?

Yet there are striking examples of the effectiveness of advertising. Honda successfully used it to change a negative image—with modest expenditures of only a few million dollars a year. And the advertising campaigns of Pepsi—the Pepsi Generation and the Pepsi Challenge—have to be models of the most effective use of advertising.

We can draw these conclusions:

> There is no assured correlation between expenditures for advertising and sales success. However, given that the other elements of the strategy are relatively attractive, advertising can be an effective tool in generating demand and bringing about attitude change.

Advertising induced consumers to go to dealer showrooms to look at the Edsel, It performed its primary objective of gaining attention and interest for the product so that consumers would examine it more closely. With the Mustang, they liked what they saw; with the Edsel, they did not—as simple as that.

Planning and budgeting advertising presents some problems. Certain advertisements and campaigns are more effective than others. Other campaigns with perhaps higher budgets somehow fall short of expectations. Therein lies the great challenge of advertising. One never knows for sure how much should be spent to get the job done, to reach the planned objectives of perhaps increasing sales by a certain percentage or possibly gaining market share. Despite the inability to measure directly the effectiveness of advertising, aggressively promoting competitors usually need to be countered, as Coors belatedly found out.

Limitations of Marketing Research

Marketing research is usually touted as the key to better decision-making and the mark of sophisticated professional management. It is commonly thought that the more money spent for marketing research the less chance for a bad decision. But heavy use of marketing research does not always help the situation, as we saw with the Edsel and Coca-Cola.

Marketing research does not guarantee a correct decision. At best, marketing research increases the batting average of correct decisions—maybe only by a little, sometimes by quite a bit. To be effective, research must be current and unbiased. The several million dollars spent on Edsel marketing research came to naught. Most of the research on consumer preferences and attitudes was done several years before the Edsel came on the market, and the decision to use the name Edsel was made despite its negative connotation to many people. From the Edsel example we can further conclude that planning and long lead time do not assure success, especially when based on faulty premises.

And the several million dollars in taste-test research for Coca-Cola can hardly reassure us about the validity of marketing research. Admittedly, results of taste tests are difficult to rely on, simply because of the subjective nature of taste preferences. But the Coca-Cola research did not even uncover the latent and powerful loyalty toward tradition, and gave a completely false ''go'' signal for the new taste.

On the other hand, it is wrong to view all marketing research and planning as useless. Some of the flawed studies might have been worthwhile with better planning. Lee Iacocca used marketing research to identify the most promising markets for the Mustang, guide the design of the car, and determine its price. Marketing research could have provided Coors with early feedback that customers did not like the hard-to-open cans and increasingly preferred low-calorie beer.

Many successful firms chronicled in this book used little formal research. The great successes of Nike and Apple relied on entrepreneurial hunch rather than sophisticated research. Ray Kroc of McDonald's recognized a good thing when he saw it, although McDonald's later relied heavily on research, especially for its site selections. Kresge's major move into its K mart also came without formal research: Harry Cunningham on his own conducted a two-year investigation that was a far cry from a formal and sophisticated marketing research study.

Why have we not seen more extensive use of marketing research? Consider the following major reasons:

1.   Most of the founding enterpreneurs did not have marketing backgrounds and therefore were not familiar and confident with such research.
2.   Available tools and techniques are not always appropriate to handle some problems and opportunities. There may be too many variables. They may be intangible and incapable of precise measurement. Much research consists of collecting past and present data, that while helpful in predicting a stable future, are of little help in charting revolutionary new ventures. The risks for such ventures must be faced by the entrepreneur in the quest for great rewards.

Unimportance of Price As An Offensive Weapon

We generally think of price promotions as the most aggressive form of marketing and the one most desirable in the eyes of society. Yet we have seen here an example of the misguided use of price as a marketing weapon. The A & P WEO campaign had strong repercussions in the food marketing industry. Food prices were reduced by A & P to almost intolerably low markups. A & P hoped to win a much greater share of the market for itself; if it drove some of its weaker adversaries out of business in the meantime, A & P would not have cared. However, the strategy had only negative consequences for A & P and the rest of the industry. A & P lost over $50 million in the first year of its WEO campaign; most other grocers also lost money. And what was gained? While consumers enjoyed somewhat lower prices, most were scarcely aware of this since wholesale prices were relentlessly going up during this time. As for winning substantial market share and holding it, this did not happen for A & P. Its problems were not solved by merely lowering prices for a few months or a year.

The major disadvantage of price as an offensive weapon is that other firms in the industry are almost forced to meet the price-cutter's prices—such a marketing strategy is easy to match. Consequently, prices for an entire industry fall; no firm has any particular advantage and all suffer the effects of diminished profits. Competitive advantage is therefore seldom won by price-cutting. Other marketing strategies more successfully enable a firm to best its competitors—strategies such as better quality, better product and brand image, better service, and improved warranties. All are aspects of nonprice rather than price competition.

At the same time, we have to recognize that in new industries, which are characterized by rapid technological changes and production efficiencies, severe price competition can be expected—and is even necessary to weed out the host of marginal operations that entered in the expectation of cashing in on a rapidly growing market. However, as Osborne learned, even a substantial position in such an industry does not necessarily protect a firm from such severe price competition that its very viability may be jeopardized.

Need for Environmental Monitoring

A firm must be alert to changes in the business environment: changes in customer preferences and needs, changes in competition, changes in the economy, and even changes in international events such as nationalism in Canada, OPEC machinations, or Japanese productivity and quality control advances. Edsel failed because it did not recognize the trend away from big, high-horsepower cars toward smaller, more economical ones. Gilbert did not recognize changes in toy marketing, which should have been obvious to any alert observer. Penney's did not comprehend that the retail environment had changed greatly over three or four decades, and that unchanging policies were no longer appropriate. Harley Davidson, Coors, and Adidas also did not heed changes, even though some of these should have been obvious.

How can a firm remain alert to subtle, insidious, as well as more obvious, changes? A firm must have *sensors* constantly monitoring the environment. The sensors may reside in a marketing or economic research department, but in many instances such a formal organizational entity is not really necessary to provide primary monitoring. Executive alertness is essential. Most changes do not occur suddenly and with no warning. Feedback from customers, from sales representatives, from suppliers; keeping abreast of the latest material and projections in business journals; and even simple observation of what is happening in stores, in advertising, to prices, and introduction of new technologies—these sources can provide sufficient information about the environment and how it is changing. Sensors of the environment can be organized and formal, or they can be strictly informal and subjective. But it is surprising and disturbing how many executives overlook or disregard—or else are not even aware of—important changing environmental factors that presage changes in their present and future business.

GENERAL INSIGHTS

Impact of One Person

In many of the cases presented in this book one person had a powerful impact on the organization. Harry Cunningham of Kresge completely turned a mediocre and conservative variety-store chain into the most aggressive and largest discounter, with a growth rate almost unparalleled in retailing. Ray Kroc of McDonald's converted a successful small hamburger stand into the world's largest fast-food franchised operation, and maintained its successful format against all comers. The accomplishments of Lee Iacocca are well known, both with the Mustang case described here, and with his later rejuvenation of Chrysler.

One person can also have a negative impact on an organization. Eugene Ferkauf was the force behind the development and growth of Korvette. He was heralded as one of the outstanding merchants in U.S. history, but he could not adapt himself or his organization to the challenges of large size. And how can we forget Adam Osborne? The impact of one person, for good or ill, is one of the marvels of history, whether business history or world history.

Prevalence of Opportunities for Entrepreneurship Today

The recent successes of Nike and Apple show that opportunities and rewards for entrepreneurship were never better. Despite the maturing of our economy and the growing size and power of many firms in many industries, there still is abundant opportunity. Such opportunity exists not only for the change maker or innovator, but even for the entrepreneur who only seeks to do things a little better than existing, and complacent, competition.

Venture capital to support promising new businesses is increasing—some $1 billion a year. In the 1980s we are in the midst of the greatest boom in new stock issues and new company formations since the late 1960s.

Of course, we know that not all of us have what it takes to be an entrepreneur. It takes more than the "great idea." Nolan Bushnell, founder of Atari in 1972 with $500, says: "A lot of people have ideas, but there are few who decide to do something about them now. Not tomorrow. Not next week. But today."[2] Dreamers do not make entrepreneurs; doers do. The great venture capitalists look at the person, not the idea. Typically they distribute their seed money to resourceful people, who are courageous enough to give up security for the unknown consequences of their embryonic venture, who have great self-confidence, and who demonstrate a tremendous will to win.

FINALLY

We learn from mistakes and from successes. Yet every management problem seems cast in a somewhat different setting, requiring a different strategy. One author has likened business strategy to military strategy:

> . . . strategies which are flexible rather than static enhance optimum use and offer the greatest number of alternative objectives. A good commander knows that he cannot control his environment to suit a prescribed strategy. Natural phenomena pose their own restraints to strategic planning, whether physical, geographic, regional, or psychological and sociological.[3]

And:

> Planning leadership recognizes the unpleasant fact that, despite every effort, the war may be lost. Therefore, the aim is to retain the maximum number of facilities and the basic organization. Indicators of a deteriorating and unsalvageable total situation are, therefore, mandatory. . . . No possible combination of strategies and tactics, no mobilization of resources . . . can supply a magic formula which guarantees victory; it is possible only to increase the probability of victory.[4]

Thus we can pull two concepts from military strategy to help guide business strategy: the desirability of flexibility due to an unkonwn or changing environment, and the idea of a basic core that should be maintained under all circumstances. The first suggests that the firm should be prepared for adjustments in strategy as conditions warrant. The second suggests that there is a basic core of a firm's business that should be unchanging; it should be the final bastion to fall back to for regrouping if necessary. Grant and Korvette abandoned their basic strengths, and had nothing to

[2]John Merwin, "Have You Got What It Takes?" *Forbes*, August 3, 1981, p. 60.
[3]Myron S. Heidingsfield, *Changing Patterns in Marketing* (Boston: Allyn and Bacon, 1968), p. 11.
[4]Ibid.

fall back on. Harley Davidson stolidly maintained its core position, even though it let expansion opportunities slither away.

In regard to the basic core of a firm, every viable firm has some distinctive function or "ecological niche" in the business environment:

> Every business firm occupies a position which is in some respects unique. Its location, the product it sells, its operating methods, or the customers it serves tend to set it off in some degree from every other firm. Each firm competes by making the most of its individuality and its special character.[5]

Woe to the firm that loses its ecological niche.

For Thought and Discussion

1. Design a program aimed at mistake avoidance. Be as specific, as creative, and as complete as possible.
2. How would you build into an organization the controls to assure that similar mistakes will not happen in the future?
3. Which would you advise a firm to be: an imitator or an innovator? Why?

Invitation to Role Play

You have been asigned the responsibility of assuring that your firm has adequate sensors of the marketplace. How would you go about developing such sensors?

[5]Alderson, op. cit., p. 101.